DAVID

Other books by this author:

Behind the Seen: God's Hand in Esther's Life . . . and Yours

David: A Heart Like His

David: Faith on the Run

Out of the Pit: Joseph's Story and Yours

Well-driven Nails

Wrestling With Angels

Larry
LICHTENWALTER

DAVID

DANCING LIKE A KING

REVIEW AND HERALD® PUBLISHING ASSOCIATION
HAGERSTOWN, MD 21740

The author assumes full responsibility for the accuracy of all facts and quotations as cited in this book.

This book was
Edited by Gerald Wheeler
Copyedited by Delma Miller
Cover designed by Luemas Design
Cover illustration by Craig Nelson/Bernstein & Andriulli, Inc.
Typeset: 11/14 Berkeley

PRINTED IN U.S.A.

09 08 07 06 05 5 4 3 2 1

R&H Cataloging Service
Lichtenwalter, Larry Lee, 1952- .
David—Dancing like a king.
1. David, king of Israel. I. Title.

221.4092

ISBN 0-8280-1771-9

DEDICATION

This book is dedicated to my father,
Thomas Phillip Lichtenwalter,
who danced through life with passion.
Who showed me how to do everything I ever did with passion.
Who was passionately pursued by God all through his troubled life.
Who wanted to die with his heart full of
what he had never had all his life.
Who fell asleep with passion for God, a dance in his eyes.
Who left a legacy of how every one of us can end well.

"Every time I think of you, I give thanks to my God"
(Phil. 1:3, NLT).

CONTENTS

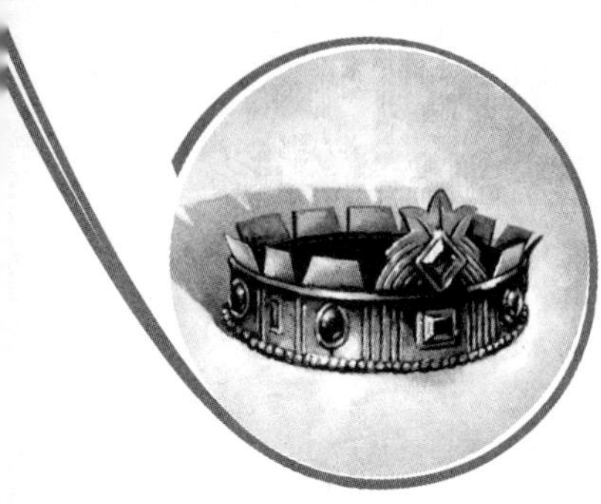

Introduction

I HOPE YOU DANCE

This morning i woke up early and stood wearing my underwear out my big open window looking over a small part of the city. i read my german bible . . . a couple chapters in psalms about singing the praises of God as long as i live. passion. passion for God, life and everything else in between. thats what david had. send me dads books about david. i feel like reading them. I love you. ehren. p.s. just a reminder that my account size is under 200."

I try to imagine the setting of this e-mail. My son is far away from home at our Adventist college in Villa Aurora, Italy. The open window. Colorful boxers. Disheveled hair. Unshaven face. Sleepy eyes. Dragon breath. Sunlight reaching in from the morning sky. The romantic touch of Florence's famous architecture. Street sounds. A cluttered, messy dorm room. My son, Ehren, learning Italian and not able to find his English translation, reads his German Bible instead. Speaking about praising God as long as one has breath—my son connects with God somewhere deep down. I sense passion in him. For God, life, and everything else in between. Every day. Always. And unrelenting. It was something that King David had. Something Ehren wants besides the $200 he reminds me about at the end. He seeks God!

I am filled with wonder. Joy, in fact. This is my son, thirsting for God! I marvel how the Lord does it—how He still awakens spiritual passion, still arouses deep longings for Himself. It is something I cannot do for myself, let alone for my son. But here it is, stirring in Ehren's heart on the other side of the ocean. And he wants more. Just as I did when, as a young person, God first awakened that thirst in my own heart. Awesome!

But I worry, realizing how fragile passion for God can be. I live in the daily awareness of how much easier it is to talk about passion than to find it or, having obtained it, to maintain it—let alone encourage it in others.[1] The Bible emphasizes a relationship with a Person rather than a doctrinal system, mystical experience, or spiritual technique. And personal relationships are never steady-state—they are always undergoing change.[2] It is no wonder, then, that a relationship with an invisible God will always include uncertainty and variability.[3] A thousand other passions can steal my energy for God: the pursuit of a career position. A hobby or recreational effort. Money. Sex. Power. Notoriety. The thrill of raw achievement.

I've watched so many glow spiritually hot, then burn out. Or simply become bored and lukewarm. "Going through the motions," they live out of religious habit more than anything else. We notice a dullness in their eyes when they talk about God, worship, or read their Bibles.

You know something is missing.

Passion is mysterious. It is hard to measure and difficult to pin down. But you know when you have it, and you are quite sure when you don't. You recognize, too, when others have it or not.[4]

And so I worry.

". . . singing the praises of God as long as i live. passion. passion for God, life, and everything else in between. thats what david had. send me dads books about david. i feel like reading them."

I wish that were enough. Just read Dad's books on David and he'd have it—or at least enough to nudge his passion a little further along or help him better understand the issues. But will he read all three volumes? By the time he gets to this part of the story (if he ever does), will he have the same interest? Will I have continued to sustain it? Carried him along in his imagination enough to take him the final lap through David's journey so that he has a sense of what's ahead for him spiritually, both by way of pitfalls and triumphs? That he, like David, can make it to the end?

Trilogies are challenging. Each subsequent piece in the unfolding story needs to maintain interest while drawing the viewer more deeply into the plot. Each volume should build anticipation and pull it all together toward a grand climax that makes it worth the long wait. The finale should be awesome in its emotional appeal and moral commentary. Unfortunately, though, not all parts of such stories are of equal value. Nor do they stir imagination or captivate in the same way. Some scenes will forever stand out above all others. So as the story line moves along, how do you sustain the energy or interest? Especially when some parts seem so mediocre in comparison to what has gone before or what still lies ahead?

These were the kind of realities that the film producers of *Matrix* and *The Lord of the Rings* series faced as they carried the imagination of their audience through a two-year viewing experience. Both film critics and viewers weighed in on the ability of the producers to make each part of the unfolding story line both stand on its own and at the same time reach powerfully forward (and subsequently, backward). People passionately (and critically) compared the second installments of these two fantasy trilogies to the first releases, stirring speculation about the ability of the third to deliver. *Matrix* supposedly started out well, but its sequels, while packed with plenty of action and special effects, didn't seem to connect in the same way as its reported spellbinding beginning. According to ticket sales and Oscar awards, *Lord of the Rings* proved to be an authentic, transfixing trilogy. J.R.R. Tolkien's Middle Earth saga is among the greatest works of imaginative fiction of the twentieth century, encompassing more than 1,100 pages. Its immense narrative power holds the reader enthralled for days and even weeks.

The ability of a trilogy writer or filmmaker to keep it up, complete the story, and end well is challenging. The first thing one asks of an adventure story is that it be varied and exciting, including high drama, suspense, mystery, poetry, and imagination. Story and characters must come across in three-dimensional reality—the real stuff of life. I think of observations from the Review and Herald book review committee on the different reactions they experienced between volumes 1 and 2 of this three-part series on David. Some sensed a difference in the passion itself by the way I wrote. One remarked that *Faith on the Run* (David's fugitive years) lacked the engaging passion of *A Heart Like His* (David's shepherd years). "First 100 pages are theologically correct, technically flawless—and totally boring. Last half of book captures the same passion I found in David 1. Add stories from real life, emotion, passion." In other words, I needed to rewrite a few things, add some more stories, and make the book more personal.

You can imagine how I felt. When *Faith on the Run* came off the press, I read it with interest. Did the energy begun with *A Heart Like His* somehow stall in this second volume, at least till you got past the first couple chapters? While I had not intended it so, I had to agree that the critics knew what they were sensing. I experienced it myself now that I wasn't so close to the act of writing itself. But then I was gently reminded by the acquisitions editor that each David volume stands on its own. Tells its own story. That *Faith on the Run* could not possibly have the same passion as *A Heart Like His,* because that's where David was now in life. The intense pressures and trials of David's fugitive years threatened to diminish his passion for God. It was a struggle. How can you write passionately about problems and failures, betrayal and compromise, and the like? The ups and downs, twists and turns, burning passion and barren desert, are part of David's story. While not particularly energizing at every turn, they are still part of the story nevertheless. That's where David was. But where was his story headed? How does it finish? What does the whole narrative say about passion for God?

These were good proddings. While my ability to deliver is still on the line, the bottom line of this trilogy is the same throughout—passion. Passion for God. What does David's *whole* story say about human passion for God? Why does it get bland at points or even downright troubling? How does it finish? Will hearing David's story somehow make any difference in our own spiritual journey? What about the final leg of his journey and mine? And what about God? What does the whole story say about Him and whether He is just as worthy of passion at story's end as at the beginning?

Spiritual passion is like a well-written trilogy (or a poorly written one that bombs). It opens with incredible potential and awesome experience with God. But then it encounters real life. That is not to say that passion for God is neither *real* nor *real life,* but that life has a way of robbing us of spiritual passion by diverting it or even killing it altogether. Sometimes we feel a difference in the passion itself, the way we live with God. It's not particularly energizing at every turn. But then again, What really is passion for God? And where are we going with it? How will we finish? What will our whole life story say about passion for God? Like a trilogy writer or filmmaker, our ability to keep it up, complete the story, and end well, is challenging. Daunting, actually, when we take time to think about it. Having tasted God's mysterious awakening touch as a young person, I feel keenly what's ahead for my son. He will experience the trilogy with its ups and downs, throbbing passion and barren desert. By God's grace I have held on to my passion for God for nearly 40 years since first pursuing that thirst. Determined never to let it go, I want it to deepen with every new morning. Every new experience of life and God. Will that be the case for Ehren? Or for you?

Thus the power of David's story and why I keep thumbing back to it, including all the triumphs and fiascoes of his royal years. How through the leadership and family ethical opportunities and dilemmas David still managed to passionately live large for God till the very end of life. I know no better model for a fervent relationship with God for the long haul. Nowhere else is there such a powerful example of passion that, once awakened, never dissipates. "David's strongest instinct was to relate his life to God. In comparison, nothing else mattered at all."[5] His was a God-saturated life. He had but one overriding passion that he was privileged to experience and one that we will close this volume with—"I will sing to the Lord as long as I live. I will praise my God to my last breath!" (Ps. 104:33, NLT).[6]

David's life is an authentic passion trilogy, demonstrating that the long march of years doesn't preclude true passion. Nor need our own initial passion for God ever diminish—no matter what life brings us. As with David, our passion for God can radiate long and deep within—until we breathe our last or Jesus comes.

Dancing Like a King will take us through a journey of David's experience as Israel's most celebrated king. It is here that we find him dancing. Not only did David *dance* when the sacred ark of the covenant symbolizing God's presence arrived with fanfare in Jerusalem—bursting with joy and cartwheeling in the streets—his whole life as Israel's king was a *dance,* so to speak, between the fine moral and spiritual nuances of the issues and decisions that confronted him as a king, a parent, a human being, a leader, a friend, and a man of faith. Sometimes David danced well. Other times he flat out blew it. Once again we will see ourselves mirrored in the episodes of this incredible man's life. Like *Faith on the Run,* not everything in this volume is exciting reading. But it's David's story. And it reveals both the realities of his heart and that of God—thus worth the read.

We'll learn, too, additional insights about passion for God. How it *dances* before God even as it *dances* the fine line of life's challenging exigencies and opportunities. I am using *dancing* here as a metaphor for walking a fine line between the moral and spiritual nuances of the issues and decisions that passion for God faces. In the process I hope you will yourself dance! That's what country pop singer Lee Ann Womack sang in her award-winning song. Named the 2000 CMA single of the year and song of the year, "I Hope You Dance" is a challenge to make the most out of life. Commenting about the choice to sit it out or dance in life, she sings, *"I hope you dance."* We must all figure out a way to keep the energy and gumption and fire alive. Each of us must cling to our sense of wonder and hope and faith and never even take a single breath for granted. As LeeAnn sings the chorus, "I hope you dance . . . I hope you dance . . .," male background voices proclaim that time constantly rolls us along. None of us wants to wonder where the years have fled. So make the most out of life—dance.

When I look back and wonder where my life has gone, I want to be able to say that I have made the most out of it—that I have truly danced, as did King David. We do it for a one-Person audience—God! I want my passion for Him to be stronger and steadier than ever before. No matter what life brings, I want it to keep burning brightly. I want to reach for God until I have no more breath in me. Till Jesus comes. For He alone is worthy of such energy, focus, love, and honor. May it ever be that God, and God alone, keeps my soul dancing.

That's why I want to hear the whole story of David. How one of the most well-documented lives in biblical history ends. God desires that we know David's life, his passion trilogy.[7] For in the end that life says something about God Himself, and why our passion for God is ever worth the journey.

---

[1] Gordon MacDonald, *Restoring Your Spiritual Passion* (Nashville: Oliver-Nelson Books, 1986), p. 10.

[2] Philip Yancey, *Reaching for the Invisible God* (Grand Rapids: Zondervan Publishing House, 2000), p. 188.

[3] *Ibid.*

[4] See my discussion of passion in Larry L. Lichtenwalter, *David: A Heart Like His—The Shepherd Years* (Hagerstown, Md.: Review and Herald Pub. Assn., 2003), pp. 12-15. In this first volume on David I outline nine facets of passion that we find expressed in David's ex-

perience with God: 1. Passion *claims it all*—one's whole being. It is what the heart seeks, but it demands the whole heart—all the heart and soul and strength and mind. It is everything or nothing. Only when passion claims the whole heart can we say that it has truly seized *us* rather than our trying to create it or fake it. 2. Passion *yields it all.* It not only *claims it all,* it presses the heart to *yield it all* as well. You cannot have passion if you are not willing to yield yourself fully to whatever that passion has been awakened toward. 3. Passion is *imaginative,* filling the heart with art. Nothing remains status quo or colorless. Rather, it produces inspiration that leads to creativity and freshness. When passion *claims it all* and *yields it all* for some compelling cause or experience or object or being or relationship, an imaginativeness frames everything one does. 4. Passion *constantly renews itself.* Yesterday's passion cannot be today's inner energy. Quickly dissipating, passion must be restored regularly. By nature passion gravitates toward whatever inspires it, thirsting for more of it—thus renewing itself. Living by your passion keeps your passion stirred. 5. Passion *hears what it wants to hear.* Endowed with selective hearing, it chooses who or what it listens to. It will not open itself indiscriminately to just any voice or influence that might sidetrack its vision, focus, or vitality. 6. Passion *has purpose,* a reason for being, an agenda—something that it is willing to spend and be spent for. Without a purpose or reason for being, passion is either impossible or empty—mere emotionalism, zeal without knowledge or real meaning or direction. 7. Passion *haunts the imagination*—our worldview. Whatever vision of reality dominates our inner private world will become our passion. Once passion for something awakens, it can so dominate our perception of reality that our imagination will be both imprinted with and centered by that very vision. 8. Passion *evokes passion.* Your drive for some cause or someone can spark a similar focus in another individual's life. That responding passion can be either positive or negative, stimulating or intimidating. We can turn people on or off, drawing them to us or driving them away from both us as people and whatever is important to us. 9. Finally, passion is *deeply personal,* because it is experienced and expressed by a personal being—you, me, or God. It involves the meaning of our lives and the purpose of our existence. Furthermore, passion is personal because it is experienced and expressed most powerfully and most perfectly when directed toward another personal being. Intimacy makes life a passion (pp. 125-127).

[5]Yancey, p. 192.

[6]While Psalm 104 names no author, we find many indications of David's touch, and the Septuagint claims it for David (see F. B. Meyer, *Gems From the Psalms* [Westchester, Ill.: Good News Publishers, 1976], p. 168; and Derek Kidner, *Psalms 73-150* [InterVarsity Press, 1975], p. 367). Because of its common framework and style—its exordium and conclusion, calling on the singer's "soul" or "whole being," to bless the Lord—Psalm 104 is often paired (as companion psalms) with Psalm 103, which clearly identifies itself as a psalm of David. While their themes are different, both Psalm 103 and Psalm 104 begin with an individual self-exhortation to praise, then develop into a communal hymn of praise, and conclude with a reiteration of its preliminary self-exhortation. Their common framework must have provided the reason for their pairing right at the beginning of a collection of songs of praise, Psalms 103-107. In Psalm 63:4 David utters similar sentiments: "I will bless You as long as I live" (NASB).

[7]Keith Kaynor, *When God Chooses: The Life of David* (Schaumburg, Ill.: Regular Baptist Press, 1989), p. 9.

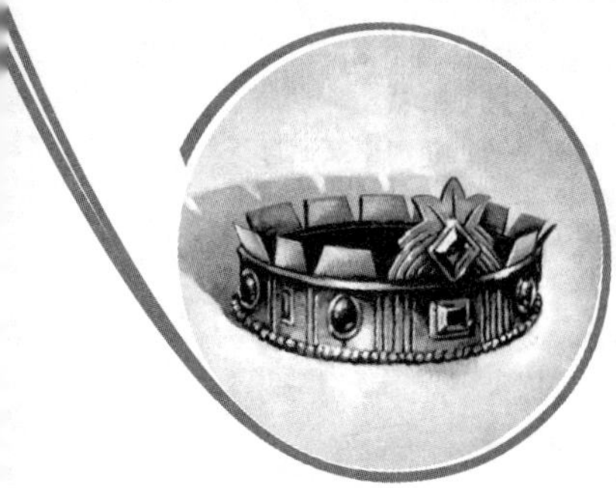

I

LET THE YOUNG MEN PLAY

2 Samuel 2:12-17; 3:1

It was a standoff, one of those stare-your-opponent-down-until-they-blink kind of moments. The armies of Abner and Joab had simultaneously converged on the strategic city of Gibeon.[1] Instead of attacking each other, though, the two forces set up their camps on opposite sides of the city's landmark pool—a hand-carved reservoir 37 feet in diameter and 82 feet deep.[2] A remarkable spiraling rock-cut staircase of 79 steps leads to the bottom where a tunnel extends another 167 feet through solid rock to a spring. The pool of Gibeon was well known for its abundant supply of water (Jer. 41:12). The two groups now sat down beside it and nervously faced each other. It was an awkward and temporary truce. The pool separated yet united the two groups, who both needed water.[3] They were two generals and their armies, each representing a king vying for undisputed control over one nation.

Saul and Jonathan were dead. David had magnificently mourned their deaths. His lament depicted his passion for God at its best, revealing him as reverent and generous. He is also king. David's long-ago anointing by Samuel as Israel's next ruler is now out in the open. King Saul no longer obstructs the way. After more than a decade of being hunted in the wilderness, living on the defensive, 30-year-old David is now in a position of strength. The tables have turned. An old regime is on its way out, and a new one is beginning.

When Saul and Jonathan perished on the battlefield, David didn't rush to the throne and assume charge. He didn't march into the land of Israel and take over the whole nation. Instead, he asked God what to do before he took a single step in his inevitable journey to the throne:

"'Shall I go up to one of the towns of Judah?' he asked.

"'The Lord said, 'Go up.'

"'Where shall I go?'

"'To Hebron,' the Lord answered" (2 Sam. 2:1, NIV).

Did you notice how David kept asking until he had a specific answer from God? How greatly we would profit if we would follow his example. He didn't want general directions—he desired God's exact will for his life. Instead of simply getting to the throne, he wanted to do it God's way. If that meant waiting longer or making some further adjustments in his life, then so be it.

God instructed him to go to Hebron, a region rich in biblical history. Located in the hill country of Judah about 19 miles south of the city of Jerusalem, the site has been occupied continuously since 3300 B.C. Some very important events have occurred there. That's where Abraham settled and built an altar to God (Gen. 13:18). There God spoke to Abraham through three visitors and told him that Sarah would bear a child (Gen. 18:1-15). Joshua gave Hebron to Caleb as an inheritance (Joshua 14:13). Evidently Hebron was a place where God was worshipped, would speak, and would empower His people. It was there that David and his family would rest awhile and put down a few roots—and God would write some new rich history on the map of Hebron through the future king of all Israel.

After he settled in Hebron, "the men of Judah came . . . and there they anointed David king over the house of Judah" (2 Sam. 2:4, NIV). At last his private anointing years earlier had become public knowledge. Only Judah crowned David, though. He had a limited reign over the people of Judah for seven and a half years (verses 1-3, 11). Somehow, ever since the conquest, the 12 tribes had always divided into two factions: Judah and Benjamin in the south, the others in the north.

David's difficult and persistent problem involved the tribes who were still loyal to Saul's family, especially that of Benjamin, which, interestingly, was in the south.[4] They continued to recognize the family line of Saul as king. Not surprisingly, at the same time some who had previously been riding on Saul's shirttails now sought to make their move. "Abner son of Ner, the commander of Saul's army, had taken Ish-bosheth son of Saul and brought him over to Mahanaim. He made him king over Gilead, Ashuri and Jezreel, and also over Ephraim, Benjamin and all Israel. Ish-bosheth son of Saul was forty years old when he became king over Israel, and he reigned two years. The house of Judah, however, followed David" (verses 8-10, NIV). Although God had given the kingdom to David, he would have to wrest it from the old aristocracy.

It was one of those "hurry up and wait" kind of moments in which David was "all dressed up with no place to go."[5] Right then he had to be content with ruling only Judah. But he didn't complain or become anxious. Still, although he waited on the Lord's leading, he didn't sit idly. Intentionally wooing supporters of the house of Saul, he reached out through diplomacy. David had heard about the brave actions of the Jabesh-gileadites who had buried Saul and his three slain sons (2 Sam. 2:4; 1 Sam. 31:11-13). Their respect for the slain king (cf. 1 Sam. 11:1-11) impressed David, and he sent messengers to the men of Jabesh-gilead expressing his appreciation for their kindness to Saul and pledging his favor to them: "May the Lord bless you for being so loyal to your king and giving him a decent burial. May the Lord be loyal to you in return and reward you with his unfailing love! And I, too, will reward you for what you have done. And now that Saul is dead, I ask you to be my strong and loyal subjects like the people of Judah, who have anointed me as their new king" (2 Sam. 2:5-7, NLT).

Field of the Swords

Since Ish-bosheth considered himself ruler not only of Gilead but all Israel (cf. verse 9), he doubtless would have regarded David's gesture to Jabesh-gilead as an open challenge.[6] But Ish-bosheth wasn't a strong leader. So Abner, the consummate opportunist,[7] and in reality the de facto leader of the north,[8] responded to David's overture to the people of Jabesh-gilead (verses 4-7).[9] He ventured south close to the borders of David's domain in Judah. Joab, however, was not about to let Abner get too close, and marched out to intercept him beyond the borders of David's territory.

And so they stared at each other across the pool. It was unthinkable that their armies would really fight. After all, they were Hebrews—brothers. This was a family matter.[10] But deep tension still existed between the two leaders. While each came with an entourage of supporters, the drama was in their more personal rivalry.[11] Failure to fight would mean loss of face for either one of them. Someone had to gain the upper hand. As they stared each other down, their followers wondered who would blink first.

Abner finally took the initiative. "Let's have a few of our warriors put on an exhibition of hand-to-hand combat," he suggested (see verse 14). Let's settle it with a little sport (he uses the Hebrew word קא׳ שֲׂצָק, which means to make sport, play, or entertain).[12] While it sounded innocent, to refuse the challenge would appear an act of cowardice.[13]

When Joab agreed, they each put forward a team of 12 men to engage in a contest of arms.[14] At a signal the two teams went at it, but instead of playing a game in which one wins and the other loses, the encounter somehow got out of hand, and they all killed each other. The contest ended almost as quickly as it had begun, with no winners. Only losers—all 24 dead. "Each one grabbed his opponent by the hair and thrust his sword into the other's side so that all of them died" (verse 16, NLT). While it was supposed to be a contest at which everyone except the participants was to be a spectator, the two watching armies—echoing modern-day fan violence—poured out of the stands onto the field into an orgy of pursuit and murder (verses 16, 17). The little sporting event at the pool of Gibeon got out of hand, setting off a fierce and bloody battle between the north and south, Israel and Judah. By the end of the day the body count was Israel 360 and Judah 20 (verses 30, 31). "Abner and the men of Israel were defeated by David's men" (verse 17, NIV). What started out as a game had turned into a free-for-all riot that ended in a massacre. So the place in Gibeon acquired the name Helkath Hazzurim—Field of the Swords (verse 16).

The most notable loss of the day was Joab's youngest brother, Asahel. The biblical author considered the death significant enough to count it as a separate casualty because of the man's prominence as a mighty warrior and whom he was related to. David had a sister named Zeruiah. She had three noted warrior sons—Joab, Abishai, and Asahel (verse 18). Each thirsted for the glory of military victory.[15]

When it became clear that his men were getting the worst of it, Abner retreated. Asahel, the youngest of Zeruiah's trio of firebrands, saw an opportunity. Determined to have the glory of slaying the leader of the opposing army, he chased the battle-hardened leader of the northern forces. Intoxicated with the prospect of instant fame, he pursued Abner with either no weapons or armaments clearly unequal to Abner's (verse 21). Nor did he stop to consider that he was much less experienced than the northern general. As they ran, Abner shouted back twice to warn Asahel to stop. He tried to talk him out of the pursuit, reminding him of the consequences (verses 20-22). But Asahel would not give up. Compelled at last to defend himself, Abner suddenly stopped and thrust the butt (the blunt, nonaggressive end) of his spear into Asahel's stomach. Though Abner probably intended only to knock the wind out of his opponent, Asahel's charge was so energetic and the general's thrust so powerful that "the spear came out through his back" (verse 23, NIV).[16] Asahel died on the spot. The gruesome sight of one of David's most honored soldiers slain in such a freakish manner caused every man to stop when he came to the place where Asahel had fallen.

"When Joab and Abishai found out what had happened, they set out after Abner. The sun was just going down as they arrived at the hill of Ammah near Giah, along the road to the wilderness of Gibeon. Abner's troops from the tribe of Benjamin regrouped there at the top of the hill to take a stand. Abner shouted down to Joab, 'Must we always solve our differences with swords? Don't you realize the only thing we will gain is bitterness toward each other? When will you call off your men from chasing their Israelite brothers?' Then Joab said, 'God only knows what would have happened if you hadn't spoken, for we would have chased you all night if necessary.' So Joab blew his trumpet, and his men stopped chasing the troops of Israel" (verses 24-28, NLT).

Not only had Abner killed Asahel in self-defense; he had even given him all kinds of opportunity to back off. But the incident had set the stage for bitter revenge. Forever remembering it, Joab would seek from then on to avenge his younger brother's death. In due time he did just that. The next chapter tells how Joab murdered Abner (2 Sam. 3:22-30) in cold blood. It happened when the northern leader let his guard down (verse 27), partly because of the peace agreement he had just negotiated between the leaders of Israel and David arranging for the peaceful transfer of power (verses 6-21) and partly because he was in a city of refuge (cf. Joshua 20:7; 21:13), in which biblical law strictly prohibited vengeful violence without due process of law (cf. Num. 35:24, 25). Joab had called the unsuspecting Abner back to Hebron. When he arrived, David's general took him aside as if to speak with him privately. But then he drew his dagger and killed Abner in revenge for killing his brother (2 Sam. 3:27). His behavior was not only unwarranted, but a flagrant violation of divine law.[17] Abner had acted with honor and deserved better. Joab, on the other hand, was a vengeful and murderous individual.

One more grisly scene rounds out this transition period in Israel's checkered history. Abner's death caused panic in Saul's camp. As the news of his death spread, two opportunists (Baanah and Recab) decided to desert to the victor's camp. The time was ripe to assassinate Ish-bosheth. They stabbed Israel's king while he slept, then cut his head off and carried the grisly proof of their deed to David in Hebron, expecting a reward (2 Sam. 4:1-12).

We read all this and think, *Such fighting and killing is senseless. Violence is a stupid way to solve problems and settle differences.* The pacifist in us would like to skip the bloody details of Israel's civil war. But the Bible student in us knows we shouldn't. Old regimes rarely crumble without bloodshed. Israel often wrote its history in blood. The civil war lasted a long time, but "David grew stronger and stronger, while the house of Saul grew weaker and weaker" (2 Sam. 3:1, NIV). We see a fact sadly reflective of human life. In the midst of every situation we will find those obsessed with trying to use it to establish their own power. They have little or no sense of God and His providential presence and care nothing about truth and honor.

They're Wearing Me Out

David's throne hung in moral balance as everyone watched him, waiting to see what he would do. *How much is he involved in all the sordid activities? they wonder. Did he order Abner's death or have Ish-bosheth assassinated? How will he treat Joab, who had served him so faithfully but had acted criminally? What about Baanah and Recab? How will he exercise his authority? Now that he no longer has to run to the Lord for refuge, does he see any need for God at all?*[18] *Will his new kingdom be any different, or will it be just a continuation of the usual power and politics?*

David himself gave the most significant insight to understand the fine line he was dancing during these pivotal and tragic events. After weeping over Abner's tomb and singing a lament in his honor—"Should Abner have died as the lawless die? Your hands were not bound; your feet were not fettered. You fell as one falls before wicked men" (verses 33, 34, NIV)—David vocalized his feelings about all that had taken place. "Do you not realize that a prince and a great man has fallen this day in Israel? And I *am* weak today, though anointed king; and these men, the sons of Zeruiah, *are* too harsh for me. The Lord shall repay the evildoer according to his wickedness" (verses 38, 39, NKJV). The New Living Translation puts it: "Even though I am the anointed king, these two sons of Zeruiah—Joab and Abishai—are too strong for me to control. So may the Lord repay these wicked men for their wicked deeds."

"They're wearing me out. I know that I'm God's anointed, that He has preserved me against formidable odds—Goliath and Saul, Philistine wars and wilderness dangers. Because of Him I can lead His people into lives of worship and love and obedience, but they are wearing me out. Their vendettas, their plots, their jealousies, their anger, their violence . . . they're wearing me out." David thus contrasted his weakness with their strength; his gentleness with their brutality; and his way (and God's) with theirs.

The two sons of Zeruiah were terrific fighting men and fiercely loyal to David's political interests. But Joab and Abishai comprehended nothing of their leader's true spirit. They couldn't emotionally, psychologically, or spiritually connect with peace and the things that had to do with peace. Instead, they sought only mastery and influence and power.[19] Constantly they sabotaged his attempts at justice and peace and love.

Thus David found himself confronted with two moral issues as he danced the fine line between God's way and the human way of doing things. First, what kind of spirit would permeate his life? What would be the nature of his leadership? What kind of strength would he use? How would he exercise authority?

Second, David realized that he had no control over what others did, whether it was Abner, Baanah and Recab, or especially his nephews Joab and Abishai. He recognized that there are moments in life in which we can control only ourselves, not others. But that, nevertheless, was important enough—controlling one's self. We must learn to master our responses and motives, our way of doing things. What kind of self-control, then, would he possess? How could he keep moral/spiritual distance from what others were doing? And how would he respond to the unmanageable actions of others?

In the opening chapters of 2 Samuel we find David's reaction to Saul's death, Abner's death, and then Ish-bosheth's death (2 Sam. 1-4). He mourned Saul and affirmed and praised the men of Jabesh-gilead for bravely honoring the former king and his family. Next he denounced and distanced himself from the behavior of Joab and Abishai. And finally he executed Baanah and Recab (having their hands and feet cut off and their bodies hung beside the pool of Hebron as a public humiliation and horror at such treachery). In the process he made a deliberate decision to create a kingdom with a completely different kind of government—one of high morals and ethics. David determined to be different.

"I am weak today, though anointed king," he declares (2 Sam. 3:39, NKJV). The passage contains allusions that we can easily overlook. In his overtures to the men of Jabesh-gilead David chose to be like God: "May the Lord now show you kindness and faithfulness," he says, "and I too will show you the same favor because you have done this" (2 Sam. 2:6, NIV). Their burial of Saul was an act of loving loyalty. In return David assured them of the Lord's kindness and faithfulness as well as his own. He intentionally selected terms taken from God's own self-description in the Torah.[20] Remember the time Moses wanted to see the divine glory? God passed in front of him, proclaiming, "The Lord, the Lord, the compassionate and gracious God, slow to anger, abounding in love and faithfulness" (Ex. 34:6, NIV). "You want to see me, Moses? This is who I am and what I am like." God says He abounds in love and is full of faithfulness, two important Hebrew terms for God: צֶסֶד (qesed), meaning kindness, lovingkindness, mercy; and וֶאֱמֶת (תֱמֶ), meaning firmness, truth. I will be that way to you, David vowed. I will show you the same favor of boundless love and faithfulness.

When Abner decided to switch his loyalty to David and take the lead in bringing the northern tribes with him, the king didn't hesitate to enact a covenant with him (2 Sam. 3:12-16). "Let's make an agreement," Abner offered, "and I will help turn the entire nation of Israel over to you" (verse 12, NLT). "Let's do it," David agreed. And so he negotiated in good faith that years of rivalry would be laid aside in the interest of peace. David hosted a covenant-making meal on behalf of Abner and his men. And he sent them on their way in peace (verses 21, 23). The Hebrew term used here is *shalom*—covenant peace. It occurs three times for emphasis (verses 21, 22, 23).

David wanted and chose lovingkindness, faithfulness, mercy, peace, and covenant. He was willing to negotiate and work at things relationally. But the sons of Zeruiah were wearing him out as they constantly made life difficult for him. Their interference destroyed what he attempted to build. They cared nothing about relationships or building bridges.[21] We can only imagine how emotionally draining it was.

"I am weak today, though anointed king. I cannot control the sons of Zeruiah. They are too much for me and wear me out." He was not able at that point to force them into line. But he could disassociate himself from them and model a totally different kind of spirit.

Rather than overlook the actions of his close relative and commanding general, David denounced and distanced himself from Joab and placed a curse on him and anyone who participated in the crime—"I vow by the Lord that I and my people are innocent of this crime against Abner. Joab and his family are the guilty ones. May his family in every generation be cursed with a man who has open sores or leprosy or who walks on crutches or who dies by the sword or who begs for food! . . . May the Lord repay these wicked men for their wicked deeds" (verses 28-39, NLT). On his deathbed the king would later cite Abner's murder as one of two reasons for ordering his general's execution: "You know that Joab son of Zeruiah murdered my two army commanders, Abner son of Ner and Amasa son of Jether. He pretended that it was an act of war, but it was done in a time of peace, staining his belt and sandals with the blood of war. Do with him what you think best, but don't let him die in peace" (1 Kings 2:5, 6, NLT).

David did three things about Abner's death: He rebuked Joab (2 Sam. 3:28, 29), honored Abner (verses 31-34), and publicly mourned him, making Joab and the whole army join him in grief (verse 35). David's actions did not go unnoticed: "This pleased the people very much. In fact, everything the king did pleased them! So everyone in Judah and Israel knew that David was not responsible for Abner's death" (verses 36, 37,

NLT). "The people notice that David is still the passionate, caring man they have known him to be. They notice David has not turned into a cynical despot, incapable of caring. They notice he has not completely capitulated to Joab, whom they perhaps fear and resent. They notice that there continues to be a human quality about David's governance that permits them to believe David is the vehicle of Yahweh's will."[22]

As David realized that he couldn't control everyone around him, he chose to mirror his thinking and ways after God. He would be different no matter what others around him were like, thus demonstrating a better way, and in the process he won the hearts of the people.

God's work can't be done other than in His way. It meant that David couldn't work through exploitation and violence or raw power and politics. As he danced his way through the moral and spiritual issues of these pivotal transitional moments, his passion for God would be his only compass. It was uncharted territory.

Peterson observes that "we find God's purposes being worked out in the precise moral and political, social and cultural conditions that we wake up to each morning, a world of shabby morality and opportunist companions, religious violence, religious propaganda—the many, many sons of Zeruiah that are too hard for us."[23] Such people want mastery, influence, and power—and nothing to do with peace and worship and the pursuit of holiness. Daily they threaten to pull the world around us down as they jockey for position.

But how will we be? What kind of spirit will permeate our life and what kind of strength will we use? How will we exercise authority? What kind of self-control will we possess? How will we distance ourselves from those who choose ways we cannot support? How will we respond to the unmanageable actions of others?

Watching David dance through these kinds of issues can help us keep our moral/spiritual bearings when any other choice would erode our passion for God.

---

[1] Gibeon was six to eight miles north-northeast of Jerusalem. Its location suggests that the city had considerable strategic importance in the struggle that emerged between David and Ish-bosheth. See P. Kyle McCarter, Jr., *II Samuel, Anchor Bible* (Garden City, N.Y.: Doubleday and Co., Inc. 1984), p. 95.

[2] Robert D. Bergen, *1, 2 Samuel* (Nashville: Broadman and Holman Publishers, 1996), p. 302.

[3]J. P. Fokkelman, *Narrative Art and Poetry in the Books of Samuel, Vol. III: Throne and City (II Sam. 2-8 and 21-24)* (Assen/Maastricht, Netherlands: Van Gorcum, 1990), p. 47.

[4]See K. Kaynor, *When God Chooses,* pp. 149-152; and Walter Brueggemann, *First and Second Samuel* (Louisville: John Knox Press, 1990), p. 220.

[5]Kaynor, pp. 145, 163.

[6]See McCarter, p. 94.

[7]As Abner establishes his king-maker role in Israel by reducing the ineffectual Ish-bosheth to a puppet figurehead, he gradually realizes that the future is with David and works out diplomatic ways of turning over the northern tribes (Israel) to David so that he can be assured a leading place in the new government. See Eugene H. Peterson, *Leap Over a Wall: Earthly Spirituality for Everyday Christians* (San Francisco: HarperSanFrancisco, 1997), p 126.

[8]Brueggemann, p. 221.

[9]The material between this passage (2 Sam. 2:12-32) and the account of David's overture to the people of Jabesh-gilead (verses 4-7) provides circumstantial information necessary to the main narrative thread, which resumes here in verse 12. See McCarter, p. 94.

[10]Their conflict was fundamentally between two families vying for undisputed control over one nation, not two nations at war with each other. The struggle between the "house of David" and the "house of Saul" was a family affair with relatives leading on both sides. See Alden Thompson, *Samuel: From The Danger of Chaos to the Danger of Power* (Boise, Idaho: Pacific Press Pub. Assn., 1995), p. 192.

[11]Brueggemann, p. 221.

[12]McCarter, p. 96.

[13]*Ibid.,* p. 222.

[14]Fokkelman notes: "And what a number! Twelve for both sides—does this mean that both sides are laying claim to the twelve tribes of Israel in its entirety? Something hair-raising clings to the use of the sacred number in an arena about to run red with blood" (p. 44).

[15]Zeruiah must have been a remarkable woman. Not only did she put iron into the lives of her sons, but to be mentioned in Scripture was rare for a woman, yet the Bible refers to her several times.

[16]Bergen, p. 304.

[17]*Ibid.,* p. 312.

[18]Peterson, p. 125.

[19]*Ibid.,* p. 130.

[20]Bergen, p. 298, note 5.

[21]Peterson, p. 128.

[22]Brueggemann, p. 231.

[23]Peterson, p. 130.

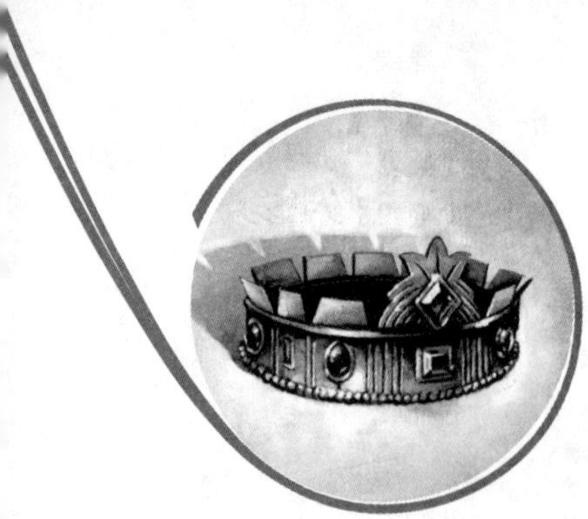

2

WHEN EVEN THE BLIND AND LAME INTIMIDATE YOU

2 Samuel 5

Jerusalem has been a prize fought over for centuries. A city imbued with the blood of ages, steeped in symbol and myth, it is sacred to Jew, Christian, and Muslim alike. While it is a place on the map like any other city, it exists more vividly, more powerfully, more *dangerously*, within the longitude and latitude of the mind.[1] Jerusalem is built with the bricks of the religious imagination. Whoever controls it will always find themselves constrained by the meaning the city has acquired during three millennia of wars, conquests, sacred happenings, and prophetic utterance.

For politicians seeking peace in the Middle East, Jerusalem is the insoluble riddle that keeps bringing the whole process crashing down.[2] When Prime Minister Ehud Barak and Palestinian leader Yasir Arafat joined President Bill Clinton at Camp David in summit talks focused on finalizing Israeli and Palestinian peace agreements during July of 2000, Jerusalem became the unsolvable problem. Barak promised his people that "Yerushalayim" would remain the "eternal and undivided" capital of Israel. Arafat demanded that the capital of the Palestinian state be located there too. The United Nations, supported by the Vatican, would have the city internationalized and under its jurisdiction. One thing is certain—there can be no enduring solution to the question of Jerusalem that does not respect the emotional attachment to the city formed by each faith.[3]

Even in David's day the city of Jerusalem was a longstanding thorn in Israel's side. Lying on the border between Judah and Benjamin, it was an enemy stronghold that no one had yet been able to conquer. Since the Israelites first arrived in the Promised Land, Jerusalem had divided Judah in the south from the other tribes in the north. The city overlooked the main inland route from north to south. With the Philistines in possession of the coastal plain, the inland route provided the only alternative for trade among the tribes.

The Jebusites, a banned Canaanite group that God had expressly told His people not to make a covenant with or to show mercy to (cf. Ex. 23:23; 33:2; 34:11; Deut. 7:1, 2; 20:17), occupied the city. Previous generations had tried to take the city and failed miserably. The book of Joshua tells us that "Judah could not dislodge the Jebusites, who were living in Jerusalem" (Joshua 15:63, NIV). Later, Judges reports that the Benjamites likewise "failed to dislodge the Jebusites, who were living in Jerusalem" (Judges 1:21, NIV). Both passages end with the unthinkable comment that "to this day the Jebusites live there" (NIV). Still there living right along side the people of Judah and Benjamin. By the time of David the Israelites had been in the Promised Land for nearly 400 years. Why had they not conquered Jerusalem?

The fact of the matter was that the city was so well fortified that "nobody bothered the Jebusites. They lived unvisited and unattacked for centuries. Philistines, Amalekites, and Hebrews waged war with one another in battle after battle, up and down the countryside, back and forth, but the Jebusites were exempt from it all. . . . Ironically, the Jebusite walled city was named Jerusalem, 'City of Peace.' And in fact the Jebusites lived quite peaceably. . . . Nobody bothered the Jebusites. Nobody, that is, until David decided to make it his capital city."[4]

Credible opposition to David's claim to kingship over all Israel died with Abner and Ish-bosheth. Making David king over all Israel thus became the northern tribes's only rational alternative. So a major portion of the combined tribes went down to Hebron to ask David to become their king (1 Chron. 12:23-40).[5] "We are all members of your family," they said. "For a long time, even while Saul was our king, you were the one who really led Israel. And the Lord has told you, 'You will be the shepherd of my people Israel. You will be their leader'" (2 Sam. 5:1, NLT). So at

Hebron David made a covenant with the leaders of Israel before the Lord. And they anointed him king of Israel (verse 3). What an exciting day. It was a sacred as well as a political moment when the people of God tell David, in effect, "Be our prince: don't change into a power-hungry king who imposes his will on the people. Be our shepherd: don't change into an ego-driven king who uses the people as food for his self-importance. Be our prince; be our shepherd."[6] That is, be the shepherd ruler God called you to be. God chose David not in spite of the fact that he was a common shepherd, but because he *was* a shepherd. We began David's passion trilogy with him as a shepherd boy. Now we see a shepherd king. He was the same shepherd, but with different sheep—God's sheep. "You will shepherd my people Israel, and you will become their ruler" (verse 2, NIV).

The now-united nation celebrated. "They feasted and drank with David for three days. . . . People from as far away as Issachar, Zebulun, and Naphtali brought food on donkeys, camels, mules, and oxen. Vast supplies of flour, fig cakes, raisins, wine, olive oil, cattle, and sheep were brought to the celebration. There was great joy throughout the land of Israel" (1 Chron. 12:39, 40, NLT).

Once the coronation festivities were over, David got on with the business of leading. Wanting to channel the energy and enthusiasm of his new subjects, he proposed a site for the nation's new capital that would capture the affection of the masses and serve as the center for its visionaries.[7] No one had ever expected that he would choose Jerusalem. After all, it was an embarrassing symbol of defeat. Nobody had seen Jerusalem as a strategic site for Israel. Nor did anyone dare to think of it in that way. But David did. He wanted to make it the center of his new kingdom. The city was a perfect location, sitting on a mountain spine connecting the northern tribes of Israel with the southern tribe of Judah and unclaimed by either. Since it belonged to none of Israel's tribes, all the tribes could have a part in acquiring it.[8] And after nearly four centuries of inability to conquer Jerusalem, victory here would be sweet. Taking Jerusalem would inflame Israel's religious imagination, setting a tone of obedience to the Lord and the desire to experience victory through God for years to come.[9]

David had staked his claim to Jerusalem years earlier when he carried Goliath's severed head there and threw it over the wall (1 Sam. 17:54).[10] Now he would follow through with his long-held dream. As his first agenda item, he would lead his people in an incredible experience of victory and faith (2 Sam. 5:6). David had a faith-based optimism—a give-me-this-mountain attitude. It would begin a dance that would prove contagious.

Taking Jerusalem would be no picnic. The new king faced some daunting geographical obstacles. The relatively small walled city perched atop the southern ridge of a steep, finger-shaped hill. Valleys surrounded it on three sides. Because of its protection by both natural and human-made defenses, the Jebusite soldiers mocked David's forces as they approached the massive city walls. "You'll never get in here," they taunted. "Even the blind and lame could keep you out!" (2 Sam. 5:6, NLT). Evidently they had held the fortress for so long and were so confident of its impregnable walls that in derision they placed a number of disabled and blind persons along the walls, boasting that even they would be strong enough to keep David and his whole army at bay.[11] Even blind and physically challenged guards could protect their city against the motley crew of soldiers David had brought.[12] The Jebusites really thought they were safe.

By the way, this reference to "the lame and blind" occurs three times in the unfolding story (2 Sam. 5:6, 8). We find David picking up on the imagery when he tells his troops, "Go up through the water tunnel into the city and destroy those 'lame' and 'blind' Jebusites. How I hate them" (verse 8, NLT). In insulting David, the Jebusites had implicitly compared themselves to "the blind and lame." David now turns their own metaphor back on them—as if to say, "you are all blind and lame and so are the gods you think will save you."[13] While it is certainly politically incorrect language by today's standards, David wasn't expressing generic prejudice against the physically challenged.[14]

Scripture tells us that David's men used the city's water shaft to infiltrate Jerusalem.[15] A narrow vertical shaft 40 feet long connected to a horizontal tunnel provided the residents of the fortress access to waters from the Gihon spring during times of siege. Since Jerusalem was located just eight miles north of David's hometown of Bethlehem, he had, undoubtedly, walked its streets as a boy and was familiar with the city. He certainly knew about the water shaft and may have even climbed it. It would be just the kind of thing a daring kid would do. Now as a military strategist, he knew that, though difficult to scale, the water shaft would prove to be the Achilles' heel of the Jebusite fortress. I can imagine Joab leading a commando raid up through that vertical rock shaft, perhaps at night when the city was asleep. The first man may have inched himself up by exerting pressure against the shaft walls with his hands and back and feet, then dropped a rope down for his buddies.

However it happened, "the conquest which had baffled the Israelites through their whole history became amazingly easy when David was king."[16] It's incredible when you stop to think about it—quick victory over an enemy that had been there a long, long time. Jerusalem had taunted David, seeking to prove his weakness by placing its weakest on the walls. Then suddenly they were vanquished. Why? How?

We find here a rich lesson of spiritual truth for us to ponder. As Epp writes: "There are habits of sin so deeply entrenched in our minds and bodies that we have struggled in vain against them from the day of our new birth. We may have felt it was no use to try to overcome these habits and that we might as well give up. . . . Just as the stronghold of the Jebusites which is typical of the power of sin in our lives, was overthrown; so will the power of sin in our life be broken and every area of it made to be under the control of our Lord and King."[17]

Can you think of an entrenched sin in your life that has been there for as long as you can remember? Some weakness that just doesn't go away? Because of it you don't feel quite right about your experience with God or the genuineness of your faith. It's like the "blind" and the "lame," the weakest of the weak, harassing you with your own weakness and failure. Whatever the thing might be, it claims to be stronger than you—in effect, stronger than your God.

Jerusalem under Jebusite control points to any stronghold of sin that has defied our very best efforts. It symbolizes that citadel of weakness that has caused us many a heartache and tear. That lingering failure or dysfunction or habit that leaves us with remorse and frustration. Sometimes it causes us to give up the fight altogether and just live in a kind of status quo equilibrium with the enemy.

In his Biblical Concepts in Counseling program, John Regier identifies 10 key areas Satan uses to defeat believers and wreak havoc within interpersonal relationships, including marriages: bitterness, rebellion, pride, immorality, temporal values, generational sins, sinful habits, occult activities, hypocrisy, and negative thought patterns. Regier suggests that we especially need to understand three areas in order to resolve personal or marital problems: (1) generational problems—family issues inherited from our parents; (2) strongholds—areas of continual struggle in which Satan has bound us and we cannot get free, aspects of life in which we experience frequent temptation and never seem to get victory; and (3) blind spots—things that we do not see, problems we don't know we have. Resolving strongholds is important, since they not only affect us but also our spouses and children. They have the ability to destroy relationships in the home. Working them out through prayer and Scripture leads to personal freedom.[18]

The sudden conquest of Jerusalem points to bold faith and the experience of victory that God seeks to bestow upon each of us. He wants to help us develop a give-me-this-mountain attitude in which we would live large for Him. Jerusalem was the place that God chose to make His name known. It would become the central place of worship for His people, the site of Solomon's great Temple. The Lord wants us to worship Him in the very place where the enemy once boasted his power against us. As I've said, Jerusalem is built with the bricks of the religious imagination. While it is a place on the map like any other city, it exists more vividly, more powerfully, more dangerously within the longitude and latitude of the mind.[19]

The Longer Stride

As it wraps up the story of the capture of Jerusalem, Scripture tells us that David "became more and more powerful" (2 Sam. 5:10, NLT). Eugene Peterson suggests that he proceeded from that moment of sweet victory with "a longer stride."[20] I like that. The Hebrew phrase uses the word כאלֹה (to walk, go, proceed) twice. The point is that David himself is in action.[21] He is changing, growing—dancing. As a result he is no longer the same. Nor are his people.

As Kaynor writes: "In establishing his capital at Jerusalem, David was not moving far from where he grew up. Bethlehem was only eight miles from Jerusalem—but what a change had come about in him! David did not move far geographically, but he had traveled a long distance politically and spiritually. He was more experienced, wise, obedient, faithful and ready to lead than when he had lived in Bethlehem."[22] Choosing to claim Jerusalem for God was an undeniable step toward that growth. These were the best years of David's life—years of dancing like a king. Before the horrible years of family crisis and personal moral failure, Israel enjoyed 13 years of excellence in leadership.[23]

Some suggest that we owe Psalm 101 to this period in David's life.[24]

> "I will sing of your love and justice.
> I will praise you, Lord, with songs.
> I will be careful to live a blameless life—
> when will you come to my aid?
> I will lead a life of integrity in my own home.
> I will refuse to look at anything vile and vulgar.
> I hate all crooked dealings;
> I will have nothing to do with them.
> I will reject perverse ideas
> and stay away from every evil.
> I will not tolerate people who slander their neighbors.
> I will not endure conceit and pride.
> I will keep a protective eye on the godly,
> so they may dwell with me in safety.
> Only those who are above reproach will be allowed to serve me.
> I will not allow deceivers to serve me,
> and liars will not be allowed to enter my presence.
> My daily task will be to ferret out criminals
> and free the city of the Lord from their grip"
> (Ps. 101:1-8, NLT).

David found himself suddenly called to administer a great nation that had been born, so to speak, in a day. The new needs demanded new expression as departments of law and justice, of finance, and of military organization rapidly came into existence and became localized at David's new capital.

I love 2 Samuel 5:12, in which we learn that after he "captured the fortress of Zion, the City of David" (verse 7, NIV), "David knew that the Lord had established him as king over Israel and had exalted his kingdom for the sake of his people Israel" (NIV). Many things must have confused David through his shepherd and fugitive years. There were so many things he did not know. Why had God chosen him? Why did Saul turn on him? Why did Jonathan have to die? When would God ever fulfill His promises of the kingdom? Why did he have to deal with the likes of Joab and Abishai and Israel experience the painful, bloody years of civil war?[25]

David had not known whether he would ever live to be king. But when God handed over the most fortified city in all Israel to him and placed favor in the heart of the king of Tyre to send him cedar logs and carpenters and stonemasons to build him a palace, David realized that the Lord had established him! No one can help dancing in such moments.

You too may be going through a confusing time—some fugitive years during which your faith is on the run. Perhaps you may not know how God is going to use a situation in your life or why certain things happen to you. But even in the midst of uncertainties you can be encouraged and strengthened by recalling what you already know about God. Perhaps you may never know in the present life the why or how, but you can always know who is faithful. And when you choose to be faithful in return, God can turn defeats into victory and establish you as well. Thus whenever through faith we overtake the strongholds of sin that have defied our very best efforts, that citadel of weakness that has caused us many a heartache and tear will then collapse. That lingering failure or dysfunction or habit that leaves us with many a feeling of remorse and frustration will be conquered. Then and then alone will we know for certain that God is establishing us. Ours will be a longer stride, and we'll dance like a king.

The Lord Did It!

But it was not over yet. The Philistines did not take the news of a united Israel lightly. Learning that Israel had anointed David as its king, they mobilized their forces to capture him (2 Sam. 5:17). When David had been a man on the run, the Philistines had been a temporary refuge. They had taken advantage of his homeless estate by using his strength. During the seven and a half years that David had been king of only Judah, he hadn't been much of a threat. Now their perception of him changed dramatically. In their opinion, if they did not deal with the Judaean newcomer immediately, it might never be possible to bring him to heel again.

Interestingly, Scripture tells us that it was the anointing of David as Israel's new king that set the Philistines off—not the capture of Jerusalem. The biblical writer, though, purposely places the capture of Jerusalem (verses 6-12) between the record of David's anointing (verses 1-3) and the story of the Philistine invasion (verses 17-25). His purpose, I believe, was to convey the idea that the capture of Jerusalem and the Philistines' advance took place at approximately the same time.[26] At least not a lot of time occurred between the two events. No sooner had David captured Jerusalem than he found himself faced with Philistine troops fanning out across the Valley of Rephaim (verse 18). The Valley of Rephaim is a steep-walled canyon less than a mile southwest of Jerusalem running in a southwesterly direction toward Kiriath-jearim and Beth-shemesh. In other words, the Philistines were practically under the walls of Jerusalem! Mark that point very carefully. "They spread themselves around a focal point where, for many decades, they had been occupants. . . . They had defied all the attempts of the people of God to throw them out since Joshua first conquered the land. But once they had been thrown out, they immediately tried to recapture the stronghold."[27] They wanted to overwhelm this new overcomer.

Capturing Jerusalem had been an offensive measure. Now suddenly David was on the defensive. The lesson is clear. Whenever we've made a significant victory in our life, taking longer strides in faith, growing spiritually and living in ways that honor God completely—then the powers of darkness will usually respond with a massive counterattack of some kind.[28] As long as we are satisfied with little things and just ruling over a portion of what God promises us (only Judah, just one twelfth), the devil will likely leave us alone. But when we start to grow and live large for God, then he fears our power and what we might soon become with God's blessings. At that point he rises up aggressively to meet it. Satan counterattacks pointedly and persistently.[29] Two battles took place in the Valley of Rephaim (verses 17, 18, 22). Both times David went to his knees (verses 19, 23).

"'The Lord has done it!' David exclaimed. 'He burst through my enemies like a raging flood!' So David named the place Baal-perazim (which means 'the Lord who bursts through')" (verse 20, NLT). The imagery is one of pent-up water bursting through a dam, or more likely, a flash flood. The Lord "burst through" with power.

David's forces pounded the Philistines so hard in the first battle that the invaders left their idols behind as they hurriedly retreated (verses 17-21). I find the record of this first defeat humorous and instructive. "They abandoned their idols there, so David and his men carried them away" (verse 21, NASB). The Chronicles record of the incident tells us that the Philistines "abandoned their gods there; so David gave the order and they were burned with fire" (1 Chron. 14:12, NASB). In reality, the powers of darkness are no match for the living God.

When the Philistines gathered the second time in the Valley of Rephaim, David again beat them back, this time pushing and pounding their routed forces all the way from Gibeon to Gezer, a westward trek of more than 20 miles (2 Sam. 5:22-25). The episode has some incredible imagery and is filled with spiritual lessons. Once again David came to the Lord in prayer (verse 23). "What do I do, Lord? Do I attack them, as before?" "'Do not attack them straight on,' the Lord replied. 'Instead, circle around behind them and attack them near the balsam trees. When you hear a sound like marching feet in the tops of the balsam trees, attack! That will be the signal that the Lord is moving ahead of you to strike down the Philistines'" (verses 23, 24, NLT). And so David waited for the rustling wind in the trees, and when he attacked, it was an overwhelming victory.

Wind is an exciting phenomenon filled with mystery. Have you ever watched it stir the trees? How a single tree or a group of trees will begin swaying with the wind while other trees right beside them remain undisturbed? Then suddenly the trees that were initially swaying with the wind lapse into stillness while some of those previously untouched begin to move? I've watched the wind dance and swirl all around a given tree, never touching it at all, yet thoroughly animating every other tree around it. And I've seen just one tree swaying in the breeze while every other tree around it seemed perfectly still. Whenever I watch or feel wind blowing, I think of the Holy Spirit. Jesus Himself made the connection: "The wind blows wherever it pleases. You hear its sound, but you cannot tell where it comes from or where it is going. So it is with everyone born of the Spirit" (John 3:8,

NIV). As I see grass bending in the wind, water churning on a lake, clouds driven across the sky, or feel the breeze through my hair, I consciously invite God's Spirit to blow through me. I've done it so many times now that it's almost automatic. The stronger the breeze, the more I find myself yearning for this mighty power of God to work in my life. Its an existential moment during which my heart and mind reach once again for the invisible God. The blowing wind often stirs great spiritual passion within me.

David had to wait and listen for the wind of heavenly feet in the balsam treetops. The wind would show David that God Himself was marching in front of his men to smite the Philistines. By deferring his attack until the Lord had gone out in front of Israel, David was charting a course for the nation that differed fundamentally from the one the people had proposed during the days of Samuel. They wanted to be like the nations with a king who would lead them in battle against their enemies (1 Sam. 8:20). But under David's leadership the Lord would go out before the nation and fight their battles.[30]

For believers to realize that the God of the entire universe is guiding their life is vital. Those who wait and listen for God's approach can truly dance.

When the enemy came to attack, we find that David went right to his knees in prayer. But God's answer and God's deliverance are different on each occasion. If David had followed the same strategy he used in the first battle, he would have missed his divine resources and would have been humiliated by defeat. "Victory of yesterday does not put into me strength for today."[31] While the enemy and the location were the same, God's directives to David were different. So many times we find ourselves in situations similar to those in which we have been victorious before. Yet we still must seek and obey the Lord.[32]

We can never rout the enemy by ourselves. It must be done through the strength of Christ. The two incidents clearly show the only way we can achieve true victory in our lives. "For the Lord God of hosts was with him" (2 Sam. 5:10, NASB). "And David realized that the Lord had established him as king over Israel, and that He had exalted his kingdom for the sake of His people Israel" (verse 12, NASB). The Lord has done it!

David captured Jerusalem (the city of the boastful Jebusites) and conquered the Philistines (who mobilized against him). As he did so, he experienced the Lord, who bursts through any situation! He learned to wait for God's leading, and in the process he danced like a king. His story is a call for us to receive the presence and power of God to meet every challenge we might face. God wants us also to dance like a king.

Do you have Jebusites occupying Jerusalem? Have Philistine troops spread out right in front of your face? Are you experiencing a second surge of the enemy's powerful threats or temptation in your life?

No matter how deep a habit has become, the power of the blood of Jesus can penetrate even deeper. Those enslavements, which have baffled all our efforts and mocked all our struggles, bringing us shame and failure time and time again, can be broken by the power of Jesus Christ.

"Remember that the temptations that come into your life are no different from what others experience. And God is faithful. He will keep the temptation from becoming so strong that you can't stand up against it. When you are tempted, he will show you a way out so that you will not give in to it" (1 Cor 10:13, NLT). "I can do everything with the help of Christ who gives me the strength I need" (Phil. 4:13, NLT). "We are human, but we don't wage war with human plans and methods. We use God's mighty weapons, not mere worldly weapons, to knock down the Devil's strongholds" (2 Cor. 10:3, 4, NLT).

The promise is sure when we submit ourselves to Christ: "When the soul surrenders itself to Christ, a new power takes possession of the new heart. A change is wrought which man can never accomplish for himself. It is a supernatural work, bringing a supernatural element into human nature. The soul that is yielded to Christ becomes His own fortress, which He holds in a revolted world, and He intends that no authority shall be known in it but His own. A soul thus kept in possession by the heavenly agencies is impregnable to the assaults of Satan. . . . The only defense against evil is the indwelling of Christ in the heart through faith in His righteousness. Unless we become vitally connected with God, we can never resist the unhallowed effects of self-love, self-indulgence, and temptation to sin. We may leave off many bad habits, for the time we may part company with Satan; but without a vital connection with God, through the surrender of ourselves to Him moment by moment, we shall be overcome. Without a personal acquaintance with Christ, and a continual communion, we are at the mercy of the enemy, and shall do his bidding in the end."[33]

It's the only way to dance!

---

[1]Kenneth L. Woodward, "A City That Echoes Eternity," *Newsweek,* July 24, 2000, p. 28.

[2]Daniel Klaidman and Jeffery Bartholet, "The Real Jerusalem," *Newsweek,* July 24, 2000, pp. 18-25.

[3]Woodward, p. 28.

[4]E. H. Peterson, *Leap Over a Wall,* p. 132.

[5]K. Kaynor, *When God Chooses,* pp. 165, 170.

[6]*Ibid.,* p. 140. See also R. D. Bergen, *1, 2 Samuel,* p. 318; and W. Brueggemann, *First and Second Samuel,* pp. 237-239.

[7]Kaynor, p. 171.

[8]*Ibid.,* p. 172.

[9]The standard for evaluating a king's reign was his obedience to the Lord (1 Kings 15:3, 11, 26; 16:2, etc.). "By David making his first recorded act as Israel's king that of fulfilling the long-neglected Torah command to dispossess the Jebusites and of reinitiating the crusade to eradicate them from the land (cf. Ex. 23:23-24; Deut 7:1-2; 20:17), he was demonstrating his continuity with Moses and establishing himself as a king devoted to the Lord's demands (cf. Deut 17:19)" (Bergen, p. 320).

[10]See my chapter "How to Carry a Giant's Head," in L. Lichtenwalter, *David: A Heart Like His,* pp. 101-113.

[11]F. B. Meyer, *The Life of David* (Lynwood, Wash.: Emerald Books, 1995), p. 143.

[12]It is possible that this mocking back and forth about blind and lame grew out of David's reference to their gods as blind and lame. See Kaynor, p. 173.

[13]See Kaynor, p. 173.

[14]J. P. Fokkelman, *Narrative Art and Poetry in the Books of Samuel,* vol. 3, p. 162. See Bergen, p. 322. Not only did David provide Mephibosheth, the nation's most famous invalid, with the practical status of a prince in Jerusalem (2 Sam. 9:10, 13), but Jesus unapologetically spoke metaphorically of excluding the morally "blind and lame" (see Matt. 13:41, 42, 49, 50; Luke 13:24-29).

[15]The Hebrew text of this verse is filled with difficulties and permits several possible translations, which include "water shaft" (NIV), "grappling-iron" (NEB), "dagger" (LXX), "trident," "joint," "neck" and "windpipe." Of all the possibilities, the NIV's rendering is the most popular today (cf. NASB, NRSV, NKJV, NLT) and appears corroborated by archaeological evidence (see Bergen, p. 321).

[16]Alan Redpath, *The Making of a Man of God* (Westwood, N.J.: Fleming H. Revell Co., 1962), p. 148.

[17]Theodore H. Epp, *A Man After the Heart of God* (Good News Broadcasting Association, Inc., 1965), pp. 118, 119.

[18]John Regier, *Biblical Concepts Counseling Workbook: Identifying and Resolving Personal and Marital Problems Biblically* (Colorado Springs, Colo.: Biblical Concepts in Counseling, 1999).

[19]Woodward, p. 28.

[20]Peterson, p. 135.

[21]Fokkelman, p. 164.

[22]Kaynor, p. 180.

[23]*Ibid.,* p. 181.

[24]See Meyer, p. 144.

[25]Beth Moore, *A Heart Like His: Intimate Reflections on the Life of David* (Nashville: Broadman and Holman Publishers, 1999), p. 136.

[26]Fokkelman, p. 170. See also McCarter's opposing discussion (P. K. McCarter, *II Samuel,* pp. 157-160).

[27]Redpath, pp. 150, 151.

[28]*Ibid.,* p. 151.

[29] *Ibid.*

[30] Bergen, p. 327.

[31] Redpath, p. 152.

[32] Kaynor, pp. 177, 178.

[33] Ellen G. White, *The Desire of Ages* (Mountain View, Calif.: Pacific Press Pub. Assn., 1898), p. 324.

3

THE THREE, THE 30, AND A BOTTLE OF WATER

2 Samuel 23:8-23; I Chronicles 11:10-12:40

Pararescue jumpers (PJs) are members of a little-known elite Air Force/Air National Guard special forces unit that performs military and civilian rescues. Their mandate is to drop behind enemy lines during war and rescue downed pilots. They're the ones who got the F-117 pilot who was shot down outside Belgrade when NATO bombed Slobodan Milosŏević's Yugoslavia. When pilots go down at sea, PJs jump with scuba gear. If planes crash on glaciers, they parachute with crampons and ice axes. And if an aircraft disappears into the jungle, they jump with 200 feet of tree-rappelling line. There is literally nowhere on earth a PJ can't go.

During peacetime PJs keep their skills sharp by performing civilian rescues—recovering victims from treacherous mountaintops or raging seas. Every time the space shuttle launched, PJs went on alert in Florida and Africa, ready to perform any rescue that might be needed. Whenever a ship of any nationality finds itself in distress off North America, PJs can be called out. They are among the most physically fit and mentally tough men in the armed forces. It is arguably the toughest program in the military, in many ways more difficult than what the Navy SEALS or Army Special Ops go through. Their training essentially combines the separate specialty schools of the Green Berets, Army Rangers, SEALS, and other elite units. Most people learned of the PJs in Sebastian Junger's *The Perfect Storm*, with its riveting account of how a helicopter of PJs from a squadron on Long Island plunged into the Atlantic during a rescue of a Japanese sailor.

It takes 18 months of full-time training to become a PJ. The first three months of training weed candidates out through sheer raw abuse. The dropout rate is often more than 90 percent. In one drill the team swims their normal 4,000-yard workout, then the instructor tosses a whistle into the pool. Ten guys fight for it, and whoever manages to blow it at the surface gets to leave the pool. Again the instructor tosses the whistle in, and the nine remaining guys fight for it. It continues on until only one man remains, and he's kicked out of PJ school.

Survivors then enter a period known as "the pipeline," in which they learn how to parachute, climb mountains, survive in deserts, resist enemy interrogation, evade pursuit, and navigate underwater at night. The schools are ruthless in their quest to eliminate people. In dunker training, for example, candidates are strapped into a simulated helicopter and plunged underwater. If they manage to escape, they're dropped in again, this time upside down. Should they still manage to get out of the simulator, they repeat the experience a third time, not only upside down but blindfolded. Candidates who make it through the pipeline still have almost another year of paramedic training, mountain climbing, desert survival, tree landings, more scuba school, tactical maneuvers, and air operations. PJs learn to parachute into the ocean at night with inflatable speedboats. Also they drop into the ocean at night with scuba gear and go straight into a dive. Deploying from a submarine by air lock, they swim to a deserted coast. In the area of weapons, they train with shotguns, grenade launchers, M-16s, and six-barreled "mini guns" that can fire 6,000 rounds a minute and cut down trees.

Finally, once they've mastered every conceivable battle scenario, PJs learn something called HALO (high altitude low opening). They jump from so high up—as high as 40,000 feet—that they need bottled oxygen to breathe. Then they free-fall for two or three minutes and release their chutes at 1,000 feet or less. This keeps them from being an easy target when they parachute into combat areas. That way, they're almost impossible to kill.[1]

The best of the best, their training regimen and gripping accounts of rescues make fascinating reading. In an age seemingly devoid of heroes, these men are the real deal, a close-knit unit bound together by selflessness and sacrifice and the intense desire both to serve their country and to live life on the edge.

David's Mighty Men

David had his own elite special forces. Large numbers of armed warriors joined him when he became king at Hebron. Soldiers from all over Israel were eager to see him become king instead of Saul, just as the Lord had promised. "All these men came in battle array to Hebron with the single purpose of making David king of Israel" (1 Chron. 12: 38, NLT). You can read the roster (1 Chron. 11:10-47; 2 Sam. 23:8-39; 1 Chron. 12:1-38). In time there emerged in his army a group of about 30 individuals who became known as David's mighty men. Among them three especially stood out as the mightiest.[2] So there were the three, and the 30, David's elite—the best of the best.

First on the list was Josheb-basshebeth, the commander of David's elite three. In fact, Josheb was the greatest of all of David's warriors because on one occasion he used his spear to kill 800 enemy warriors singlehandedly (2 Sam. 23:8). The second most-honored warrior was Eleazar, the son of Dodai the Ahohite. He and David had been abandoned in the middle of a barley field when the entire Israelite army retreated during an intense battle with the Philistines at Pasdammin. In a remarkable show of courage and strength, Eleazar stood his ground with David. Intense and unrelenting, he stopped fighting only when he was too tired to lift his sword any more and muscle cramps literally froze his hand to his sword (verses 9, 10; 1 Chron. 11:12-14). Finally, there was Shammah. His retreating cohorts had also stranded him in the middle of a field. But like Eleazar, in a courageous one-man stand he held his ground and beat back the advancing Philistines (2 Sam. 23:11, 12).

Next came a list of David's renowned 30 mighty men (verses 18-39), warriors highly celebrated in Israel but not as renowned as the three. Scripture has singled out two for their extraordinary exploits and leadership. The first was Abishai (verses 18, 19), Joab's brother, Zeruiah's son, and David's nephew. Abishai's prestige resulted from his heroic exploits on the battlefield that gave him a reputation on a par with the three, though he never attained the status of becoming one of the three. But he was captain of the 30, and if, as some suggest, the three were a subgroup of the 30, he could have been captain of the three as well.[3] Probably Abishai was David's most ruthless aide.[4] He was the one, you remember, who wanted to impale the sleeping Saul with a single blow. And it was Abishai who saved David's life when a Philistine giant named Ishbi-benob came after the king, intending to kill him. Already weary from fighting, David found himself engaged in battle with the huge warrior. It was an unequal match in which David would likely have lost. But Abishai saw the situation and came at once to his leader's help (2 Sam. 21:15-17). Elsewhere Scripture credits Abishai with numerous daring and brilliant military activities.[5]

Benaiah, another much-renowned warrior, chased a lion down into a pit on a snowy day. Despite the snow and slippery ground, he caught the beast and killed it. On another occasion Benaiah found himself confronted by an impressive Egyptian mercenary armed with a spear. With only a club in hand Benaiah went after the man, wrenched the spear out of his hand, and used it to kill him. Because of his bravery and skill (and perhaps because he was also a Levite—a member of the priestly community),[6] Benaiah became head of David's bodyguard (the Secret Service). While not among the three, he was held in greater honor than any of the 30 (2 Sam. 23:20-23).

Like the Pjs, these were the best of the best. The gripping accounts of their exploits provide fascinating reading. They were the Steven Seagals, the Schwarzenegger Terminators, the Rambos of their day, forming a close-knit unit bound together by skill, bravery, and an intense desire both to serve their country and to live life on the edge.

Raising Up Giant Killers

It's easy to read this stuff and conclude that David lived in a gung-ho macho world of blood, power, violence, and force.[7] Undoubtedly such things were part of his experience. The question, though, is why the Holy Spirit made sure this list of David's mighty men got included in the biblical record. Was it to glorify power, violence, coercive force—to wow us with macho page-turning material?

The answer appears, I believe, in the fascinating little story tucked in the middle of this parade of mighty men. It records an episode that occurs during one of the two invasions of the Philistines mentioned in the previous chapter (2 Sam. 5:17-21; cf. 2 Sam. 23:13-17; 1 Chron. 11:15-19).[8] As we have already learned, when the Philistines awoke to the fact that all Israel had united under David and that he had captured Jerusalem, they realized that it was necessary for them to make an immediate all-out effort to crush him before he had time to become too strong for them to handle. So they gathered all of their forces and invaded Judah, marching up toward Jerusalem through the Valley of Rephaim. Evidently David wasn't about to let himself be caught in a defensive standoff with the Philistines at Jerusalem and decided to move his base of operations to a place called "the stronghold" (2 Sam. 5:17, NKJV). "The stronghold" was the name earlier given for David's wilderness hideout at the cave of Adullam (2 Sam. 23:13, 14; 1 Chron. 11:15, 16). It included the sentry system, the water supply, the escape routes, and the lookout posts and other military secrets that had enabled David to elude King Saul for so many years. Located west of Jerusalem, it would actually place David closer to the enemy.

Sometime during the two battles with the Philistines in the Valley of Rephaim the Three (Josheb-basshebeth, Eleazar, and Shammah) journeyed to David's wilderness stronghold at Adullam for a meeting with him (2 Sam. 23:13). Their visit came at a time when the Philistines had stationed a detachment of soldiers at Bethlehem, the king's hometown (verse 14). Evidently the Philistines weren't sure where David was and wanted to taunt him and lure him out of hiding by showing up at his birthplace (2 Sam. 5:17).[9]

Perhaps David was tired of living in a cave again. Or it could have been that the site had no natural water supply close by or the water in the cave was somewhat stagnant or bad-tasting. Whatever, the king became thirsty and offhandedly expressed his desire for some water from the well in Bethlehem (2 Sam. 23:15). Surely he never intended anyone to take his request seriously. It was clearly not a command or even a call for volunteers—merely a wish! Just a longing, but the elite Three heard it and immediately determined to deliver water as a gift from the Bethlehem well as soon as possible. Living up to their reputation for fearless action, they set out to fulfill their leader's desire. We thrill at the story of how they fought their way through the Philistine lines, entered the occupied city of Bethlehem, drew the *brand-name water* David had been craving for, and, fighting their way back the same way they came, carried it back to David. It was a perilous journey of at least 25 miles (verse 16).

"This is an example of the exploits of the Three," we read at the end (verse 17, NLT). It was the kind of stuff these action heroes did. But why? What motivated them? Was it the adrenaline rush of living on the edge? the testosterone high of proving you're a cut above everyone else? that you're the strongest? the bravest? Or was there something profoundly deeper? David's men were utterly devoted to him. Regarding his wish as their command, they secured the water from Bethlehem at great risk to themselves.

But obviously David was as devoted to them. In fact, he was more sensitive than anyone might expect in such a moment. We would assume that he would be grateful, but he was far more than that. Their feat so moved him that he could not bring himself to drink the water. Rather, he poured it out on the ground as a drink offering to God (verses 16, 17). David discerned immediately that the water, acquired at great risk and with the utter devotion of his men, had within it the tremendous bonding power of sacrament. He knew that to drink it would violate something holy that bound him to his men.[10] To David, the Bethlehem water symbolized the risk of death that they had literally faced. "This water is as precious as the blood of these men who risked their lives to bring it to me," he said (verse 17, NLT). Israel's king knew devotion when he saw it. He appreciated the fact that no human being was worthy of the intense devotion these three men had given to him.[11] And so David enacted a deep solidarity with them by pouring the water into the earth.

No wonder his men stood in awe of him. Here was a greater reward than had he drank the water. Deep down the three wanted more than the mere pleasure of seeing their leader imbibe *brand-name water* from a well. Or a few pats on the back or greater status. Rather, they coveted close relationship with David—sought intimacy with him. Why? Because David was a person of passion and excellence and skill. And they wanted to be both like and with him. As leadership guru John Maxwell notes: "When a leader reaches out in passion, he is usually met with an answering passion."[12] People with passion ignite others, inflaming their imagination. They attract and influence others. David was a man of passion and excellence and skill, a *giant killer* who attracted giant killers. No fewer than five of his "mighty men" also became giant killers, just like David, their leader.

In one sense what the three did was the height of folly. But it was striking proof of the enthusiasm that David inspired in his followers.[13] It was their personal response to him as a leader,[14] an expression of their deep admiration and devotion.

In his book *Developing the Leader Within You* Maxwell outlines five levels of leadership influence. At the bottom is *positional* leadership in which people follow because they have to. The next level is the *permission* level in which people serve a leader because they want to. Here you have developed a relationship with them to the point at which they open themselves to be led. Real leadership begins with the heart. The third level of leadership influence is the *production* level. In it people accept your leadership because of what you have done for the organization. They like what's happening and thus admire you. Then there is the *people development* level at which people follow because of what you have done for them personally. They, not just the organization, are different because of you. It is at this level that individuals become intensely loyal. Finally, we reach the personhood level in which others serve because of who you are and what you represent.[15]

David's elite mighty men had come to admire him for what he was doing for God's people. They were intensely loyal to him because they knew he was calling something greater out of them than they had ever previously experienced. Who he was and what he represented and stood for—morally and spiritually—awed them. David was a man with a passion for life and excellence and, most of all, for God. He was dancing like a king, and that's what they wanted to be—not king . . . but like him. Dancing!

I believe this parade of mighty men and the episode of devotion tucked in the middle of it points to the kind of experience God wants every generation of His people to have. He seeks men and women of such moral and spiritual passion and impact that they elicit the very best out of those around them. The church of God would see more such mighty men and women—both the three and the 30—if its leaders were men and women of passion and spiritual moral impact.

Who are the people of spiritual influence around you? What great things do you see taking place through the lives of others, such as the prayer warriors or those whose ministry seems to be doing something, going somewhere? What in their lives especially touches the younger generation? Isn't it passion, integrity, competence, and results?

Just as it requires a giant killer to produce other giant killers, so it takes a leader to raise up other leaders. Only a person who impacts other lives can inspire others to become a person of great influence. And you can never become such a person if you don't have a passion for excellence in all you are and do for the Lord. As "[leaders] cannot give to others what they themselves do not possess,"[16] so we cannot inspire others beyond where we are ourselves. A fire in the heart lifts everything in your life.[17]

The Ultimate Passion

An important facet of this list of mighty men deserves our attention—Scripture credits the victories of these mighty men to the Lord, not to the soldiers themselves or even David.[18] Twice in this parade of mighty men the writer tells us that the Lord brought about a great victory (verses 10, 12). The author narrates in a way that reflects a powerful theological awareness.[19] We find here a unique blend between human skill and divine enablement—human passion and divine empowerment. Today we might be tempted to view these mighty men as action heroes or killing machines. Modern Rambos or Terminators. But God was at work in their lives in a powerful way. Yes, they trained and practiced and got themselves in shape. Each of them pursued excellence in every aspect of their field. But in the end it was God who gave them the edge, not their might, weapons, or strategy. It was the power of God.

I believe that divine energy creates the ultimate passion. Incredible things happen when the passion of God dominates our imagination. Down through the ages ordinary and somewhat unskilled people have caused remarkable things to happen in their worlds when divine passion has dominated their being. They took risks, overcame obstacles, and set standards that leave us breathless. David had that kind of passion. So did the three and the 30.

A story tells of a young man who approached the Greek philosopher Socrates and casually stated, "O great Socrates, I come to you for knowledge." The philosopher took the young man down to the sea, waded in with him, and then dunked him under the water for 30 seconds. When he let the young man up for air, Socrates asked him to repeat what he wanted. "Knowledge, O great one," he sputtered. The philosopher put him under the water again and held him even longer. After repeated dunkings Socrates asked, "What do you want?" The young man finally gasped, "Air. I want air." "Good," answered Socrates. "Now, when you want knowledge as much as you want air, you shall have it."

When we long for the kind of spiritual passion that will honor God and make us people of impact and influence badly enough, God will award it.

Our passion for greatness for God comes by being around the one who generates that passion. For the three it occurred as a result of being in the presence of David. In the intimacy of their relationship with him they found themselves deeply stirred by a mere wish. The desire of the king came through like a command to the devoted. The passion it generated moved them from a listening mode to an action one. Intimacy with a leader generates passion, and intimacy with God can produce even greater passion. "Convictions generated from a genuine encounter with the living God create the passion to act and the strength to carry out that action."[20] Such intimacy makes it possible to hear even God's wishes.[21]

As I sit here I wonder what wishes God might have that I could gain a passion for.

---

[1] See Sebastian Junger, *The Perfect Storm* (New York: HarperPaperbacks, 1997), pp. 223-227; Jack Brehm and Pete Nelson, *That Others May Live: The True Story of a PJ, a Member of America's Most Daring Rescue Force* (Crown Publishers, 2000).

[2] Holmes Rolston, *Personalities Around David* (Richmond, Va.: John Knox Press, 1968), p. 60. It's possible that the Thirty was an institution, not just a list, and its membership must have changed from time to time with deaths and replacements. See P. K. McCarter, Jr., *II Samuel,* p. 500.

[3] R. D. Bergen, *1, 2 Samuel,* pp. 470, 471.

[4] W. Bruggemann, *First and Second Samuel,* pp. 349, 350.

[5] He accompanied David on a stealthy foray into Saul's camp (1 Sam. 26:6-12); commanded most of David's forces on an Ammonite campaign (2 Sam. 10:10), led one third of David's troops against Absalom's rebels (2 Sam. 18:2), received command of David's troops in quelling Sheba's revolt (2 Sam. 20:6), and killed 18,000 Edomites in the Valley of Salt (1 Chron. 18:12).

[6] Bergen, p. 471.

[7] Brueggemann, p. 350.

[8] Rolston, p. 87. Both stories take place in the Valley of Rephaim at a time when David was at war with the Philistines rather than when he was a fugitive from Saul.

[9] The Hebrew word used in 2 Samuel 5:17 is הסאקב בקש—"to search"—suggesting that the Philistines didn't know where David was and were seeking him. See Bergen, p. 470, for discussion on the Philistine detachment at Bethlehem.

[10] Brueggemann, p. 349.

[11] G. MacDonald, *Restoring Your Spiritual Passion,* p. 210.

[12] John C. Maxwell, *The 21 Indispensable Qualities of a Leader* (Nashville: Thomas Nelson Publishers, 1999), p. 81.

[13] Rolston, p. 89.

[14] *Ibid.*

[15] John C. Maxwell, *Developing the Leader Within You* (Nashville: Thomas Nelson Publishers, 1993), pp. 5-13.

[16] Maxwell, *The 21 Irrefutable Laws of Leadership* (Nashville: Thomas Nelson Publishers, 1998), p. 136.

[17] *Ibid.*, p. 85.

[18] Brueggemann, p. 347.

[19] *Ibid.*

[20] MacDonald, p. 214.

[21] *Ibid.*, p. 211.

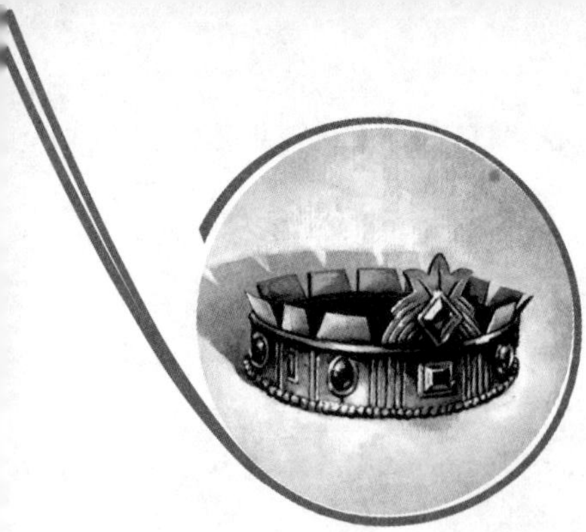

4

TO MOCK, TO DANCE, TO DIE

2 Samuel 6:1-23; 1 Chronicles 13:1-14; 15:1-29

The story of David and the ark of the covenant opens a Pandora's box of issues that many of us would rather just leave alone. We get nervous about such things as dancing before the Lord with all our might (2 Sam. 6:14, 16). After all, is dancing really legitimate, especially as an act of worship? Are we to incorporate it into our religious experience, as some suggest today? What about the enthusiasm and shouting? Or the music? Scripture's list of instruments can be disconcerting, especially the percussion and rattles and cymbals (verse 5). And what about Uzzah's death? One of the hardest sentences to read in Scripture is how the Lord's anger blazed out against the man for touching the ark. "And God struck him dead beside the Ark of God," we're told (verse 7, NLT). All he wanted to do, it seems, was to keep it from falling off the cart it rode on and getting damaged. It's difficult to fit the incident in with our usual picture of God.

But we cannot deny or ignore the event. The ark of God was the occasion for death, dance, and mockery. The story contains aspects that none of us seem to be able to account for satisfactorily. And yet its thrust and meaning are blazingly obvious—there is a right way to approach the living God . . . and there is a way that can get you killed. And even when you're doing it right, some people will think you're doing it wrong.

Once David had conquered Jerusalem and defeated the Philistines, what should he do next? He set out with 30,000 men to an even more important task—to bring the ark of God to Jerusalem (verses 1, 2). A sacred chest made of acacia wood overlaid with gold—three feet nine inches long, two and a quarter feet wide, and two and a quarter feet high—it had been a part of Israel's wilderness tabernacle. Its upper surface or lid, the mercy seat, was solid gold and surrounded with a rim of gold. Two gold rings fastened on each side of the ark allowed the Levites to insert two gold-covered poles in order to carry it. Posted on both sides of the mercy seat were two solid gold cherubim, their faces turned toward each other and looking down. Their wings spread over the top of the ark, forming the throne of God, while the ark itself represented his footstool (Ex. 25:10-22). When carried about by its poles, the ark was wrapped in a veil of badger's skin and blue cloth. The sacredness of the object reflected the reality of God's holy presence, sovereign will, and atoning grace.

At this point the ark had been sitting 30 years in the house of the old priest Abinadab in the village of Kiriath-jearim. During the time of Saul any emphasis on the tabernacle and the ark of God had faded away. Now as Israel's new leader, David wanted to put the ark and the service of the tabernacle back in its rightful place. "Let us bring the ark of our God back to us, for we did not inquire of it during the reign of Saul" (1 Chron. 13:3, NIV). *"Back to us,"* David says. Because it was their new capital, David concluded that Jerusalem was to be a place where God would be worshipped and where He would be Israel's true leader. Transporting the ark from its obscure storage site to its new place of prestige and significance was an enormously important event for David.[1] By bringing it to Jerusalem, David would be making both a theological and a leadership statement.

So it all started out with good intentions. The journey to Jerusalem began with a great pageant—soldiers, musicians, and much fanfare. It would be a significant moment in Israel's life and future. The event would bring God back into focus in the nation's everyday life.

God in a Box

Then Uzzah perished. He reached out to steady the ark, and God struck him dead (2 Sam. 6:6, 7). With his death the joy of the throng suddenly evaporated, and the procession stumbled to a halt. One can imagine people hurrying to Uzzah's side as the harps, cymbals, and other instruments became silent. People milled around to see what had happened. Then the crowd slipped away lest something happen to them as well. Dancing suddenly turned to mourning. It was total disaster.

Imagine being emotionally geared for a great celebration, only to encounter disaster instead. Uzzah's death would have been shocking under the most somber of circumstances, but can you imagine the impact in the midst of such celebration? David must have felt as if he had fallen off an emotional cliff. Instinctively he felt two powerful emotions: anger and fear (verses 8, 9). First, David was angry at God. Uzzah's death had utterly ruined the king's festival. Suddenly he discovered that the procession was, in a radical sense, not *his* celebration. Forced to cancel the whole enterprise, David had to slink away. Such things would never please any leader.[2]

But he was also afraid of God (verse 9). Abruptly he had a feeling that his own heart might not be all that right with the Lord.[3] Had he been in danger? The thought of bringing the ark to Jerusalem now made him nervous. Suddenly he didn't want the ark to get any closer to Jerusalem lest something worse happen—to himself or others (verse 10). David had seen the death, but at that point he didn't know what had led up to it.

"Why did Uzzah die?" everyone kept asking "What happened?" What had ruined an event that had started out with such apparently good motives?

Maybe it was Uzzah's fault. Perhaps he had spoiled it for everyone. Scripture does tell us that "the anger of the Lord burned against Uzzah, and God struck him down there for his irreverence" (verse 7, NASB). That's it! Uzzah was irreverent. But how? And why? When the oxen stepped in a rut and stumbled and the cart lurched and the ark began to slide off, the man instinctively reached out to steady it. Wouldn't you have done the same if you had been there? However, his reflex action didn't seem to be the mistake of a moment. It was a piece of his lifelong perspective of God.[4] His automatic response to steady the ark actually expressed what he really thought about God. Uzzah had spent his whole life taking care of the ark—managing God, so to speak. Unwittingly, in the process he had put the Lord in a box. God needed to be managed, protected, cared for. The man's experience teaches us that it's fatal to take charge of God.[5] To feel that you need to take care of Him, protect Him, oversee Him, as if He or His work required our oversight.

We are also told that the "transgression of God's law had lessened his [Uzzah's] sense of its sacredness, and with unconfessed sins upon him he had, in face of the divine prohibition, presumed to touch the symbol of God's presence."[6] Unconfessed sins? In the vicinity of the holy but untouched by the holy? It's one thing to transgress God's law; it's another not to feel sorrow for it, repent, or confess. Apparently Uzzah regarded the holy as always something external that never really made a difference in his life.

Not-So-Little Details

But it wasn't just Uzzah that caused the celebration to come to a halt. His death resulted from a series of decisions involving seemingly little things that God had been very clear and detailed about. First, David had 30,000 chosen soldiers to protect the assembly and the ark (verse 1).[7] Sounds to me as if he too may have had God in the box! Or at least the military parade was a major focus of the day. The show of arms, the pageantry, the music, and their king rather than their holy God, were the people's center of attention.

When we read the story carefully, we can get the sense that God has been relegated to the back seat (verses 1-7)—there for the ride on a new cart. Up until the moment Uzzah dies God is only peripheral. It is the physical ark that is in focus, not God Himself. The people are more aware of King David than the Lord. The music and pageantry—not divinity—are at the center of their attention. When we read the passage in terms of frequency of words—modifiers, verbs, and subjects—it suggests that in this first attempt to bring the ark to Jerusalem, David and God are on an even footing.[8] The Lord does not appear as standing on His own. But with the death of Uzzah, God is no longer in the box. No longer framed in by human attitudes, perceptions, values, and standards, suddenly He is the subject who acts.[9] The Lord will not allow Himself to be put in a box, whether constructed of crafted wood or hewn stone or brilliant ideas or fine feelings or culture. We don't take care of God—He takes care of us.[10] God is fully able to protect the ark (1 Sam. 5:3-12; 6:19, 20; 2 Sam. 6:7).

Second, David did not allow Scripture to guide his thinking in either the transfer of the ark or his plans for the celebration of its installation in

Jerusalem. Later he will explain the various mistakes: "It was because you, the Levites, did not bring it up the first time that the Lord our God broke out in anger against us. We did not inquire of him about how to do it in the prescribed way" (1 Chron. 15:13, NIV). "Instead of asking God, we used our own reasoning," David declares. According to the regulations of the kings of Israel, they were to hand-copy the law of God personally so that they would know every line. Because David and those around him hadn't been reading their Bibles, their thinking about how to move the ark was fuzzy. In the process the king and Israel's spiritual leaders unwittingly allowed a compromising method that followed the thinking of a counterfeit and distorted religion—they set the ark of God on a new cart (2 Sam. 6:3). David along with the Levites ignored the Mosaic directions for handling the ark and substituted the latest Philistine technological innovation—an oxcart. The Philistines had used a new cart when they returned the ark to Israel years before after they had captured it in battle (1 Sam. 6:1-9). The idea of a new cart pulled by oxen came from their priests and diviners. The whole idea reflected their theology.[11] A new cart meant one that had not been polluted by previous secular use.[12] The concept makes sense, doesn't it? You don't want to put something sacred on a cart that has hauled manure or trash or common things.

So putting the ark on a new cart was a sign of honor for the holy object. But as respectful and well-intention as David's effort might be, it still violated clear biblical guidelines (Num. 4:15; 7:9). At the base of each of the four corners of the ark, you will remember, was a fixed ring of gold. Through the rings would be slipped gold-plated poles by which the entire chest was to be carried so that no human hand would ever touch the ark itself. Those poles were never to be removed (Ex. 25:15). Interestingly, they were so long that when the ark rested in the Most Holy Place, they pushed out the inner veil separating the holy place from the Most Holy Place, creating a kind of curtain horseshoe around the golden altar of incense—almost making the golden altar and the ark one (1 Kings 8:8). Which, by the way, is why the book of Hebrews can portray the golden altar as being one with the ark in the Most Holy Place, while in reality it was in the holy place (Heb. 9:1-5). In addition, God clearly stated that only the Levites were to handle the tabernacle furniture, and they were to carry the poles on their shoulders (Num 7:9; 1 Chron. 15:15; 2 Chron. 35:3).

Every aspect of Israel's worship was important to God, even how His people transported the ark from one place to another. And that's where David got into trouble. He wasn't careful about the details or keeping divinely established precepts and principles in mind. David chose the quickest way to get the ark to Jerusalem—on a new cart instead of taking the time to think things through or check things out with God's Word. The people of God would not have been in danger had they carried it exactly as He had commanded. But David took a pragmatic approach, one that seemed to fit the expediency of the hour.[13]

Ellen White agrees: "David and his people had assembled to perform a sacred work, and they had engaged in it with glad and willing hearts; but the Lord could not accept the service, because it was not performed in accordance with His directions. The Philistines, who had not a knowledge of God's law, had placed the ark upon a cart when they returned it to Israel, and the Lord accepted the effort which they made. But the Israelites had in their hands a plain statement of the will of God in all these matters, and their neglect of these instructions was dishonoring to God."[14] What kind of plain statements do we have in our hand? I wonder. Evidently, glad and willing hearts are not enough when God has already outlined His will.

No Longer Awed?

So the ark must not be presumed upon, taken for granted, or treated with familiarity. The background of this tragedy involves the loss of a sense for the holy—the holiness of God. Our story hints at it in 2 Samuel 6:2 when it says, "Bring up from there the ark of God which is called by the Name, the very name of the Lord of hosts who is enthroned *above* the cherubim" (NASB). Think about that description of the ark. Read it in a couple different translations. It speaks of the very name of the Lord enthroned above the cherubim. Rarely do we find so much emphasis on details of narration unless there is a vital point in them.[15] Here is what everyone was missing—God's holiness. In the end, the death of Uzzah was a dramatic demonstration of the Lord's zeal to protect His holiness—His name that expresses who He really is: holy, almighty, exalted above the cherubim. Brueggemann captures it well when he writes, "When people are no longer awed, respectful, or fearful of God's holiness, the community is put at risk."[16]

I discern a similar loss of the sense of awe of the presence of God among His people today. At the moment the focus is on His closeness and immanence—the loving God who dwells within. We don't hear much anymore about the holy God who is transcendent, unapproachable, and pure. In some ways we have domesticated Him, made Him "user-friendly." But in the process we have lost an awareness of the awesomeness of His presence and an appreciation of our finiteness before Him.

More and more of us restrict our understanding of worship to the context of who we are and of our culture and what is meaningful to us. What meets our needs. But worship really takes place where God is—around Him, not us. Only when we find ourselves truly drawn away from where we are and who we are and what is important to us will we ever truly worship. Only a renewed sense of the holy can ever produce that kind of experience in our lives.

The people were to treat the ark with care because God is a holy being. We cannot tone down the holiness of God to suit our desires or our ideas about Him and His worship. When we tamper with His holiness, we invite judgment. While it may not kill us physically, it will destroy us spiritually. Isaiah had a vision of God in all His holiness, and he trembled. Daniel fainted in the presence of the holy Lord. John fell as one dead when he came into the presence of the resurrected Lord. We must have a clean heart and a clean life, one washed in the blood of Christ . . . before we can be in the divine presence (Ps. 24:3-10). This is not perfectionism, or rabid "holiness," as in the contemporary Christian milieu. Rather it is a proper sense of our place before God. As the biblical writer asserts in Hebrews 12:28, 29: "Let us show gratitude, by which we may offer to God an acceptable service with reverence and awe; for our God is a consuming fire" (NASB). "Let us be thankful and please God by worshiping him with holy fear and awe," the New Living Translation reads.

"The Lord did that because we didn't seek Him," David said about Uzzah's death. "We didn't consult Him first. Nor did we take the time to adjust our thinking and decisions and perspectives to His. Assuming that we thought we knew His will, we dashed off and did it. Because we winged it, we missed it." Sincerity is not enough.

The world's system says, "Don't worry about those little details." David thought the same thing. We've all heard people declare that it's what's in the heart that is most important. If we are sincere, we can worship God in many different ways. Some might wonder what difference it makes how we serve the Lord just so we serve Him with all our heart and strength. But David and the people of his time found out there was a difference. They presumed upon the Lord and didn't take Him seriously. "Who cares about little ringlets and little golden poles that go through ringlets? God does. If He didn't, He wouldn't have said anything about it. And because He cares, we must also care."[17]

On Shoulders of Living Men

After he cooled down, David began asking, "Why did this happen?" All who saw Uzzah die on the road and those who learned about it later must have wondered what went wrong. The man's fate, like earlier deaths, evoked an awestruck question on the king's lips: "How can the ark . . . come to me?" (2 Sam. 6:9, NIV). As David feared the Lord on that day he literally experienced a new spiritual depth. Furthermore, it prompted him to study Scripture and examine his own heart. He began to make adjustments in his life and become a different kind of leader. From now on he would pay attention to the details. I think one reason his passion for God never waned was his unwillingness to turn from the Lord, even when he was struggling with negative emotions. David allowed his anger and fear to motivate him to seek more insights into the heart of God, and in the process to draw closer to Him in humility, confession, and surrender. It's the only way to dance. We need to follow David's example by allowing our questions and confusion to drive us to seek God.

Meanwhile the king received word about the exciting things taking place in the home of Obed-edom the Gittite. Uzzah's instant death made everyone so nervous that they wanted to keep the ark at a distance. Who would want the potential for a similar outburst from God in their backyard? Like everyone else, David feared the ark, so he parked it at the closest place he could find—the home of Obed-edom the Gittite (verse 10)—and left for Jerusalem. But while everyone else faded away with fear, Obed-edom welcomed the sacred symbol as the pledge of God's favor to the obedient.[18] He saw it as the symbol of divine favor to the obedient. God's gracious presence, His holiness, were there for the obedient. Obed and his family hosted the ark for three months, and during that time "the Lord blessed Obed-Edom and all his household" (verse 11, NKJV). Evidently others expected the worst, so when they witnessed incredible blessings instead, rumors began to spread. In time David learned about it. "The Lord has blessed the house of Obed-edom and all that belongs to him, on account of the ark of God," they reported (verse 12, NASB). Evidently God didn't want David to lose interest in having the ark in Jerusalem, so He blessed Obed's house. It provided proof that God is pleased with those who would be near to Him in *His* way.

And it worked. David found his imagination stirred again. "I want God's blessings," he said to himself. "And I want God's blessings on Israel." "So David went down and brought up the ark of God from the house of Obed-Edom to the City of David with rejoicing" (verse 12, NIV). Notice that the second try results in joy and rejoicing. When David resolved to make a second attempt, he removed his royal robes and attired himself in a plain linen ephod (verse 14; 1 Chron. 15:27). He had learned a vital lesson. Now the only focus was on the Lord. He would be the sole object of attention and reverence.[19] Israel would look beyond themselves, beyond the ark. "Oh, worship the Lord in the beauty of holiness! Tremble before Him, all the earth" (Ps. 96:9, NKJV). "Give to the Lord the glory *due* His name; bring an offering, and come before Him. Oh, worship the Lord in the beauty of holiness!" (1 Chron. 16:29, NKJV).

Dancing Like a King

This time David put the ark on the shoulders of living men, and he offered sacrifices along the way. And he danced. The Hebrew words for "dance" mean to whirl or leap and make merry like children skipping (2 Sam 6:14, 16; 1 Chron. 15:29). It reminds me of the time my surprised son Ethan raced around a tent I pitched in the backyard. "I'm so happy. I'm so happy. I'm so happy," he repeated again and again as he ran and leaped. When the ark, the symbol of God's presence, finally arrived in Jerusalem to the accompaniment of a brass band and the shouts of a huge crowd, David totally lost control. Bursting with joy, he cartwheeled in the streets.[20] The king was excited that sacrifice had provided a way for him and his people to be in the presence of the holy God.

Ellen White tells us that David's dancing was "in reverent joy before God."[21] She explains that "the music and dancing in joyful praise to God at the removal of the ark had not the faintest resemblance to the dissipation of modern dancing. The one tended to the remembrance of God and exalted His holy name. The other is a device of Satan to cause men to forget God and to dishonor Him."[22] Furthermore, she refers to the entire second attempt to bring the ark to Jerusalem as a series of "solemn ceremonies" that made lasting impressions upon the people of Israel and aroused a deeper interest in the sanctuary service and kindled anew their zeal for the Lord.[23]

The story displays both liturgical and social extravagance. We find music, shouts of praise, continual sacrifices—and dance. Everyone celebrates with a piece of bread, a portion of meat, and a cake of raisins (2 Sam. 6:19).

On the one hand, the holiness of God demands incredible respect, reverence, obedience, awe, and surrender. On the other hand, that same holiness can be the occasion for incredible joy. When we obey, we feel a great sense of freedom.[24] God's holiness can literally release us when in His grace our hearts have been prepared with awe. David's dance was an expression of joy and freedom experienced in a context of careful obedience emerging out of the study of Scripture.

But the king soon found himself in trouble. His dancing and clapping and leaping caught the attention of Michal, his wife, as she looked out the window. The sight of Israel's ruler doing somersaults in a scanty robe scandalized her. David was in total movement, symbolizing total surrender before God, as he worshipped with abandon, almost oblivious to everything around him. Totally liberated in spirit, he danced through the streets of Jerusalem "with all his might" (verse 14). An awesome scene, it reminds us of the time Mary Magdalene poured the fragrance of abandoned worship on Christ's feet (John 12:1-8). But people often misunderstand such ecstatic worship.[25] Michal could neither experience nor appreciate the moment. "When she saw King David leaping and dancing before the Lord, she despised him in her heart" (2 Sam. 6:16, NIV). In effect she placed herself outside of what was happening and isolated herself from everyone.[26] Contempt, jealousy, and hatred filled her heart. Later when David came home to "bless his household," Michal met him with ridicule and condemnation (verse 20). "How glorious the king of Israel looked today!" she railed. "He exposed himself to the servant girls like any indecent person might do!" (verse 20, NLT). But David refused to allow her to quench his spirit. "It was before the Lord," he replied (verse 21). It was as if he were saying, "How dare you! My worship was not for you; it was for the Lord!" Her scolding must have stung his heart. Yet we can sense his reaction from his resolve: "I will celebrate before the Lord" (verse 21, NIV). "I will be even more undignified than this, and will be humble in my own sight. But as for the maidservants of whom you have spoken, by them I will be held in honor" (verse 22, NKJV). "Whether or not my family does, whether or not my friends do, whether or not this nation does, I will celebrate and make music before the Lord."[27]

In this story we've gone from celebration to mourning back to rejoicing, from anger and fear to worship with abandon, holy awe, and deep humility. The incident presents two different kinds of celebration, stemming from the same motives but resulting in different attitudes and behaviors. It shows both how not to worship and how to do it. How we can have right motives, good intentions, and love the Lord, but be dead wrong. David's first attempt to transfer the ark led to dancing and singing that presumed upon God's presence. But in the second attempt the dancing and singing respond to the assurance that our holy God is graciously present.

Where are your eyes today? On the Lord or on others or ceremonies or icons or innovation or self? Is your God in a box? Do you have unconfessed sins? Are you right with Him? Are you in touch with the holy and what God is really like? Does reverence fill your life? Do you listen carefully to Holy Scripture? Do you worship with abandon? Or are you nervous about what others might think or say or do? Are you worried about how someone else worships? Jealous perhaps, and removed from the genuineness of it all?

Our contemporary society assumes that we can believe anything we want as long as we are sincere—a loving God will not reject us. That we can worship any way we want as long as we are sincere. God looks on the heart, not the form. But the story we've just read shifts the balance in another direction—toward unchangeable principles that cannot be touched or changed, all founded upon the holiness of God. "God is not harsh; He is holy. He is not selfish; He is sovereign. He is not unfeeling; He is all-knowing."[28] He wants us to be different from the world and establish our life and worship on His Word. Such worship will be based on sacrifice and an intimate experience with Him. As with David, we need to come to know and respect Him. And with Israel's king, we will love Him more. Passion grows out of a sense of the holiness of God. And so does dancing like a king!

We would miss a blessing if we did not conclude with David's words in Psalm 30—a psalm written for temple worship:

> "You turned my wailing into dancing;
> you removed my sackcloth and clothed me with joy,
> that my heart may sing to you and not be silent.
> O Lord my God, I will give you thanks forever"
> (Ps. 30:11, 12, NIV).

We will never be fully released to dance before the Lord until we've learned to wail. And we'll never know what it means to experience being clothed with joy until we've allowed God to remove our sackcloth. It's part of the passion—and the dance.

---

[1] W. Brueggemann, *First and Second Samuel,* p. 249.

[2] J. P. Fokkelman, *Narrative Art and Poetry in the Books of Samuel,* vol. 3, p. 189.

[3] See Ellen G. White, *Patriarchs and Prophets* (Mountain View, Calif.: Pacific Press Pub. Assn., 1890), p. 706.

[5] Kaynor suggests that three factors should have caused Uzzah to make the right choice: examples from history, the sovereignty of God, and Scripture. See K. Kaynor, *When God Chooses,* p. 189.

[5] E. M. Peterson, *Leap Over a Wall,* p. 150.

[6] White, *Patriarchs and Prophets,* p. 706.

[7] F. B. Meyer, *The Life of David,* p. 148. See P. K. McCarter, *II Samuel,* p. 168.

[8] Fokkelman, pp. 181-188.

[9] *Ibid.,* p. 188.

[10] Peterson, p. 150.

[11] Fokkelman, p. 186.

[12] McCarter, p. 169.

[13] Charles R. Swindoll, *David: A Man of Passion and Destiny* (Dallas: Word Publishing, 1997), p. 148.

[14] White, *Patriarchs and Prophets,* pp. 705, 706.

[15] Fokkelman, p. 180.

[16] Brueggemann, p. 249.

[17] Swindoll, p. 150.

[18] White, *Patriarchs and Prophets,* p. 706.

[19] *Ibid.*, pp. 706, 707.
[20] P. Yancey, *Reaching for the Invisible,* p. 190.
[21] White, *Patriarchs and Prophets,* p. 707.
[22] *Ibid.*
[23] *Ibid.*, p. 711.
[24] Swindoll, p. 152.
[25] B. Moore, *A Heart Like His,* p. 143.
[26] Fokkelman, p. 196.
[27] Moore, p. 144.
[28] *Ibid.*

5

GOD IN THE MUSIC BOX MIRROR

I Chronicles 16:1-43

En route home from some evangelistic meetings in the Ukraine, my two older sons and I spent a couple days touring Berlin. One of those days found us down at the historic Brandenburg Gate and walking the swanky *Unter den Linden* boulevard that approaches this celebrated landmark from the East. By the time we had reached the Brandenburg Gate we had been walking for hours, and two things were on our mind—eating and finding some gifts for family back home. So we wandered down the *Unter den Linden,* filled with its pricey shops, restaurants, embassies, and hotels.

One of the shops we stepped into was a toy store filled with all kinds of playthings, knickknacks, dolls, and toy soldiers made from wood. It was not exactly what we were looking for! No one we knew would want a wooden toy, even if it was from Germany. So we turned to leave when I spied the upper level. Going up the narrow stairs, I found it jammed full of high-quality (and high-priced) stuffed animals, Hummels, porcelain figurines, and elegant music boxes. The music boxes caught my eye. Not that I particularly like music boxes or could afford to buy one if I did. But they were captivating. The elegant inlaid boxes of different shapes and sizes and artistry beckoned me to pick them up and listen. Surely something this graceful had to make music just as charming. So I opened a few just to listen to their melodies, admire the inlay and artistry, and take in the ambience of it all as decorated box and enchanting music converged to create a sense of haunting beauty. Quality music boxes seek to create a mood, an impression, an idea. They reflect some aesthetic quality or value or message.

For a few moments I imagined buying one for my wife, Kathie. It would express the kind of specialness I wanted to show her and the sweetness I wanted her to experience. Surely they were beautiful. And she loves music. Wherever I travel I try to bring her back something musical or to add to her Kindermusik noise collection of drums, flutes, rattles, shakers, chimes, and such.

David loved music too! We learned that from his shepherd years when he played soft music for Saul's hard heart. There we discovered the incredible healing power of music as well as the ethics of music—the link between art and heart, that music is not neutral, that instrumentation is an important consideration in terms of both context and purpose, that excellence in musicianship is essential, and that the personal moral and spiritual experience of the music maker is indispensable. We also got a feel for the creative side of passion for God. That's because passion by nature is imaginative and creative. It fills the heart with art. People with passion have a thousand ways to say something, write something, do something, experience something—whether it be poetry, music, architecture, sculpture, art, prose, design, computer programming, speaking, loving, and even to being evil and expressing wickedness. In this context we observed how for David music became a form of both expressing his inner self and communicating his experience with God. It became a forum for riveting truths about God and life in his imagination. His passion with music extended throughout the entirety of his life.[1]

It should not surprise us then that once David settled the ark safely in Jerusalem he began to pour out a steady stream of praise songs for the chief musician and the tabernacle orchestra (1 Chron. 16:7-36). In the process the king focused on the responsibility of music and its blessing in the worship of God. He understood the need to perform it properly in divine worship.[2] Who was to take responsibility for leading music? When and how should God's people use it? They were important questions that David provided answers for. He also understood how much of a blessing the wonder of music could be both in the expression and experience of worship as it "displayed the joy of Israel under the blessings of God."[3] David recognized the power of music to express the personal journey of the soul and articulate how wonderful and majestic and gracious the living God of heaven really is. And he clearly discerned how music leadership was necessary for public worship. Music expresses the creativity of passion, as we learned in our study of David's shepherd years.[4]

So we find David commissioning musicians to perform a music ministry at the new but altarless location of the ark (1 Chron. 16:4-6, 37, 41, 42). Evidently the tabernacle remained in Gibeon, where Zadok and his fellow priests attended to the morning and evening burnt offerings in accordance with the law of the Lord (verses 37-43). The musicians in Jerusalem were to be engaged in song and music in caring for the ark. Their music ministry was "before the ark of the Lord" (verse 4) as they gave expression to Israel's praise (verses 4, 41). We need to note that the general context of the scriptural account we are studying here focuses on music and not with the sacrificial aspects of priestly duties, mentioning only the priestly task of blowing the trumpets before the ark of the covenant.

Ellen White informs us that "the solemn ceremonies attending the removal of the ark had made a lasting impression upon the people of Israel, arousing a deeper interest in the sanctuary service and kindling anew their zeal for Jehovah. David endeavored by every means in his power to deepen these impressions. The service of song was made a regular part of religious worship, and David composed psalms, not only for the use of the priests in the sanctuary service, but also to be sung by the people in their journeys to the national altar at the annual feasts. The influence thus exerted was far-reaching, and it resulted in freeing the nation from idolatry."[5]

Like a music box in which packaging and music converge to create a mood, an impression, an idea—reflecting some aesthetic quality or value or message—so the music David envisioned would lead to moral and spiritual formation in light of the vision of God it would provide. As William and Aida Spencer note: "Psalms and other scriptural songs are particularly honored in the Bible as vehicles of specific revelation, sometimes as prophecies (see Ps. 2, 16, 22, 69). Often psalms provide insights into God's nature. In the *music box mirror* of these songs, God's nature is reflected."[6] In other words, Scripture sets theology to music. Music that conveys praise enables divine truths to take firmer root in the hearts of God's people. Theology put to music functions as encouragement, giving new strength to the weary and fresh hope to the disheartened.[7] David understood the nature and the necessity of music in worship. What he did with it says volumes about his vision of worship as much as it does of music itself.

Putting Off Our Shoes

We would miss a blessing (and the point of this chapter) if we did not spend a few moments reflecting on David's awe-inspiring music box mirror found in 1 Chronicles 16:8-36. The first official psalm of thanksgiving to the Lord that he presented to Asaph and his associates, it was commissioned on that jubilant day when the ark arrived in Jerusalem and David danced with abandon before God (verse 7). When we open the music box of this psalm, remembering the context of its composition, we find some incredible images of God that invite our worship. I hope you don't skip over it! Let its imagery about God fill your imagination and mirror back to you who He is as you read it out loud.

> "Give thanks to the Lord and proclaim his greatness.
>   Let the whole world know what he has done.
> Sing to him; yes, sing his praises.
>   Tell everyone about his miracles.
> Exult in his holy name;
>   O worshipers of the Lord, rejoice!
> Search for the Lord and for his strength,
>   and keep on searching.
> Think of the wonderful works he has done,
>   the miracles, and the judgments he handed down,
> O children of Israel, God's servant,
>   O descendants of Jacob, God's chosen one.
> He is the Lord our God.
>   His rule is seen throughout the land.
> He always stands by his covenant—
>   the commitment he made to a thousand generations.

This is the covenant he made with Abraham
  and the oath he swore to Isaac.
He confirmed it to Jacob as a decree,
  to the people of Israel as a never-ending treaty:
'I will give you the land of Canaan
  as your special possession.'
He said this when they were few in number,
  a tiny group of strangers in Canaan.
They wandered back and forth between nations,
  from one kingdom to another.
Yet he did not let anyone oppress them.
  He warned kings on their behalf:
'Do not touch these people I have chosen,
  and do not hurt my prophets.'
Let the whole earth sing to the Lord!
  Each day proclaim the good news that he saves.
Publish his glorious deeds among the nations.
  Tell everyone about the amazing things he does.
Great is the Lord! He is most worthy of praise!
  He is to be revered above all gods.
The gods of other nations are merely idols,
  but the Lord made the heavens!
Honor and majesty surround him;
  strength and beauty are in his dwelling.
O nations of the world, recognize the Lord,
  recognize that the Lord is glorious and strong.
Give to the Lord the glory he deserves!
  Bring your offering and come to worship him.
  Worship the Lord in all his holy splendor.
Let all the earth tremble before him.
  The world is firmly established and cannot be shaken.
Let the heavens be glad, and let the earth rejoice!
  Tell all the nations that the Lord is king.
Let the sea and everything in it shout his praise!
  Let the fields and their crops burst forth with joy!
Let the trees of the forest rustle with praise before the Lord!

For he is coming to judge the earth.
Give thanks to the Lord, for he is good!
His faithful love endures forever.
Cry out, 'Save us, O God of our salvation!
Gather and rescue us from among the nations,
so we can thank your holy name and rejoice and praise you.'
Blessed be the Lord, the God of Israel,
from everlasting to everlasting!
And all the people shouted 'Amen!' and praised the Lord"
(1 Chron. 16:8-36, NLT).

First, this music box psalm encounters us with the holiness of God. Then it calls us to "worship the Lord in all his holy splendor" (verse 29; see Ps. 29:2; 96:9). "Worship the Lord, majestic and holy," the Contemporary English Version reads (1 Chron. 16:29). "Everyone on earth, now tremble!" it adds (verse 30, CEV).[8] The psalm defines worship here as giving to God, not getting from Him. Scripture depicts worship as God-centered. It is "to the Lord." We give thanks "to the Lord" (verses 8, 34, NIV) and sing praises to Him (verses 9, 23). What matters not just most, but completely and finally, is God—who He is and the sort of relationship He establishes with human beings. The Hebrew word for worship means to "bow down," to "surrender." Those who so submit are to do so because God is holy and because they find themselves overwhelmed by the splendor of His holiness. As His people we are to boast in His holy name and give thanks to His holy name (verses 10, 35). "Exalt the Lord our God, and worship at His holy hill; for the Lord our God is holy," Psalm 99:9 tells us (NKJV). The holiness of the Holy One is both the reason for and the object of worship.

As Trevethan observes: "Holy is the most intimately divine word in the Bible. It is that in God which marks him off as God. To say that he is holy is to say that he is God."[9] "The awesome reality of the holiness of God is at the very heart of worship. Realization of the Lord's holiness always moves people to worship him."[10] "Worship is controlled by its object, the Holy One himself. Because he is holy, his holiness becomes the center and circumference of worship."[11]

Holiness is so vast and foreign to us that the task of grasping what it means seems almost impossible. Scripture presents the true and living God as beyond our imagining—"To whom then will you compare me, or who is my equal? says the Holy One" (Isa. 40: 25, NRSV). In our modern world "God shrinkers have been at work . . . , scaling down the Holy One to the measure of the human mind and experience."[12] And, I would add, also to fit tastes and values and passions. When was the last time you bowed down to the Holy One? Have you been siding with the God shrinkers by giving Him only what you like. Or perhaps even your spiritual leftovers?

But scriptural songs—the music box mirrors—summon us back to a sense of the holy. To worship Him in the beauty of holiness. As worshipers the Bible calls us to separate ourselves from sin, rebellion, and idolatry.[13] "Just as he who called you is holy, so be holy in all you do; for it is written: 'Be holy, because I am holy'" (1 Peter 1:15, 16, NIV). Life before the Holy One and worship before the Holy One go together.

David composed three of his greatest psalms for the occasion of bringing the ark to Jerusalem: Psalm 15, Psalm 24, and Psalm 68.[14] Both Psalm 15 and 24 connect the worship of God with character and life. If we would have fellowship with God, then we must see that His holy character becomes ours through the grace of the Holy Spirit. We must watch our walk, work, and talk if we would have fellowship with a holy God.

As we read Psalm 68 we can almost mark the successive divisions of the melody as corresponding to the several stages of the march from the house of Obed-edom to the newly acquired Mount Zion—Jerusalem (verses 24, 25).[15] We see a fanfare of praise (verses 1-6), the march of God (verses 7-10), the rout of kings (verses 11-14), the mount of glory (verses 15-18), the heirs of victory (verses 19-23), the cavalcade of Israel (verses 24-27), the homage of nations (verses 28-31), and the closing fanfare of praise (verses 32-35).

Second, this music box mirror points to where worship truly takes place. Today we live in an age in which we view worship as taking place in the context of our experience, our culture, our values, and our needs, likes, and tastes. We see God coming to us rather than our going to Him. But Scripture declares, "Come before him" (1 Chron. 16:29) and "tremble before him" (verse 30, NIV). True worship is oriented toward God, not humanity. I find it interesting that the music part of the worship that

David established in Jerusalem was "before the ark" (verses 4, 6, 37). The important thing about the ark was not the object itself but the truth it stood for. The ark was the visible symbol of the divine presence. Where do we worship? Wherever God is—before Him. Psalm 99:5 declares that we are to "exalt the Lord our God, and worship at His footstool; Holy is He" (NASB). Four verses later the same psalm exhorts us to "exalt the Lord our God, and worship at His holy hill; for holy is the Lord our God" (verse 9). Did you catch the link between where we are to worship and the holiness of God? We come to where He is. He doesn't come to where we are. We enter His presence, not Him to ours!

Scripture also teaches us that what we do in our worship is part of the larger expression of worship in heaven and earth. Creation forms one grand worshipping community. We have the privilege of joining the worship that is in heaven (Heb. 12:18-29; Eph. 3:14-21; Rev. 4; 5).

The question we must keep asking ourselves is Who's presence do we focus on in worship?

Carefulness in Preparation

We can see why David focused so much energy on the responsibility of performing music properly in the worship of God. His musical contribution to worship points to how "music ministry is to be conducted by people who are trained, dedicated, and spiritually minded."[16] Music ministry around the ark and at the Temple and other worship moments was to be "performed by experienced and mature Levites who were trained musically, prepared spiritually, supported financially, and served pastorally."[17] Their task was to lead and train in worship (1 Chron. 15:16; 16:1-6, 42; 23:3-5; 25:1-7). While excellence was demanded (1 Chron. 15:22), the intent involved more than just performance. The music itself was an act of worship. The musicians were leaders in the act of worship. The same principles apply to ministers of music today.

This view of the holiness of God and our coming to worship at His own footstool also helps us understand why questions of sources and style are important when it comes to worship and worship music. While David's vision for music included singers as well as instrumentalists—and the musical instruments he used included the full repertoire of instrumentation in his day: percussion (castanet, tambourine, timbrel, cymbal, and triangle); strings (harp, lute, lyre, and 10-stringed instruments); and winds (flute, horn, trumpet)—he clearly understood that worship music had to be in keeping with the nature of God Himself.

We've already learned how David's experience with bringing the ark to Jerusalem teaches us that (1) there is a right way to approach and worship God; (2) there is a way that can get you killed; and (3) even when you are doing it right, someone will think you are doing it wrong. Remember where the Israelites got the idea of transporting the ark on a new cart? It came from the Philistines. The Philistine priests and diviners originated the idea in the first place. And it made sense. You don't put something sacred on something that belongs to everyday life. Let's show respect by putting the ark on a new cart, the Israelites reasoned. And the idea sounded good. But it wasn't good enough. God had a different idea—a very particular way in fact. And it was consistent with His holiness. Only after Uzzah died did they carefully study their Bibles and realize that they hadn't asked the Lord for His input. Now they realized that while they were very sincere and had good motives and made great music, sincerity and good motives and great music didn't cut it. Handling the ark, worshipping before it, singing and making music around it all called for an incredible level of consistency with the holiness of God. It had to reflect who God was and how His creation should approach Him.

I believe David's instruction in setting up an official music ministry reflected his understanding of the holy, and of the utmost carefulness and absolute reverence by which everything involving this music needed to be done in the act of worship. And I don't think it accidental that this episode includes the report of how he appointed Zadok and his fellow priests at the tabernacle at Gibeon to attend to the morning and evening burnt offerings in accordance with "all that is written in the law of the Lord, which He commanded Israel" (1 Chron. 16:40). While the immediate context here involves the sacrificial duties of the tabernacle at Gibeon, the larger context and story includes music at the ark. Even at Gibeon the services had music (verses 41, 42).

Stephani correctly asserts that "music styles are value-laden. They are veritable embodiments of beliefs."[18] "Styles of music are artistic embodiments of significant worldview factors in belief systems of individuals and cultural communities."[19] "That which rules the heart forms the art."[20] "In any culture there is an observable human quest for compatibility between fundamental beliefs and the character of art utilized in religious setting."[21] As Seventh-day Adventist Christians we have a moral responsibility to seek not only fitting lyrics for our songs but a musical style that legitimately expresses our understanding of God and of life.[22]

Historically, music and morality have had an intimate connection.[23] The ancients understood that music affects the will, which in turn influences character and conduct.[24] Music dictates feelings, communicates apart from words, is a form of emotional expression, and is conditioned by message. According to Best, "music has no interior beacon that guarantees permanent meaning. Unlike truth, which is transcultural, absolute, and unchangeable, music can shift in meaning from place to place and time to time. Of all the art forms, music is inherently the most flexible."[25] "Even though music is wordless and deedless, the people making it and the contexts in which it is made are not. The more a piece of music is repeated in the same context, the more it will begin to 'mean' that context. Music is the most context friendly of all the arts. It attaches itself quickly, spongelike, to whatever surrounds it."[26] Like the neutral letters in the alphabet that take on incredible meaning as a given writer combines them into words, phrases, and sentences—that can then be evaluated as refined and decent or crude and rude, reverent and respectful or blasphemous, appropriate or inappropriate, right or wrong, and so on because of the ideas they encapsulate—in the same way the musician can arrange individual tones and notes and lyrics in ways that demand the same objective moral/spiritual evaluation.[27]

I believe we're in danger of allowing the world around us to dictate music choices and worship experiences, telling us what is acceptable or meaningful. We need to remember that the "Word of God is not context absorbing; it is context disturbing. It does not change with the context. Rather, the context must change because of its presence."[28] David taught us how to set theology to music and how it is the governing factor in the creation of both worship and its accompanying music. Our worship music is to be God-centered, not self-centered. Remember, we worship at His footstool, not ours.

And All the People Said

I can almost imagine passionate David dancing in his heart and soul as he wrote and or commissioned these vibrant worship songs. It is what passion for God does, what dancing like a king means. "The Spirit of divine inspiration had rested upon the king," Ellen White informs us.[29] And so this incident touches on the role of music in our worship experience. Not only does it provide themes for our own worship, it points to the only legitimate object of our worship—God. It reminds us how our hearts should overflow with worship, thanksgiving, and praise—dance.

Scripture tells us that upon hearing how this first psalm of music conveyed praise and worship, "all the people shouted 'Amen!' and praised the Lord" (1 Chron. 16:36, NLT). In other words, the people enthusiastically endorsed the sentiments expressed in that music. Or to put it another way, they entered into that experience of worship. The joy and desires expressed by the psalm were not David's alone. The entire assembly joined him, saying, "Amen. Praise the Lord."[30] In much the same way, Scripture invites all of us to share the enthusiasm for the worship of God and the gathering of His people in His presence. We too must dance.[31]

Whenever I join the seminary's Worship and Church Music class (required of all M.Div. students) as a guest speaker, I share pastoral perspectives on worship, including the ethics of worship, the role and structure of worship committees, visualizing and planning worship, the people of worship, the relation of art and heart in worship, the Word of worship, etc. Usually I end my two-period-long presentation with a section I call "Worship and You." Here I make a couple points and ask a penetrating question. First, I assert that some people will often worship in spite of you, and some will worship with you (they are worshipping alongside you). Still others will worship because of you (they may have come empty, with no passion, but they see it in you and draw spiritual life and energy for God from you). Then comes my question: "What about your worship?" Here I tell how we can get so busy leading worship and preaching that we fail to enter the sacred experience ourselves. How we don't tune in to the children's story or special music or whatever because we're busy leading worship or thinking about our sermon. The reality too often is that worship can be taking place all around us and, preoccupied with the things of worship, we can be oblivious to it. We are not connecting with the holy God, who can make our soul dance like a king. It's up to you!

---

[1]See "Soft Music for a Hard Heart," in L. L. Lichtenwalter, *David: A Heart Like His,* pp. 50-65.

[2]He made it clear which families of priests and Levites were to play instruments and sing (1 Chron. 6:33; 15:16, 19, 22, 27; 16:4, 7, 42; 25:1-31). Beyond this, David gave attention to such practical matters as the skills and training of Levitical musicians (1 Chron. 15:22; 25:7), as well as their rotation of responsibilities (1 Chron. 25:9-31; cf. 2 Chron. 34:12). Furthermore, he facilitated a wide range of instruments to be used in worship (1 Chron. 13:8; 15:16). Chronicles gives us insight into some details of how and when such music was performed in worship (2 Chron. 5:11-14; 7:6; 23:18; 29:27, 28; 30:21), including music employed to lead Israel into battle (1 Chron. 25:1; 2 Chron. 13:12, 14; 20:21, 22) and to celebrate victory (2 Chron. 20:28). Such descriptions point to the responsibility to perform music properly in the worship of God (see Richard L. Pratt, Jr., *1 and 2 Chronicles* [Mentor, 1998], pp. 26, 27).

[3]Pratt, p. 139.

[4]Lichtenwalter, pp. 62-64.

[5]E. G. White, *Patriarchs and Prophets,* p. 711.

[6]William David Spencer and Aida Besancon Spencer, *God Through the Looking Glass: Glimpses From the Arts* (Grand Rapids: Paternoster Press [Baker Books], 1998), p. 52. (Italics supplied.)

[7]Leslie C. Allen, *1, 2 Chronicles* (Waco, Tex.: Word Books, Publisher, 1987), p. 118.

[8]The psalm given here contains material found in three well-known psalms: Psalm 105:1-15 (verses 8-22); 96:1-13 (verses 23-33); 106:1 (verse 34); and 106:47, 48 (verses 35, 36). The call to worship in the beauty of holiness comes directly from Psalm 96.

[9]Thomas L. Trevethan, *The Beauty of God's Holiness* (Downers Grove, Ill.: InterVarsity Press, 1995), p. 13.

[10]*Ibid.,* p. 244.

[11]*Ibid.,* p. 247.

[12]*Ibid.,* p. 33.

[13]Donald M. Williams, *Psalms 1-72* (Waco, Tex.: Word Books, Publisher, 1986), p. 221.

[14]F. B. Meyer, *Gems From the Psalms* (Westchester, Ill.: Good News Publishers, 1976), pp. 25, 39, 110.

[15]*Ibid.,* p. 110.

[16]Samuele Bacchiocchi, "Biblical Principles of Music," in *The Christian and Rock Music: A Study of Biblical Principles of Music,* ed. Samuele Bacchiocchi (Berrien Springs, Mich.: Biblical Perspectives, 2000), p. 231.

[17]*Ibid.*

[18]Wolfgang H. M. Stephani, "Music and Morality," in *The Christian and Rock Music: A Study on Biblical Principles of Music,* p. 358.

[19]*Ibid.,* p. 360.

[20]*Ibid.,* p. 357.

[21]*Ibid.*

[22]*Ibid.,* p. 359.

[23]Samuel Bacchiocchi, "An Overview of the Music Debate," in *The Christian and Rock Music: A Study of Biblical Principles of Music,* p. 22.

[24]Stephani, p. 348.

[25]Harold M. Best, *Music Through the Eyes of Faith* (New York: HarperSanFrancisco, 1993), p. 54.

[26] *Ibid.*

[27] See Stephani, p. 359.

[28] Best, p. 55.

[29] White, *Patriarchs and Prophets,* p. 708.

[30] Pratt, p. 145.

[31] One of the controversial questions regarding appropriate contemporary worship is Is there a place for dance in worship? Shall we dance? Dance was definitely part of the overall experience that helped establish renewed interest and respect in worship at the time of David. He was not an exhibitionist, as some would claim. Michal's problem had to do with where she was spiritually, not with any action on her husband's part. Others present that day didn't interpret David's dance the way she did. It was part of an experience that deepened their sense of worship. Obviously his dance wasn't part of the tabernacle service, but it was squarely in the context of worship and sacrifice. It was "to the Lord" and unlike the kind of dance found in the surrounding pagan culture or when Israel danced before the golden calf. Not romantic or sensually oriented dancing, it was more likely a march with rhythmic cadence. Is there a place for dance in worship? Shall we dance? Scripture appears to nod yes. There is a place for rhythmic movement of body in the context of religious music and worship. We need to allow for sacred space, sacred time, sacred art, sacred music, and sacred dance.

6

WHEN GOD SAYS NO

2 Samuel 7:1-29

John Wesley Powell and W. J. McGee were the best of friends. Both were on the cutting edge of research in all areas of science in the early years of our young nation. And both were naturalists who had a vision for understanding and protecting our environment. One day they made a playful but bizarre wager. Powell bet his brain was larger than McGee's. A friend of presidents and the Paiute Indians, Powell had led the first expedition on the rapids of the Colorado River through the Grand Canyon. As a gifted naturalist he had opened the eyes of our young nation to the promise and limitations of Western lands. He had a vision for the American West. In 1888 Powell joined 32 others in establishing the National Geographic Society with McGee as a founder and president.

Powell's stature was quite modest in comparison to McGee's bearlike build. But he figured his brain was bigger, so he challenged McGee. The latter accepted the challenge, and the two men left instructions in their wills for a renowned surgeon to perform the necessary measurements. And when that moment of measuring came, Powell's brain weighed in at 1,488 grams—5 percent larger than McGee's, winning his bet.

A scientist to the end, Powell had willed researchers his brain. You can find it in a back corridor office of the Smithsonian's National Museum of Natural History, resting in one of those old-fashioned specimen jars.

Powell always thought big. That was his way—he was a visionary. McGee wrote of his friend, "Things large to others were small to him. Things great to him were past the reach of most others."[1] He was a man who's thinking and vision soared far beyond what most brains do. Yes, his brain was physically larger. It weighed more than McGee's. But Powell thought large, too. He dreamed big. And he always did something with his dreams.

David too was a dreamer. His thinking and vision soared far beyond that of others to encompass some great things for God and His people. We have already seen how he envisioned the Jebusite-controlled Jerusalem—that symbol of defeat and status quo with the enemy—as the capital city of his new kingdom. Nobody had seen Jerusalem as a strategic site or dared to think of it. But David did.

Israel's king also envisioned Jerusalem as a center of worship! That is why he moved the ark to his capital city. David had a vision for music and art in worship, as well. He went out of his way to make Israel's worship experience so God-focused that the people's lives would never be the same again—in character and in dance.

Because vision has a way of unfolding and expanding in the mind of such dreamers, David's thoughts kept mulling over the idea of God's presence in Jerusalem. When he had settled into his new palace and was enjoying a period of rest from all his enemies around him, the king became absorbed with a new and even bolder idea. He had subdued his enemies, and life was calm. He was basking in the splendid palace that Hiram, king of Tyre, had created for him. The one who had once found refuge in a cave now sat enthroned in a magnificent palace. But as he looked around he kept thinking, *There's something wrong with this picture.* Evidently it began to bother him that the ark of God resided in a tent, while he lived in a beautiful cedar-paneled palace. It seemed inappropriate to David for an underling to be living in greater luxury than his divine Master. Not feeling right about it, he wondered whether he was giving God second place and himself first. So he got the idea in his mind to build a permanent residence for God—something even more magnificent than his own palace. As conviction and excitement about the project began to build in his heart, he talked it over with his pastor, Nathan the prophet. "Look!" David said. "Here I am living in this beautiful cedar palace, but the Ark of

God is out in a tent!" (2 Sam. 7:2, NLT). "I don't feel right about this. I fear I am giving God second place and myself first place."

Now, pastors love such moments—those turning points when a person moves from receiving to giving. When people catch some vision of doing a great thing for God—whether building, or ministry, or mission. Nathan, like most pastors, must have spent much of his life being approached by people who were after something from God and wanted his assistance in getting it. Asking Him for help in time of need is our basic and most honest stance before God. Even David was a master at imploring God for what he needed—for help, refuge, healing, salvation, deliverance, forgiveness, mercy, the life of a son, the Holy Spirit.[2] So when David started talking about doing something big for God, Nathan got excited. It was like a breath of fresh air. He instinctively endorsed the king's proposal wholeheartedly. There was no need to even think about it. After all, it was a great idea. It was for God, it was big, and it was definitely needed.[3] "Go, do all that is in your heart, for the Lord is with you" (verse 3, NKJV), he told David.

Every time I read this passage I'm filled with awe and begin to wonder about the level of my thinking for God. Is it just ordinary, or is it *big*? Do I envision doing something great for God? Do my thoughts reach past what most have in view? Is my dream for God's work and His honor so compelling that I am willing to do something about it? Even to making it real? Am I willing to spend and be spent until the power of God's gracious presence flows through me and I see things happen? Giving God second place is a common practice with many of us. As with David, I want to dance—for God.

In *The Acts of the Apostles* Ellen White writes how "the apostle Paul in his ministry among the churches was untiring in his efforts to inspire in the hearts of the new converts *a desire to do large things for the cause of God.* Often he exhorted them to the exercise of liberality."[4] Great things for the cause of God! How big do I see? David's dream for doing big things for God grew out of the contrasts he observed between his own apparent affluence and the seeming meagerness of God's work or His visual prominence in Israel's life. It emerged out of the love he had for God and the passion he had to honor Him with his whole life. The king wanted to do something for God, who had done so much for him. The Lord had blessed him with a place of honor and peace. Now he sought to glorify Him with a place of honor and peace. Just as David didn't want to give God seconds, neither do I.

Something Bigger in Mind

But that is not where our story leaves us. While David's dream is exciting and surely models what it means to dance like a king, it's neither the heart of the account nor the major lesson we are to walk away with. Rather, we run into an incredible and surprising reversal—we discover God dreaming even bigger things for him. Here is a story about dreaming great things for God and discovering that the Lord has even more magnificent ones in mind for us.

That night God gave Nathan a reason to pause as the Lord assessed the king's proposal in a quite different light than the prophet had. So Nathan went back to him the next morning and essentially withdrew the building permit. "Why would a prophet of God discourage well-intended work for God? In the midst of the epidemic of *disobedience* and *sloth* and *inertia* that prevails most of the time among God's people, why would anyone say no to an obviously God-blessed, God-ardent David? Why throw a wet blanket on a blazing fire? All that enthusiasm for God, all that energy ready to be poured into doing something for God—and instead of affirming and guiding, saying no."[5] Why?

Evidently, God felt that David's building plans for Him would somehow interfere with His building plans for David.[6] God had something else in mind—something grander, even more wonderful and enduring. Listen: "Go and tell my servant David, 'This is what the Lord says: Are you the one to build me a temple to live in? I have never lived in a temple, from the day I brought the Israelites out of Egypt until now. My home has always been a tent, moving from one place to another. . . . Now go and say to my servant David, "This is what the Lord Almighty says: I chose you to lead my people Israel when you were just a shepherd boy, tending your sheep out in the pasture. I have been with you wherever you have gone, and I have destroyed all your enemies. Now I will make your name famous throughout the earth! And I have provided a permanent homeland for my people Israel, a secure place where they will never be disturbed. It will be their own land where wicked nations won't oppress them as they did in the past, from the time I appointed judges to rule my people. And I will keep you safe from all your enemies. And now the Lord declares that he will build a house for you—a dynasty of kings! For when you die, I will raise up one of your descendants, and I will make his kingdom strong. He is the one who will build a house—a temple—for my name. And I will establish the throne of his kingdom forever. . . . my unfailing love will not be taken from him as I took it from Saul, whom I removed before you. Your dynasty and your kingdom will continue for all time before me, and your throne will be secure forever"'" (verses 5-16, NLT).

I find it interesting that "the message that Nathan delivers to David is dominated by a recital of what God *has done, is doing,* and *will do.* God is the first-person subject of twenty-three verbs in this message, and these verbs carry the action. David, full of what he's going to do for God, is now subjected to a comprehensive rehearsal of what God *has done, is doing,* and *will do* for and in David. What looked yesterday like a bold Davidic enterprise on behalf of God now looks picayune."[7] *Our dreams for God can never outstrip His dream for us!*

What is God saying? "David, I've gifted you and chosen you to lead My people—not build a temple." As Bergen observes, "David did not need to construct an impressive but lifeless building in which the Lord could dwell; the Lord had already constructed an impressive living building in which to dwell, and that edifice was the life of David. Though the ark resided in a lifeless tent of skin, in a very real sense the Lord resided in the living tent of David."[8] And God had not finished adorning His earthly dwelling place. He would make the king great. The greatness, the house that God had in mind, had to do with character and reputation—with spiritual and moral influence—more than it did with any material blessing or earthly reign. His words to David about erecting Him a house remind me of the "living stones" that Peter speaks about: "As you come to him, the living Stone—rejected by men but chosen by God and precious to him—you also, like living stones, are being built into a spiritual house to be a holy priesthood, offering spiritual sacrifices acceptable to God through Jesus Christ. . . . But you are a chosen people, a royal priesthood, a holy nation, a people belonging to God, that you may declare the praises of him who called you out of darkness into his wonderful light. Once you were not a people, but now you are the people of God; once you had not received mercy, but now you have received mercy" (1 Peter 2:4-10, NIV).

The structure God wanted to construct was more important than the one David had in mind. In fact, the Lord questioned the desirability of anyone erecting a permanent building in which He might dwell. "I have never lived in a temple, from the day I brought the Israelites out of Egypt until now. My home has always been a tent, moving from one place to another," God declared (2 Sam. 7:6, NLT). In other words: "My presence among My people has been real and certainly impressive without a building. Even in the absence of an impressive edifice that people can see, My presence is discernible. Especially, David, when I act through leaders such as you."

So God said no to David's grandiose dream! But His refusal came in such a gracious way—*padded* by *positive* statements, *assurances* of love, *reminders* of past mercies, and *promises* for the future—that no sting remained in the refusal.[9] So indirect was God's answer that we must read the chapter carefully to see a clear no to David's plans. The chronicler's account of this episode, however, says it more openly: "You shall not build Me a house to dwell in" (1 Chron. 17: 4, NKJV).

When we dream large things for God, we need to grasp the reality that He already has in mind more wondrous things for us! God wants to fill our empty hands in ways that we would never believe (Eph. 3:20)! Long before anything we might ever do for Him, God has already done mighty things for us. And He will continue to do so in the future.

Sitting Down

What would you do if God said to you some of the same things he did to David? How would you feel? Have you experienced a time when you were so overwhelmed with both the person of God and His actions in your life that you simply didn't know what to do?

David's response to the Lord's magnificent declarations was awestruck humility. After hearing the Lord's words, he entered the sacred tent that housed the ark and simply sat down (2 Sam. 7:18).[10] Note the sharp contrast between the time that David danced exuberantly before the ark and how he now humbly seats himself to pray, next to the ark.[11] It may be the single most critical act that David ever did. He sat *before God.* According to Peterson, "by sitting down, David renounced royal initiative, abdicated kingly authority, got himself out of the driver's seat, and deliberately and reverently placed himself before God his King."[12] Furthermore, his sitting down was an act of worship! David came to meet purposefully with the Lord—to be conscious of His presence and worship Him.[13] I imagine a long period of silence as he just sat there with a lot on his mind.

Finally the king prays a powerful prayer full of God. Seventeen times he refers to God by name. "Who am I, O Sovereign Lord, and what is my family, that you have brought me this far? And now, Sovereign Lord, in addition to everything else, you speak of giving me a lasting dynasty! Do you deal with everyone this way, O Sovereign Lord?

"What more can I say? You know what I am really like, Sovereign Lord. For the sake of your promise and according to your will, you have done all these great things and have shown them to me.

"How great you are, O Sovereign Lord! There is no one like you—there is no other God. We have never even heard of another god like you! What other nation on earth is like Israel? What other nation, O God, have you redeemed from slavery to be your own people? You made a great name for yourself when you rescued your people from Egypt. You performed awesome miracles and drove out the nations and gods that stood in their way. You made Israel your people forever, and you, O Lord, became their God.

"And now, O Lord God, do as you have promised concerning me and my family. Confirm it as a promise that will last forever. And may your name be honored forever so that all the world will say, 'The Lord Almighty is God over Israel!' And may the dynasty of your servant David be established in your presence.

"O Lord Almighty, God of Israel, I have been bold enough to pray this prayer because you have revealed that you will build a house for me—an eternal dynasty! For you are God, O Sovereign Lord. Your words are truth, and you have promised these good things to me, your servant. And now, may it please you to bless me and my family so that our dynasty may continue forever before you. For when you grant a blessing to your servant, O Sovereign Lord, it is an eternal blessing!" (2 Sam. 7:18-29, NLT).

It's the second-longest monologue Scripture recorded from David's lips—198 words in all. Only his psalmodic recitation in 2 Samuel 22:2-51 exceeds the length of this prayer. One of the most beautifully reverent passages in all the Bible, it is also one of the most tender, affectionate portrayals of a relationship between God and one of His children. The passage allows us to see into David's very heart and mind. We receive a private view of his attitude toward God.[14] The prayer reveals what passion for God is really like and all about.

David knew what it was like to have intimate communion with God. Now, dreaming of doing something big for God, he realizes that the Lord had something far more important in mind for him. When he thinks about all that God has done, is doing, and has promised to do, the king finds himself literally overwhelmed by grace. "Who am I, O Sovereign Lord, and what is my family, that you have brought me this far?" he asks (2 Sam. 7:18, NLT). "Do you deal with everyone this way?" he wonders out loud (verse 19, NLT). "You know what I am really like," he confesses (verse 20, NLT). "Dream or no dream, I'm a blessed person," he concludes.

Overwhelmed by grace and seating oneself before the Lord—here is the heart of worship: ascribing to God all that He is and does and reminding ourselves of His unfathomable value. Then, as we remember that in reality we deserve none of His goodness and blessings, we value more and more highly our relationship with Him.

Whenever I read this story I think of the apostle Paul: "By the grace of God I am what I am, and His grace toward me was not in vain; but I labored more abundantly than they all, yet not I, but the grace of God *which was* with me" (1 Cor. 15:10, NKJV). I am what I am because of the grace of God!

When I think over my life, I see only a little backwoods country farm boy running through tall field grass carrying my .22 rifle. I lived in a humble home built sometime around 1860 in the hills of upstate Pennsylvania. It had no running water, just an outhouse. We bathed in washtubs and hung our clothes on the line after washing them. But God has brought me so far. I am what I am because of His grace. Everything I am and have and have done is His doing. Sometimes I just sit, like David, amazed at degrees and books and influence and world travel and inner peace and awesome hope. Wow! I have so much to thank God for. And He's not finished!

Beyond the personal privileges, there are the awesome realities of redemption that God pours out to me and to you through Jesus. Every time I read Ephesians 1, I am reminded of God's gracious and kind purpose for me—"to be holy and without fault in his eyes" (Eph. 1:4, NLT), to experience "every spiritual blessing in Christ" (verse 3, NIV), to "have redemption through his blood, the forgiveness of sins" (verse 7, NIV), and to "be marked in him with a seal, the promised Holy Spirit, who is a deposit guaranteeing our inheritance until the redemption of those who are God's possession" (verses 13, 14, NIV). And there is so much more! God's vision for me and you is so vast. "'For I know the plans I have for you,' says the Lord. 'They are plans for good and not for disaster, to give you a future and a hope'" (Jer. 29:11, NLT).

On the day I left for my very first evangelistic crusade in the Ukraine, I gave my wife, Kathie, a pile of gifts, one to open every Friday night while I was gone. And one to open on our twentieth wedding anniversary. I wanted her to know that she was special to me during the seven weeks we would be separated. Also I wanted her to know, too, that I was not taking the weeks she would have to be a single parent for granted. One of those gifts was an old-fashioned canning jar filled with dazzling colored marbles that I had found in an antique store. The moment I saw it I remembered a story that I had read of an 89-year-old man who kept a bottle filled with colorful marbles. Whenever something good happened in his life, he'd drop a colorful marble into the bottle. Now that bottle was filled to the very top—a vivid kaleidoscopic reminder of life's blessings. Should he feel a little low or discouraged, he would gaze at that jar of brilliantly colored memories. The sparkling jar of marbles never failed to cheer him up![15] It's amazing how simple little colored spheres can be so captivating. I wanted that little jar of "cat's eyes" and "milkies" to symbolize the collection of our blessings and privileges. God had been so good!

And whenever I stop to look at my jar of marbles, I am overwhelmed. As I sit before the Lord and rehearse His blessings, I am filled with awe. That's what this story about—coming to the point at which you realize that God has been filling your hands in ways that you find hard to believe.

Do you ever "sit down before the Lord"? Maybe you haven't heard what God has done, is doing, and promises to do for you. Perhaps you have heard, but it hasn't sunk in yet. Or maybe up till now it hasn't mattered all that much to you. It is important that every once in a while we sit down and take a look at our lives and count our blessings. Who are we to have been blessed by God the way we are? we must continually ask ourselves. This is what it means to dance like a king as we find our minds stirred by the incredibly gracious goodness of God.

When David prayed, "Who am I" and "You know what I'm really like," he realized how undeserving he was of God's grace. I want to answer the question he put to God as he mused on God's gracious blessings to such an undeserving fellow as himself—"Do you deal with everyone this way, O Sovereign Lord!" (2 Sam. 7:19, NLT). What do you think? Certainly He has with me!

When God Says No!

When I read this story in the life of David, I can't help wondering whether he was wrong to dream such a dream—wrong in thinking of building a temple. Actually, it is not a question of being wrong but rather of accepting God's no and living with the mystery of His will. Accepting that He may have something else totally in mind altogether. Notice what Solomon years later said about his father's experience: "My father David had it in his heart to build a temple for the Name of the Lord, the God of Israel. But the Lord said to my father David, 'Because it was in your heart to build a temple for my Name, *you did well to have this in your heart.* Nevertheless, you are not the one to build the temple, but your son, who is your own flesh and blood—he is the one who will build the temple for my Name'" (2 Chron. 6:7-9, NIV).

God says to David, "You did well that it was in your heart." It wasn't something wrong. The Lord commended him for it, for having a heart that sensitive to Him and that desired to construct a house of worship for His glory. "It's not My plan for you to build Me a house," God says, "but I commend you for such a thought."

This brings us back to our need to let God ultimately lead in everything we do for Him. Sometimes the dream is from God; other times it's not. Perhaps we may have great motives and are as sincere as we can be, but we may not be going about things the way God has shown. The fact of the matter is that "our plans are not always God's plans. He may see that it is best for us and for His cause to refuse our very best intentions, as He did in the case of David [who wanted to build a house for God]."[16] "When God says no, it means He has a better way, and He expects me to support it."[17] Thus when God says no, it is very important to trust Him. His refusals hold potential blessings—provided we can trust and ward off a sour spirit. Since David could not do what he wanted to do, he decided to do what he could do. As a result he began to make preparations for the Temple. Can you take a no from God? And are you willing to do what you can do for God right now? He knows what is best for all of us. Remember His promise to David: "I will be with you forever."

The dialogue between David and Nathan, between God and Nathan, and then Nathan and David is insightful. Sometimes even a fellow believer can offer wrong advice. We are wise to make sure that whatever they might suggest fits with God's Word and will. Nathan's initial response to David was mistaken. "Whatever you have in mind, go ahead and do it, for the Lord is with you" (2 Sam. 7:3, NIV). But God taught both the king and His prophet a gentle lesson on making assumptions.

To David, God said, "Don't conclude that every bright and noble idea in a godly man's mind, or his support of what you want to do, is from Me." Good ideas and My ideas are often completely different.

And to Nathan, God explained, "Don't assume that a leader I have chosen is always right." I may be "with" that leader, but he or she can still make decisions "without" Me! Perhaps, too, as Beth Moore suggests, God wanted to dissuade the prophet from thinking David's actions were always right. He was preparing Nathan in advance for a time when he might have to confront and rebuke David.[18]

Dreaming big things for God and discovering that He has even bigger things in mind for you—wow! But what about those of us who don't dream big for God?

Let's return again to the awesome Scripture we touched on earlier: "'For I know the plans I have for you,' says the Lord. 'They are plans for good and not for disaster, to give you a future and a hope'" (Jer. 29:11, NLT).

> "Marvelous grace of our loving Lord,
> Grace that exceeds our sin and our guilt! . . .
> Grace, grace, God's grace,

Grace that will pardon and cleanse within,
Grace, grace, God's grace,
Grace that is greater than all our sin!"

---

[1]"John Wesley Powell: Vision for the West," *National Geographic,* April 1994, p. 114.

[2]E. H. Peterson, *Leap Over a Wall,* p. 158.

[3]Building a temple was logical in light of the needs created by growth of the capital city. About 26,000 Levites and priests were serving the religious life of the nation. Having a facility commensurate with the portion of religious personnel that served in Jerusalem made sense. See Keith Kaynor, *When God Chooses,* pp. 202, 203.

[4]Ellen G. White, *The Acts of the Apostles* (Mountain View, Calif.: Pacific Press Pub. Assn., 1911), p. 342. (Italics supplied.)

[5]Peterson, p. 160. (Italics supplied.)

[6]*Ibid.*

[7]*Ibid.,* p. 161. (Italics supplied.)

[8]R. D. Bergen, *1, 2 Samuel,* p. 339.

[9]Kaynor, p. 203.

[10]Bergen, p. 342; J. P. Fokkelman, *Narrative Art and Poetry in the Books of Samuel,* p. 236.

[11]Fokkelman, p. 236.

[12]Peterson, p. 162.

[13]Kaynor, p. 206.

[14]*Ibid.,* p. 201.

[15]"Knuckle Down With the 'Marble Lady,'" *Reminisce,* January/February 1993, pp. 22, 23.

[16]Ellen G. White, *The Ministry of Healing* (Mountain View, Calif.: Pacific Press Pub. Assn., 1905), p. 473.

[17]C. R. Swindoll, *David: A Man of Passion and Destiny,* p. 166.

[18]B. Moore, *A Heart Like His,* p. 147.

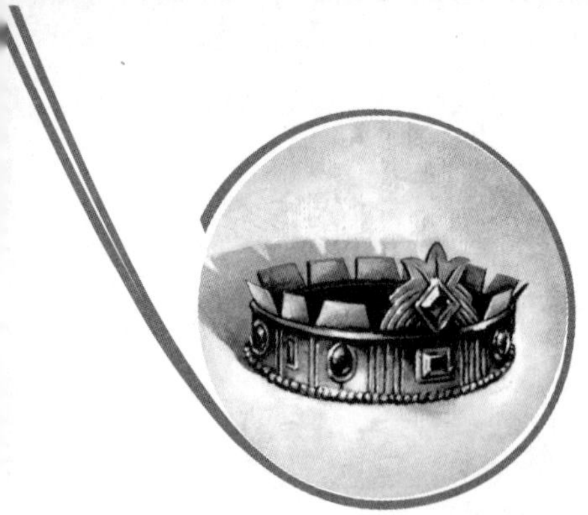

7

GRACE FOR A NO-NAME DEAD DOG

2 Samuel 9:1-13

In 1698 the French imprisoned a mysterious man in the Bastille. Almost no one seemed to know who he was, although inmates of the French prison were usually important people who had fallen out of favor with King Louis XIV. The man had been a captive of the government since at least 1687, and for all that time an iron mask hid his face. Supposedly the prisoner ate wearing the mask, slept in the mask, and eventually died with the mask still on. Two musketeers stood by him at all times, ready to kill him if he removed his mask.

The mysterious masked man reportedly died in 1703, but rumors and speculation about his strange existence continued to circulate. The king's sister-in-law, Princess Palatine, mentioned the story in a letter to her aunt in 1711. The philosopher and writer Voltaire, who himself had been confined to the Bastille, referred to the man in the iron mask in his later writings and dropped broad hints about the prisoner's possible identity. In 1789 journalist Frederic-Melchior Grimm claimed that a royal valet had revealed to him that Louis XIV had an identical twin. The twin's father, Louis XIII, feared the brothers would grow up to fight over the throne, so he sent the second-born baby away to be raised in secret. The boy went to a nobleman's household that treated him with great respect, but no one ever told the child who he really was. As a young man he saw a portrait of his brother and guessed the truth. The authorities immediately arrested him, and he spent the rest of his life as the man in the iron mask.

No one knows for sure who the prisoner was, but his dangerous identity must have been the whole point of the mask, so the twin brother theory is as good as any. That's why the French novelist Alexandre Dumas worked the twin brother theory into its best-known and popular version of the old tale—*The Man in the Iron Mask.*

Dumas' version of the legend portrays a character difference between identical twins. The brother on the throne was despotic, spoiled, and known for his cruel fits of rage. The people of France suffered under his leadership. The brother in the iron mask, however, was gentle, selfless, and humble—the very kind of king people longed for and would love to serve. So Dumas' famous Three Musketeers facilitate a switch, replacing the despotic king by his gentle, selfless sibling. A spirit of love and kindness would now rule France.

As with any leader, David had to decide what kind he would be. What would characterize his rule—power or love? cruelty or gentleness? severity or grace? self-absorption or selflessness? Would he manipulate others so that he could be in complete control? Or would he be open and generous? What would he choose as the course of his life and leadership?[1]

He answered those questions as he looked for a way to keep a promise he made with his best friend, Jonathan. Bringing Jonathan's son, Mephibosheth, before him, he had to decide whether to execute him as a threat to his power or honor him by keeping his promise of love. Speaking of the shattered house of Saul, David asked, "Is there anyone belonging to Saul's family left, to whom I might show faithful love for Jonathan's sake?" (2 Sam. 9:1, New Jerusalem). When the king inquired whether there were any members of Saul's family whom he could love in Jonathan's name left, he was asking, in effect, "Is there anyone left in the enemy camp whom I can love?" David was looking for an *enemy* to love.[2]

Why did David want to do this? I think he looked around the kingdom and thought of the man who first planned to share it with him—Jonathan. He missed his best friend. Jonathan wasn't there to enjoy the blessings of God with him. Plus, David had made a promise. In fact, he had made two promises. Back when he was still running for his life from Saul, the former king's son said to him, "If it please my father *to do* you harm, may the Lord do so to Jonathan and more also, if I do not make it known to you and send you away, that you may go in safety. And may the Lord be with you as He has been with my father. If I am still alive, will you not show me the lovingkindness of the Lord, that I may not die? You shall not cut off your lovingkindness from my house forever, not even when the Lord cuts off every one of the enemies of David from the face of the earth" (1 Sam. 20:13-15, NASB).

It was the custom in Eastern dynasties that when a new king took over, he would have all the family members of the previous dynasty exterminated to remove the possibility of revolt. So Jonathan was saying, "David, when you get to the throne, will you show my family grace? Will you preserve our lives? Will you take care of us and protect us?" David agreed without hesitation. His love for Jonathan prompted him to make a promise—a covenant. "So Jonathan made a covenant with the house of David, saying, 'May the Lord call David's enemies to account.' And Jonathan had David reaffirm his oath out of love for him, because he loved him as he loved himself" (verses 16, 17, NIV). What the two men vowed was that "*whatever* happened, love—not power—would characterize their relationship; love, not vengeance; love, not convenience."[3] "We have made a pact in the Lord's name," Jonathan said. "We have entrusted each other and each other's children into the Lord's hands forever" (verse 42, NLT).

Later, you may recall, after David spared Saul's life in the cave at Engedi, Saul said to him, "'And now I realize that you are surely going to be king, and Israel will flourish under your rule. Now, swear to me by the Lord that when that happens you will not kill my family and destroy my line of descendants!' So David promised" (1 Sam. 24:20-22, NLT).

David had made promises to both Jonathan and to Saul. Now we find him remembering those vows. As he turned them over in his mind he wanted to keep them. During a time of great success, having captured the affection and the loyalty of his nation—when he was on top spiritually, militarily and financially—he thinks of the shattered house of Saul and his best friend, Jonathan. It is an important moment for David. Remembering promises and keeping them are vital dimensions of character. In his book *Losing Our Virtue* David Wells connects keeping a promise as part of one's moral orientation and being consistent with who a person is.[4] "Without being bound to the fulfillment of our promises, we would never be able to keep our identities; we would be condemned to wander helplessly and without direction in the darkness of each person's lonely heart, caught in its contradictions and equivocalities," Hannah Arendt writes in *The Human Condition.*[5] Thomas Bolt's brilliant movie about Sir Thomas More has a scene in which More explains to his daughter Margaret why he cannot go back on an oath he took: "When a man makes a promise, Meg, he puts himself into his own hands, like water. And if he opens his fingers to let it out, he need not hope to find himself again."[6] "We will create ourselves in the commitments we dare to make and care enough to keep,"[7] says Smedes. In her *Personal Commitments* Margaret Farley asserts that "the ultimate meaning . . . of the promise I make today can be clear only at the end of my life; and the meaning of my life at its end will be different because I made this promise today."[8]

When I make a commitment, I place myself in a stream that flows in a certain direction. But I won't know for sure until I get to the end what it really meant when I entered the stream. What finally comes of our commitments really depends on a thousand small choices we make in the process of keeping them. That's where David now found himself . . . down the stream . . . making choices. Lewis Smedes correctly asserts that "none of us is ever more God-like than when we simply make and simply keep commitments to each other."[9] We are most like God when we keep our promises. He is a promise-making and promise-keeping deity. "The Lord of the covenant is a God of promise. His promises are secured in His Being. God's promises are certain. He fulfills His promises in His own time and in the way He intends."[10] The Lord had made incredible promises to David (as we learned in the previous chapter) and had kept every one thus far! It was clear to David what the Lord was like. Now the king wanted to be like God—a promise keeper.

While David sought to be a promise keeper for Jonathan's sake, he also intended to be a grace giver. "Is there no one left, belonging to Saul's family, for me to treat with God's own faithful love?" he asks Ziba, a former servant of Saul (2 Sam. 9:3, New Jerusalem). "I want to show God's faithful love," he says. Here he employed the Hebrew word *chesed* that the Old Testament used to designate the way God loves. No single word is adequate to capture its meaning in translation. So we revert to adjectives to bring out the distinctive quality and broad reach of such love: steadfast love, loyal love, covenantal love, merciful love, lovingkindness, love that graces. "Is there anyone still living in the family of Saul to whom I could demonstrate the same kind of grace that God has demonstrated to me?" That's the idea turning over in David's mind.[11]

David longed to demonstrate love that is undeserved, unearned, unconditional, and unrepayable. He desired to be an agent of God's grace, mercy, and love to some undeserving person. Anybody! In this way David wanted to be like God. That's the kind of leader he sought to be. God was the promise-keeping and grace-giving God. The Lord's way would be the pattern for his leadership. What passion for God—what a way to dance!

The Analogies of Grace

"Is there anybody still living who ought to be the recipient of my grace?" Well, his servants found someone. Saul's former steward, Ziba, revealed the long-kept secret of someone who had been hidden since childhood. "There is still a son of Jonathan who is crippled in both feet. . . . Behold, he is in the house of Machir the son of Ammiel in Lo-debar" (verses 3, 4, NASB). If you read between the lines and follow the story of Ziba as it unfolds, you get the distinct impression that he wasn't all that excited with David's idea. The steward purposefully shares two pieces of information about the individual but not his name. Ziba doesn't divulge a name at first, just information with a subtle message. First, the unnamed descendant has serious disabilities in both feet. Second, he lives in an obscure little village on the edge of Israelite territory called Lo-debar. The name of the place says it all. Lo-debar means "no pastureland" or "barren place" in Hebrew.[12] It's as if Ziba is saying that the person dwells in a place of stark poverty, obscurity, and insignificance. What's his point? "David, you really better think twice before you do this, because this guy's not going to look very good in your court. He doesn't fit the surroundings, this throne room, this beautiful new home in the city of Jerusalem. You know, David, he has a serious disability."[13] The guy's really a reject, a nobody not worth your time and energy. Physical deformity was a great source of shame in the ancient world. Ziba's reply intimates an agenda or at the least some qualms about whether Jonathan's son would qualify for anything the king wanted to do.

But grace isn't picky. It doesn't stop to consider if we fit in or are worthy. Grace ignores where we've come from, our status, gender, ethnic background or pedigree, our failures and mistakes, our idiosyncrasies, or even the hurt we or someone connected to us may have caused. That's the point of this story. As Ellen White writes: "Grace is an attribute of God exercised toward undeserving human beings. We did not seek for it, but it was sent in search of us. God rejoices to bestow His grace upon us, not because we are worthy, but because we are so utterly unworthy. Our only claim to His mercy is our great need."[14] What Ziba implied about this unnamed descendant of Jonathan is the very reason for David's love. And God's love for you and me.

And so we find a strong and famous king stooping down and reaching out to one who represented everything David was not! "Then King David sent and brought him from the house of Machir the son of Ammiel, from Lo-debar. Mephibosheth, the son of Jonathan the son of Saul, came to David and fell on his face and prostrated himself. And David said, 'Mephibosheth.' And he said, 'Here is your servant!' David said to him, 'Do not fear, for I will surely show kindness to you for the sake of your father Jonathan, and will restore to you all the land of your grandfather Saul; and you shall eat at my table regularly.' Again he prostrated himself and said, 'What is your servant, that you should regard a dead dog like me?' . . . So Mephibosheth ate at David's table as one of the king's sons" (verses 5-11, NASB).

By the way, David didn't ask how Mephibosheth became disabled in both feet. But we are curious, and we find the answer in 2 Samuel 4. When Mephibosheth was 5 years old, news reached Saul's palace in Gibeon that the Philistines had killed the king and Prince Jonathan in the battle of Jezreel. The panic was immediate and total. The royal house and everyone in it realized that they likely faced destruction either by the conquering Philistines or by David who was not only the major contender for the throne at that time, but had been pursued by Saul for more than a decade. Not knowing exactly what to expect from Saul's enemies except the worst, all the servants in the palace ran for their lives. Five-year-old Mephibosheth's nurse grabbed him on the run and then tripped. The fall broke both his ankles (verse 4). His bones knit badly, and he was never again able to walk well.

Because his life would have been in danger if anyone knew that he was the only living heir of the once-great house of Saul, Mephibosheth grew up with his royal identity suppressed and all the privileges of royalty denied him. He lived in obscurity and poverty, both conditions aggravated by his lameness.[15] No wonder he referred to himself as "a dead dog." He felt less than human. Such things don't make people feel very good about themselves. Mephibosheth undoubtedly grew up with a deep sense of victimization and anger. Probably he heard embittering stories about David, tales that cast the new king as the villain.[16] Saul's grandson had to find someone to blame for his situation and condition. The hostile, uncaring world he knew had the face of David.[17]

Ever fearful of his life, Mephibosheth lived with the dread of that knock at his door by an emissary from the king. The day that he would be discovered. But that's exactly what happened. Strangers arrived in Lodebar asking for him. When they found him, they told him that the king wanted him in Jerusalem. From his perspective he could put only one interpretation on that summons: David was searching the land from top to bottom, looking for any trace of Saul's descendants, determined to eliminate any possible challenge to his kingdom. Terror must have filled his heart. *Well, this is it,* he thought.

We can understand, then, the fear that gripped Mephibosheth when the servants brought him into David's presence. He almost certainly expected the worst—death. The only thing he could do was fall on his face in uncontrollable terror. Observing his trembling fear, David addressed him by name, "Mephibosheth!" He recognizes him as a person—he isn't a nameless exile anymore. Saul's grandson has a name, and David knows it. Mephibosheth gets his identity from love. He is named by grace.[18]

This reminds me of what Smedes so powerfully writes in his book *Shame and Grace.* The book has a chapter entitled "Singing 'Amazing Grace' Without Feeling Like a Wretch." You know the line from the song: "Amazing grace, how sweet the sound, that saved a wretch like me." Well, Smedes asks an interesting question: "How does grace make us feel?" "Now, I may be a wretch that grace has saved, but since I am saved, do I still feel like a wretch?" So, Smedes suggests, when grace comes to us graciously, it heals. But when offered ungraciously, it shames. You can tell that grace is gracious if it makes you feel better for having it. While you may be a wretch, true grace doesn't make you feel like one. "The question is: are we accepted by grace only in spite of our unworthiness or are we also accepted precisely because we are worthy? A grace that makes us feel worse for having it is an ungracious grace and therefore not really grace at all. If grace heals our shame, it must be a grace that tells us we are worthy to have it."[19] That's an interesting twist, don't you think?

"When we feel like wretches saved by grace we do not deserve," Smedes adds, "we may also discover a worth within that makes us worthy of the grace that saved us."[20] "Grace graciously given honors our worth as it overlooks our undeserving."[21] "Grace does not make me feel less; it makes me feel worthy."[22] That's how God treats us. Marvelous, isn't it? How many times, though, have we forgiven someone but said, "Don't you ever do it again!" How many times have we thought we were being bighearted, only to have the person we've been bighearted to go away feeling really bad. Why? Because now they're living under our bighearted thumb and consider themselves shamed. David, though, knows what God's grace is all about. He has experienced it again and again. He wants to be a grace-giver like God. To offer grace that recognizes and builds up Mephibosheth as a person.

But Saul's grandson can't stop shaking. "I'm your servant," he answered.

"Don't be afraid," David continued, "for I will surely show lovingkindness to you for the sake of your father Jonathan, and will restore to you all the land of your grandfather Saul; and you shall eat at my table regularly." Mephibosheth couldn't believe what was he was hearing. The watchword of his life since he had been a little boy had been anonymity. He had never wanted to be found, certainly not by the king who had succeeded his grandfather. For a usurper to discover his whereabouts usually meant instant death. Now he hears his name—on the lips of the king. And what does he hear? Grace! Once more he fell to the ground. "Should the king show such kindness to a dead dog like me?" he exclaimed. "He uses the most descriptive words he could think of for a contemptuous, despicable, worthless creature. 'I'm just a dead dog, living in Lo-debar. Why not just leave me alone in my misery?'"[23]

Remember when you felt that way about yourself or said such a thing to God? Here is a man who is of no benefit to the kingdom as far as physical strength is concerned. But stooping in grace, David brings Mephibosheth into his own home and treats him like one of his own sons.

What a fantastic account of grace![24] As Yancey writes: "Grace means there is nothing we can do to make God love us more. . . . And grace means there is nothing we can do to make God love us less. . . . Grace means that God already loves us as much as an infinite God can possibly love."[25] "Grace does not depend on what we have done for God but rather what God has done for us."[26]

Paul summarized it well in his letter to Titus: "Once we, too, were foolish and disobedient. We were misled by others and became slaves to many wicked desires and evil pleasures. Our lives were full of evil and envy. We hated others, and they hated us. But then God our Savior showed us his kindness and love. He saved us, not because of the good things we did, but because of his mercy. He washed away our sins and gave us a new life through the Holy Spirit. He generously poured out the Spirit upon us because of what Jesus Christ our Savior did. He declared us not guilty because of his great kindness. And now we know that we will inherit eternal life" (Titus 3:3-7, NLT).

And grace won Mephibosheth's heart: "Through reports from the enemies of David, Mephibosheth had been led to cherish a strong prejudice against him as a usurper; but the monarch's generous and courteous reception of him and his continued kindness won the heart of the young man; he became strongly attached to David, and, like his father Jonathan, he felt that his interest was one with that of the king whom God had chosen."[27]

Graced People Grace

"Is anyone still alive from Saul's family? If so, I want to show God's kindness to them in any way I can." Why did he do it? Why would David lavish such love on Mephibosheth? It's a question of grace asked by a grateful person.[28] Himself overwhelmed by the Lord's goodness and grace, David was reflecting on all his blessings and how far God had brought him. "Who am I, and what is my family, that You have brought me thus far?" "I am what I am by the grace of God." "If there is any goodness now found in me, I deserve none of the glory; grace gets the credit."

We learn grace by being graced, and we offer grace because we have been graced. Grace begets grace. Only the experience of being graced makes it possible for us to give grace, just as only the experience of being forgiven makes it possible for us to forgive. "Grace alone melts ungrace."[29] David simply wanted to do what God had done for him.

He was doing the work of a king,[30] exercising his power by looking for ways to love. That's the kind of passion for God I want in my life!

The king was so overwhelmed by and immersed in God's grace that years later he extended grace to Mephibosheth a second time. David had fought for his life during Absalom's rebellion. He had escaped from Jerusalem in disgrace, cursed and maligned, with only a few faithful followers. During his flight from Jerusalem Ziba showed up without Mephibosheth. When David asked, "Where's Mephibosheth?" Ziba said in effect, "Saul's grandson has betrayed you. He's a traitor, having seen a chance at becoming king and grabbed for it. But I'm on your side." Without asking any questions, David accepts Ziba's story as true and on the spot decrees that all of Mephibosheth's assets are now the steward's (2 Sam. 16:1-4).

Days later, on the return to Jerusalem following Absalom's defeat, David hears a very different story. Mephibosheth comes out to meet him all disheveled, with beard ragged and clothes looking as if they've been slept in (2 Sam. 19:24). "'Why didn't you come with me, Mephibosheth?' the king asked him. Mephibosheth replied, 'My lord the king, my servant Ziba deceived me. I told him, "Saddle my donkey so that I can go with the king." For as you know I am crippled. Ziba has slandered me by saying that I refused to come. But I know that you are like an angel of God, so do what you think is best. All my relatives and I could expect only death from you, my lord, but instead you have honored me among those who eat at your own table! So how can I complain?' 'All right,' David replied. 'My decision is that you and Ziba will divide your land equally between you.' 'Give him all of it,' Mephibosheth said. 'I am content just to have you back again, my lord!'" (verses 25-30, NLT).

So who's telling the truth, Ziba or Mephibosheth?[31] Surprisingly, David accepts both men back into his city and household. His love is large enough to handle faithlessness, fecklessness, lies, and hypocrisy.[32] No wonder some have called David the greatest lover and the greatest forgiver in the Bible. He gave grace to Mephibosheth from a position of strength and used that strength to love generously. Later he gave grace to Mephibosheth while fatigued from battle, having barely survived the worst rejection and betrayal of his life. Is Mephibosheth one more who has betrayed his love? Who knows? If his own son, Absalom, did, why wouldn't Mephibosheth lay claim to the throne as well? But David persists in his love no matter what.

That's grace . . . amazing grace.

Is There Anyone . . . Anybody?

"Is there no one left, belonging to Saul's family, for me to treat with God's own faithful love?" David asks (2 Sam. 9:3, New Jerusalem). "Anyone? Anybody?"

I have two questions:

First, Is there someone you need to forgive, be gracious to, show God's love to? Grace is not something simply to be claimed—it is meant to be demonstrated, shared, used as a basis for friendships, and drawn upon for sustained relationships.[33] It should dominate our marriage, our home, our leadership—in fact, every aspect of our lives in relation to others.

Second, Yancey writes, "Grace comes free of charge to people who do not deserve it and I am one of those people."[34] Have you experienced God's grace? Are you so overwhelmed by and immersed in it that you find yourself compelled to offer it to someone else? We are like Mephibosheth, caught up in the disability of sin, alienated from God, unworthy, a dead dog. In his story we can see an image of ourselves. And, like Jonathan's son, apart from Christ we are broken, outcast, and crippled in both feet. But in Christ we can put our feet under His table as His child. None of us would have learned to walk with God on healthy feet had we never experienced sitting at His table with impaired feet. Our emotional and spiritual healing has come from approaching God in our damaged state and believing that we are His son or daughter and worthy of His love.[35]

How does God want you to manifest His grace just now? Who is there for you to extend divine grace to right now? Your spouse? A parent? One of your children? A friend? A colleague at work? Even your pastor? Our world is full of people starving for grace. Perhaps you are one of them. And perhaps you know one of them.

When David considered the course of his life and leadership, he chose faithfulness and grace. And he danced like The King!

---

[1]E. H. Peterson, *Leap Over A Wall,* p. 174.

[2]*Ibid.*

[3]*Ibid.*

[4]David F. Wells, *Losing Our Virtue: Why the Church Must Recover Its Moral Vision* (Grand Rapids: William B. Eerdmans Pub. Co., 1998), pp. 144, 145.

[5]In Lewis B. Smedes, *Caring and Commitment: Learning to Live the Love We Promise* (New York: Harper & Row, Publishers, San Francisco, 1988), p. 44.

[6]In Smedes, p. 45.

[7]*Ibid.*

[8]In Smedes, p. 39.

[9]*Ibid.*, p. 148.

[10]Gerard F. Hasel and Michael G. Hasel, *The Promise: God's Everlasting Covenant* (Nampa, Idaho: Pacific Press Pub. Assn., 2002), p. 48.

[11]Charles R. Swindoll, *The Grace Awakening* (Dallas: Word Publishing, 1990), p. 66.

[12]F. W. Krummacher, *David, King of Israel* (Grand Rapids: Kregel Publications, 1994), pp. 257, 258.

[13]C. R. Swindoll, *David: A Man of Passion and Destiny,* p. 172.

[14]E. G. White, *The Ministry of Healing,* p. 161.

[15]Peterson, pp. 170, 171.

[16]White, *Patriarchs and Prophets,* p. 713.

[17]Peterson, p. 171.

[18]*Ibid.*, p. 175.

[19]Smedes, *Shame and Grace; Healing the Shame We Don't Deserve* (New York: Harper Collins Publishers, 1993), p. 119.

[20]*Ibid.*, p. 120.

[21]*Ibid.*

[22]*Ibid.*, p. 122.

[23]Swindoll, *The Grace Awakening,* p. 69.

[24]Various writers draw creative parallels between the details of Mephibosheth's situation and human lostness on the one hand, and between David's actions and God's gracious work to redeem us on the other. While some details get pressed to the verge of allegory, the story itself is an incredible mirror of divine love. For such analogies of grace, see: Swindoll, *The Grace Awakening,* pp. 70-72; *David: A Man of Passion and Destiny,* pp. 176-178; A. Redpath, *The Making of a Man of God,* pp. 185-193; Krummacher, pp. 256-265.

[25]Philip Yancey, *What's So Amazing About Grace?* (Grand Rapids: Zondervan Publishing House, 1997), p. 70.

[26]*Ibid.*, p. 55.

[27]White, *Patriarchs and Prophets,* p. 713.

[28]Swindoll, *The Grace Awakening,* p. 65.

[29]Yancey, *What's So Amazing About Grace?* p. 90.

[30]Peterson, p. 172.

[31]The Scripture appears ambiguous on this and leaves it to the individual reader to decide whether Ziba or Mephibosheth is telling the truth in this incident. The closing words of Mephibosheth, though, have a ring of genuineness. If we accept them as the answer of an honest man, we can know that in the heart of the son of Jonathan there resided deep and genuine love for David. It would be in keeping with what Ellen White says about

Mephibosheth's loyalty to David. See Peterson, pp. 177, 178; Redpath, pp. 191, 192; H. Rolston, *Personalities Around David,* p. 41.

[32] Peterson, p. 178.

[33] Swindoll, *The Grace Awakening,* p. 60.

[34] Yancey, *What's So Amazing About Grace?* p. 42.

[35] B. Moore, *A Heart Like His,* pp. 159, 162.

8

ONCE UPON A ROOFTOP

2 Samuel 11:1-17, 26, 27

Malcolm Muggeridge tells a story in his autobiography *The Wasted Years* about a moment of intoxicating temptation that he yielded to. He was in India teaching journalism, far away from his wife and family. While away from home he had nursed the thought in the back of his head that if the opportunity ever presented itself, he would be intimate with another woman, just for the experience. Early each morning he rose and went swimming in the Ganges River. One day he saw a woman bathing herself in the river, quite a distance away. *This is it,* he thought to himself. *I'm a wealthy Englishman. She is a poor Indian. What could it hurt? Who will know?* As he began to swim upstream to her, he struggled, not just against the water, but against the current of his conscience. "Malcolm," a voice inside him said, "don't do it." But then another voice countered, "This is your chance. It's now or never."

He continued to swim toward the bathing woman, staying underneath the water until he was only a few feet away. When he surfaced, it was he, not she, who experienced the shock of a lifetime. Muggeridge came up out of the water and looked into the eyes of a woman who was . . . a leper. The disease had eaten her nose away, sores and white blotches covered her skin, and the ends of her fingers were gone. She looked more like an animal than a human being. Immediately he thought, *What a wretched woman she is,* but almost at the same moment the devastating truth overwhelmed him: *What a wretched man I am!*[1]

The woman David saw bathing and reached for was no ghastly leper. Scripture tells us that Bathsheba was "very beautiful" (2 Sam. 11:2). When the Bible states that a woman is beautiful, we can be assured that she is indeed fabulous. And when it claims that she's very beautiful, we can be sure she's a knockout, gorgeous, physically attractive beyond description. But no matter how ravishing Bathsheba might have been to behold and caress, the devastating truth about the moral and spiritual character of David's inner private world was unmistakable. It was he who was leprous and wretched.

During the spring of the year when David's army was besieging Rabbah he for some reason stayed behind rather than participate with his troops in the field. (The usual practice in the ancient world was for rulers of a country to personally lead their armies into battle.) One afternoon, while walking on the palace roof that overlooked the courtyards of nearby houses (as is still the case today when one stands on the site of the City of David in Jerusalem and faces the village of Silwan on the opposite side of the Kidron Valley), David saw a woman bathing on a nearby rooftop. She was extraordinarily beautiful. Quickly he sent for her and made love with her. Bathsheba's husband, Uriah, was off fighting in the army. As far as David was concerned, the event was over. But a month or so later she notified David, "I'm pregnant" (verse 5).

Good at dealing with problems, David handled this one by sending for Uriah and giving him a month's leave—time off to spend with his wife. "He'll never know the child is mine," the king reasoned (verses 6-8). But the husband was a loyal soldier who didn't feel good about enjoying his wife while his fellow soldiers were roughing it out on the battlefield. So he didn't go home and instead slept on the palace porch. Next the king devised a plan to blur Uriah's thinking. He purposely got the soldier drunk, hoping he would stumble on home and have a night with his wife. But again David's strategy failed. Even in his drunken stupor Uriah would not leave the palace.

Desperate to hide his sin, David now made an incredible decision. He would have Uriah killed—"legitimately," that is—in battle. The king dispatched Uriah back to battle with a letter to Joab, the general, instructing the officer to place Uriah in the thick of the fighting where he would almost certainly become a casualty. Joab, relishing such intrigues, carried out the instructions. Uriah perished in the next day's battle. Word came back to David reporting the event. After the time of mourning was complete, the king married Bathsheba.

Sinning With the "Best of 'Em"

At the end of this terrible episode we read 15 simple words: "But the thing that David had done was evil in the sight of the Lord" (verse 27, NASB). "In that brief statement we see the raw, open sewage of David's life."[2] We aren't prepared for such a David! Have you been keeping count of his sins? Lust, abuse of power,[3] adultery, gross hypocrisy,[4] treacherous duplicity,[5] and murder. He was sinning with the "best of 'em." When believers yield control of their lives to their sinful nature, they can be just as conniving, ruthless, and self-serving as any non-Christian. David's sinful nature surged past his spiritual nature, his passion for sex past his passion for God.

Few things frighten me more than this episode of David's life. We too could be persons of character and integrity and yet, without apparent warning, destroy our ministries, our marriages, our influence, our spiritual power, and ourselves through the choice to gratify our sudden lusts. Like David, a few short verses could record the story of our own downfall.

How could a person—someone after God's own heart—fall to such a level? From what heights of blessing is it possible for a man or a woman to tumble? To what depths of sin can an individual descend, even with all the spiritual background David had?[6]

If you are honest about your own heart, it's not hard to understand. In a sense, 2 Samuel 11 humbles us all![7] This chapter warns us about our own sinful nature. We learn that no situation in life, no office to which even God may call a person, no depth of spirituality or any admiration from others can make someone immune from the attractions of sin. After having risen with David to the pinnacle of his life—great days of victory, spiritual leadership, grace, and dancing like a king—suddenly we find ourselves hurled down into an abyss. The Bathsheba incident pulls back the curtain and reveals the human heart, leaving us stunned and wondering how David could have plummeted so deeply. After all, we are not examining the life of a wild rebel or a sexual pervert—this is David! It leaves us breathless.

Brueggemann puts our dilemma well: "We are now at the pivotal point in the narrative plot of the books of Samuel. We are also invited into the presence of delicate, subtle art. We are at the threshold of deep, aching psychology, and at the same time we are about to witness a most ruthless political performance. In this narrative we are in the presence of greatness. For David and for Israel, we are at a moment of no return. Innocence is never to be retrieved. From now on the life of David is marked, and all Israel must live with that mark. We pause before this artistic rendering, because this text, like none other we have considered, has the power and the subtlety to address us. If we face this text at all, we are soon invited behind all the critical, scholarly questions to face the harder questions of human desire and human power—desire with all its delight, power with all its potential for death. . . . The writer has cut very, very deep into the strange web of foolishness, fear, and fidelity that comprises the human map. This narrative is more than we want to know about David and more than we can bear to understand about ourselves. We might wish the story about David could be 'untold.'"[8]

The story of David and Bathsheba leaves us with a lingering question: "What is my own heart capable of doing?"

All interpreters recognize that 2 Samuel 11 marks the turning point of David's fortune.[9] As Polzin puts it: "At the center of the story of David we find something much more akin to the busting of a bubble than to the relaxed deflation of a balloon. The tragic turn of events that follows chapters 11-12 is but a consequent reverberation of the explosive events of these earlier chapters."[10] What we observe in this incident has profound implications for every one of us in light of choices we might make.

The Moment of Maybe

But how did David come to this point in his life? Some suggest it was midlife crisis.[11] The king was now 50. Or was he a workaholic, investing his energies disproportionately: career, relationships—personal and spiritual? After all, he did have a remarkable ability to give himself completely to the task at hand. He was passionate about anything he set his mind on. Had he in the process distanced himself from his wives and family? Was he a stranger to them, and they with little feeling for him? Did David take the time to establish a relationship that involved authentic intimacy, emotional closeness, and accountability with any other person after Jonathan's death? Was he physically and emotionally worn out (burned out), having neither the inner strength nor the spiritual resources to resist? Was he overcome more out of an inner emptiness than any evil desire? Did he struggle with impotency, feeling as if he was losing his libido?

Without doubt, while Joab and the armies of Israel were laying siege to Rabbah, David was idling away his time in the palace. (As we observed before, this was unusual in the ancient world. Nations expected their leaders to be in the forefront of battle.) He now had leisure he was not equipped to enjoy. As Chafin points out: "He was a man of action with a bit of time on his hands, a warrior who now took naps in the afternoon, and he may have felt the need for some excitement, for a new interest, or for an escape."[12] Ellen White implies that he was drifting spiritually. "It was now, while he was at ease and unguarded, that the tempter seized the opportunity to occupy his mind. . . . When in ease and self-security he let go his hold upon God, David yielded to Satan and brought upon his soul the stain of guilt."[13]

Adultery is never a spontaneous and totally unexpected act. People don't wake up in the morning and say to themselves, "I'm going to commit adultery today." A longer drama always precedes it, at the beginning of which we are not yet helpless. When a Christian succumbs to any sin for that matter, it is seldom a sudden thing—rather it is the culmination of a series of small temptations. Sin traps us because we haven't developed the ability to recognize temptation the moment it first whispers its beguiling suggestions. Nor have we considered the consequences of such small beginnings. Walter Wangerin calls the first subtle temptation a "moment of maybe." "Early on in an extramarital affair," he writes, "there often comes a moment of 'maybe.' Even when that friendship is altogether innocent, your friend may send the signal, or you may sense the feeling, or further possibility. It occurs in a glance more meaningful than mere friends exchange. It arises from a touch, a hug, a brushing of flesh that tingled rather more than you expected—and you remember the sensation. . . . In that moment nothing more is communicated than this: *our friendship could turn into something else.* Neither of you need say, or even think, what that 'something else' might be. . . . It is precisely here that the drama toward adultery begins. Whether it also ends here, or whether it continues hereafter, is a terribly critical question. For a door has opened up.

"If, in this moment, you do nothing at all, then you enter the door. If you make no decision (privately but consciously) to close the door and carefully to restrict this relationship, the drama continues. For though a promise has not been made in the moment of 'maybe,' it hasn't been denied either. And though you may not yet love each other, neither have you said no to love. You permit, by making no decision at all, the 'maybe.' And 'maybe' takes on a life of its own."[14]

"When a desire is born in us, we have a choice. When it exists still in its infancy, we have a choice. We can carefully refuse its existence altogether, since it *needs* our complicity to exist. . . . Or else we can attend to it, think about it, fantasize it into greater existence—feed it! . . . But if we do the latter, if we give it attention in our souls, soon we will be giving it our souls. We've lost free will and the opportunity to choose. The desire itself overpowers us, commanding action, demanding satisfaction."[15]

Scripture puts it bluntly: "One is tempted by one's own desire, being lured and enticed by it; then, when that desire has conceived, it gives birth to sin, and that sin, when it is fully grown, gives birth to death" (James 1:14, 15, NRSV).

Now I want to ask a couple questions. First, did David and Bathsheba know each other before their night of adultery? Commentators divide on the issue, but I think there exists a strong case for saying yes. Several factors suggest that David had some awareness of her before his evening stroll on the roof. We catch a hint of it in the answer his attendant gave when David asked about her: "Is this not Bathsheba, the daughter of Eliam, the wife of Uriah the Hittite?" (2 Sam. 11:3, NKJV). In other words, "the woman's married." He knew exactly what David was thinking. But notice the men in Bathsheba's life that the servant takes pains to point out. She was the daughter of one of David's best fighters, Eliam, a member of the 30 mighty men (2 Sam. 23:34), and she was the wife of Uriah, one of his inner circle of honored 30 soldiers as well (verse 39). As the daughter of Eliam, Bathsheba would have been the granddaughter of Ahithophel, one of David's most trusted and wise counselors (2 Sam. 16:23; 23:34).[16]

David's frequent association with such prominent individuals makes it almost certain that he did know Uriah's gorgeous wife prior to seeing her bathing on the roof.[17] It is even likely that the king had known her as a girl.[18] His question about her identity does not mean that he had never seen her before. It rather deals with positive identification. Then consider Joab. One gets the distinct impression from his response to David after he received Uriah's death order that he knew the king had an interest in the soldier's wife.[19] The general was no fool. He figured it all out in a few milliseconds and let David dangle (2 Sam. 11:18-21).

My point? The "moment of maybe" for David started long before. Her charming personality, quick mind, and beautiful face had previously caught his interest. The sight of her undressed or undressing and then bathing herself on the roof was the last attraction that pushed him over the brink. Interestingly, while his grab for her cost him dearly, she did become the woman of his life. From this point on Scripture mentions no other women in connection with him (except Abishag the Shunammite, sent to keep the aged David warm at night).

My second question is just as intriquing. Was Bathsheba an innocent victim of David's abuse of power or was she, too, "hot to trot"? Did she flaunt herself? Did she come to him because she was naive or simply lacked the will to resist the powerful king's request? Was she taken in by the king, and wondered what it would be like to be with him? If they knew each other before, did she keep the door open at the "moment of maybe"? Here's how Raymond Brown answers such disturbing questions: "When we read this terrible story we instinctively think of the offence as David's sin, but this attractive woman cannot be entirely excused. Bathsheba was careless and foolish, lacking in the usual Hebrew modesty, or she certainly would not have washed in a place where she knew she could be overlooked. From her rooftop she would often have looked out to the royal palace and must have known that she could be seen. It is not enough merely to avoid sin ourselves. The New Testament insists that Christians must ensure that they do not become a stumbling block to others (Rom. 14:12, 13). If David had gone to war he would not have seen Bathsheba that night. If she had thought seriously about her action she would not have put temptation in his path."[20]

Some Bible scholars go so far as to suggest that Bathsheba may have been trying to seduce David.[21] It's feasible, since she no doubt had noticed the king on many occasions strolling on his rooftop. Perhaps she purposefully sought to attract his attention. Being able to overcome her husband's death so quickly suggests that Bathsheba already had a very strong attachment to David (2 Sam. 11:27).[22]

Even she may have experienced the "moment of maybe" long before. Thus she apparently came without hesitation and offered no resistance to David's desires. From the viewpoint of the biblical writer, however, the burden of the sin lays squarely on David alone. It is his story—his dirty dance![23]

Areas of Private Neglect

Opening the door of "maybe" is only part of moral failure. Usually we have areas of private neglect that predispose us to the "maybe"—that nurture "maybes" in our thinking. David encouraged the door of "maybe" through the sensuality he had indulged through the years. He didn't fall suddenly—he had sown seeds of fleshly gratification 20 years before that night with Bathsheba. Areas of private neglect in his character were now beginning to take their toll. Earlier in 2 Samuel we read how he had kept acquiring more concubines and wives (2 Sam. 5:13) in direct contradiction to God's commandment that stated a king was not to multiply horses, material wealth, or wives lest it turn his heart away from the Lord (Deut. 17:14-17).

We read past the passages about David accumulating concubines and wives and write it off as cultural. The bottom line, however, had to do with sensual indulgence. David fostered in himself a habit of sensual excess that predisposed him to that kind of temptation.[24] The fact is that a full harem of women does not satisfy the passion—it only increases it. Lust began to erode his integrity. David's multiple wives made him even more susceptible to the charms of the mysterious beauty bathing next door. The affair with Bathsheba was the climax of 20 years of moral looseness and sensual gratification. The door of "maybe" opens easily after this kind of self-indulgence and moral laxity.

We need to consider still another principle of inner moral wellness. Job put it succinctly: "I made a covenant with my eyes not to look with lust upon a young woman" (Job 31:1, NLT). Since a connection exists between what we allow ourselves to behold and what goes on in our heart, we need to draw some boundaries on the things that enter our hearts through our senses. "There is danger in some of the things we see. And the danger may increase the longer we gaze at them. We cannot avoid seeing some improper things, but we can refuse to look a second time."[25] David could either turn away to safeguard himself, or he could "get an eyeful" and bring darkness to his soul. As Jesus says, the eye is the lamp of the heart. If it is dark, our whole inner private world can become darkened (Luke 11:34).

In their book *Every Man's Battle* authors Arterburn, Stoeker, and Yorkey talk about "bouncing your eyes" and "starving your eyes." "Bouncing your eyes" means that when your eyes bounce toward a woman, they must bounce away *immediately*. Such "bouncing the eyes" would include our response to lingerie advertisements, female joggers in tight nylon shorts, billboards with scantily clad women, beer-and-bikini commercials, movies rated PG-13 and higher, etc. "Starving your eyes" means that we control the amount of sexual images entering our eyes and mind via music, videos, magazines, TV—whatever. Besides these two intentional habits one has to corral the mustang mind. In the end it's a victory that must take place within the heart.[26]

And it is not just a male thing! Shanon Ethridge's volume *Every Woman's Battle* highlights the need for a woman to guard not just her body, but her mind and heart as well. She dispels the myth that women don't really struggle with sexual sin. It is a myth that causes many women to remain vulnerable through unhealthy thoughts, attitudes, and flirtations with men. Many women feel a double shame, because if they feel sexually tempted, they assume they must already be guilty and that no one would really understand their struggle.[27]

When you stop to think about it, the most important sexual organ is the mind. Sexual impulses first begin there. Thought is the source of our action. Our bodies are merely servants of our minds. Not only are we what we think; we do what we think. Human sexual morality is the sum of a continuous series of thoughts, choices, decisions, and actions, including all those tiny indulgences and minuscule compromises. Like a photographic plate accumulating light to form an image, our moral mind is the cumulative result of all we expose it to—whether godly or ungodly. God calls us to be pure not just behaviorally, but in our hearts, in our imaginations, in our desires and passions—in our innermost selves. That's what Jesus had in mind when He said that "anyone who even looks at a woman with lust in his eye has already committed adultery with her in his heart" (Matt. 5:28, NLT).

My point here is that there are some things that we just cannot allow our minds the luxury of thinking about or playing with. I term it *pictureless* pornography! It includes immoral relationships and perspectives. And there are some things we cannot permit ourselves the freedom to read, see, hear, experience, speak about, or wear (and perhaps individuals to be around), because they foster a distorted sexual identity. None of us is mature enough to watch just any movie or television show, read any book, listen to any music, or surf any Web sites without being affected in a negative way.

Furthermore, I hear God telling us that some things just need to be left unheard, unseen, unread, unexperienced, unspoken, unvisited, unimagined—unknown. "I want you to be wise in what is good and innocent in what is evil," Paul urges (Rom. 16:19, NASB). I call it the principle of moral innocence.[28] We need to maintain a level of innocence when it comes to evil. God summons us to a high level of moral accountability in such matters. It's a prescription for people concerned about good habits of the heart—people who want to see God crush Satan under their feet (Rom. 16:20).

James declared that "one is tempted by one's own desire, being lured and enticed by it; then, when that desire has conceived, it gives birth to sin, and that sin, when it is fully grown, gives birth to death" (James 1:14, 15, NRSV).

What Is My Heart Capable Of?

A woman in my congregation found herself strongly tempted to smoke after nine months of "breathing free." Attending a professional convention, she had forgotten that like most conventions the 15-minute breaks between presentations featured uptight people standing around drawing in smoke and puffing it out slowly. With each puff they would throw their shoulders way back and then drop them while exhaling, almost as if relaxing. Finally she went to a more removed and deserted lobby to get away from the smoking. To her surprise, she found an abandoned pack of her once-favorite brand of cigarettes lying there on the table. Luckily, they weren't the size she had usually smoked, and she stomped out immediately. The next day she came back to that same deserted lobby to get away from the pressure she felt from the smokers, only to find another forgotten pack of her once-favorite brand of cigarettes. This time they were *her* size, and it freaked her out. The woman came back from that convention thoroughly unsettled and confided in me that she thought she had dealt with smoking and was now free of it. But her struggle wasn't over. She had to win the war one victory at a time for who knows how long.

Have you ever noticed that books and movies and TV programs revolve around certain themes? It's the "same ole same ole," just with new characters. Sin stories after a while tend to sound pretty much alike—including our own. After observing the human condition for a while, we find that in regard to sin we're mostly watching reruns.[29]

Second Samuel 11 is a rerun. We need to be careful that we ourselves are not drawn into the sin of this affair by romantic—and false—notions. Thus we cannot afford to justify their behavior through sympathy. In our culture we defend immoral behavior with the excuse that two people were "in love." Even if two people are emotionally entangled, we can't call self-gratification and breaking promises to God and others love. Nor can we lend this scene the sympathies we are tempted to offer "victims" of passion in romance novels and movies. The trashy romance we're reading about here is down in the bottom of the barrel, down there with all the sticky stuff and the stench—the place we find ourselves when the line between wanting and getting erodes. Perhaps we may wish we could get everything we want—until we look at David and Bathsheba. The gap between wanting and getting is where we must flex the muscles of self-control to protect ourselves and others. David had risen to a position in which his every wish was someone else's command. He had ceased to hear a very important word—one without which integrity or moral purity cannot be maintained—the word *no*.[30] The king was probably like most of us. He could say no to some things rather easily, but he had great difficulty with others. I wonder about those "others" in my life that I find it hard to say no to. And you?

Second Samuel 11 is a chapter that humbles us all. The story pulls back the curtain and reveals the human heart. Stunned, we wonder how David could have made such a mess of things. The incident tells us more than we want to know about him and more than we can bear to understand about ourselves. Perhaps we wish the story could be "untold."[31] It should leave us with the lingering question "What is my heart capable of doing?"

None of us is completely beyond the sin of adultery. But two kinds of people are in greatest danger: those who think that they could never be tempted and those who are presently being tempted. Every one of us is vulnerable to some form of moral failure or sin. May we cast ourselves on the mercy of God and find grace to help in our time of trouble—big trouble (Heb. 4:16).

With these sobering thoughts we must listen carefully to God's Word:

"Watch and pray, lest you enter into temptation," Jesus says (Matt. 26:41, NKJV).

"Keep your heart with all diligence, for out of it spring the issues of life," we read in Proverbs (Prov. 4:23, NKJV).

"If you think you are standing strong, be careful, for you, too, may fall into the same sin. But remember that the temptations that come into your life are no different from what others experience. And God is faithful. He will keep the temptation from becoming so strong that you can't stand up against it. When you are tempted, he will show you a way out so that you will not give in to it" (1 Cor. 10:12, 13, NLT).

"Yet I still dare to hope when I remember this: The unfailing love of the Lord never ends! By his mercies we have been kept from complete destruction. Great is his faithfulness; his mercies begin afresh each day" (Lam. 3:21-23, NLT).

"God, examine me and know my heart, test me and know my concerns. Make sure that I am not on my way to ruin, and guide me on the road of eternity" (Ps. 139:23, 24, New Jerusalem).

Sinning doesn't take much imagination, but forgiveness and salvation, that's a different story. Every time it happens, it's fresh, original, catching us by surprise.[32] "We have a finite number of ways to sin; God has an infinite number of ways to forgive,"[33] Peterson writes.

In anticipation of our next chapter I want to share something I found in a section of an old worn, yellow book called *Making of a Man of God,* by

Alan Redpath. I don't ever want to forget the words I found there. I hope you'll spend some moments in prayer after you read it.

"David was called 'a man after God's own heart.' That was the caliber of the man, the height to which he had risen. He had become king of all Israel, and he had defeated all his enemies. He had risen now to the peak of his life and career—when suddenly the devil tripped him up.

"Oh, from what heights of blessing it is possible for a man to fall! To what depths of sin a man can descend, even with all that spiritual background! The higher the pinnacle of blessing, authority, and publicity he has attained by grace, the deeper and more staggering can be his collapse. There is never a day in any man's life but that he is dependent upon the grace of God for power and the blood of Jesus for cleansing."[34]

"If we learn about the heinousness of David's sin—and we leave it at that—we have learned little, because we know it; but if we learn about the mercy of God, then we surely have learned something tremendous."[35]

---

[1]As told by Ed Young, *Been There. Done That. Now What?: The Meaning of Life May Surprise You* (Nashville: Broadman & Holman Publishers, 1994), pp. 43, 44.

[2]C. R. Swindoll, *David: A Man of Passion and Destiny,* p. 193.

[3]The subtle repetition and wordplay of the Hebrew word *send* yields insights into David's abuse of power. By following the use of this verb, we can trace David's descent into calculating cruelty and ruthless exercise of power. The passage begins with the phrase "David *sent* Joab" (2 Sam. 11:1); it picks up momentum when "David *sent*" to inquire about Bathsheba (verse 3); the plot thickens when "David *sent*" and got Bathsheba (verse 4). Next follow a cluster of "sendings": "So David *sent* . . . word to Joab: '*Send* me Uriah the Hittite.' And Joab *sent* him to David" (verse 6, NIV). The king then writes a letter to Joab ordering Uriah's death and "*sent* it by the hand of Uriah" (verse 14). After he had accomplished his cover-up, "David sent" for Bathsheba again and married her (verse 27). See E. H. Peterson, *Leap Over a Wall,* pp. 183, 184.

[4]When David asked Uriah about the welfare of Joab and the other soldiers as well as the state of the war (2 Sam. 11:7), he didn't really care about the soldiers or the progress of the war or how Joab was doing. Not for a moment. It's an ad lib, designed to make him look compassionate and interested. He's merely setting Uriah up. See K. Kaynor, *When God Chooses,* pp. 229-231; Swindoll, *David: A Man of Passion and Destiny,* p. 190.

[5]Uriah was one of David's 30 mighty men, someone who had served David with loyalty and passion. What makes David's scheme so diabolical is that the king knew Uriah would not retreat in battle. He was too loyal, having already proved that point when he wouldn't go home to his wife. Nor would he read the letter that he carried ordering his death. In fact, David actually used Uriah's commitment to him as the king of Israel in order to take his life. When push came to shove, the loyalty wasn't reciprocal. David's self-serving interests would take precedence over fidelity.

[6]A. Redpath, *The Making of a Man of God,* p. 197.

[7]Kaynor, p. 224.

[8]W. Brueggemann, *First and Second Samuel,* pp. 271, 272.

[9] A. Thompson, *Samuel: From the Danger of Chaos to the Danger of Power,* p. 225.

[10] Robert Polzin, *David and the Deuteronomist: A Literary Study of the Deuteronomic History* (Bloomington, Ind.: Indiana University Press, 1993), p. 119.

[11] Richard Exley, *Deliver Me* (Nashville: Thomas Nelson Publishers, 1998), pp. 208-210.

[12] Kenneth L. Chafin, *The Communicator's Commentary: 1, 2 Samuel* (Dallas: Word Books, Publishers, 1989), p. 301.

[13] Ellen G. White, *Patriarchs and Prophets,* p. 718.

[14] Walter Wangerin, Jr., *As for Me and My House: Crafting Your Marriage to Last* (Nashville: Thomas Nelson Publishers, 1987), pp. 196, 197.

[15] *Ibid.,* p. 195.

[16] See R. D. Bergen, *1, 2 Samuel,* p. 364.

[17] Kaynor, p. 233.

[18] Ellen White makes a clear connection between Bathsheba and Ahithophel as her grandfather and comments on Ahithophel's revenge for David's breaking friendship boundaries. "'And David went up by the ascent of Mount Olivet, and wept as he went up, and had his head covered, and he went barefoot: and all the people that was with him covered every man his head, and they went up, weeping as they went up. And one told David, saying, Ahithophel is among the conspirators with Absalom.' Again David was forced to recognize in his calamities the results of his own sin. The defection of Ahithophel, the ablest and most wily of political leaders, was prompted by revenge for the family disgrace involved in the wrong to Bathsheba, who was his granddaughter" (*Patriarchs and Prophets,* p. 735).

[19] Kaynor, p. 233.

[20] Raymond Brown, *Skillful Hands: Studies in the Life of David* (Fort Washington, Pa.: Christian Literature Crusade, 1972), p. 99.

[21] G. G. Nicol, "Bathsheba, a Clever Woman?" *Expository Times 99* (September 1988): 360-363.

[22] Kaynor, p. 241.

[23] F. B. Meyer, *The Life of David,* p. 166.

[24] *Ibid.*

[25] Kaynor, p. 226.

[26] Stephen Arterburn, Fred Stoeker, and Mike Yorkey, *Every Man's Battle: Winning the War on Sexual Temptation One Victory at a Time* (Colorado Springs, Colo.: WaterBrook Press, 2000).

[27] Shanon Ethridge, *Every Woman's Battle: Discovering God's Plan for Sexual and Emotional Fulfillment* (Colorado Springs, Colo.: WaterBrook Press, 2003).

[28] The Greek *akeraious* means "innocent, guileless, pure" (Matt. 10:16; Phil. 2:15), "unravaged" or "unharmed"—that which is still in its original state of intactness, totality, or moral innocence.

[29] Peterson, p. 190.

[30] B. Moore, *A Heart Like His,* pp. 170, 171.

[31] Brueggemann, p. 272.

[32] Peterson, p. 190.

[33] *Ibid.*

[34] Redpath, p. 197.

[35] *Ibid.,* p. 196.

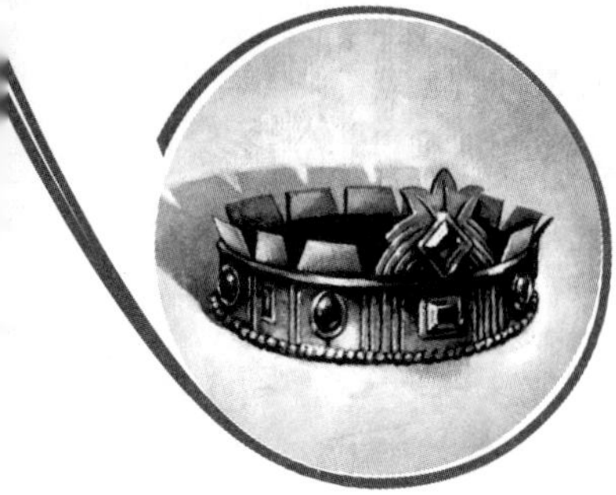

9

CHICKEN SOUP FOR THE SOUL

2 Samuel 12:1-14

The runaway best seller *Chicken Soup for the Soul*[1] captured the imagination of millions with its message of hope and inspiration. Like grandma's warm and soothing chicken soup when you're feeling yucky, this treasury of 101 inspirational stories was cooked up to "open the heart and rekindle the spirit." Stories can be therapeutic as well as captivating. So much so that Canfield and Hansen have since released multiple volumes of their *Chicken Soup for the Soul,* including ones for men and women and teenagers and the Jewish—you name it!

Besides being therapeutic, stories are one of the most powerful ways of teaching values and opening the door to new possibilities. Capturing our interest and holding our attention, they stir emotions and help us remember. They affect us in ways that abstract precepts and propositions never do. Their meaning slips past our conscious mind and its defenses and touches us on a level we can't explain. Often we don't see what is coming in the story, and when we do, it's too late. We're hooked.

For nearly a year David was able to cover his sin of adultery and murder—refusing to acknowledge it to himself, to the Lord, and to the people of Israel. Then one day a strange thing happened. David's pastor, Nathan, showed up and preached him a sermon. At the moment the king had no idea that he was listening to a sermon. After all, he wasn't sitting in a pew and Nathan wasn't standing in a pulpit.[2] It was just a story—a captivating yarn about some rich guy with large flocks of sheep cruelly and arrogantly taking the pet lamb of the poor man living down the street. Then he slaughters the lamb and serves it up to his guests, leaving the poor man heartbroken at the loss of his precious daughter-like lamb that would sleep in his arms (2 Sam. 12:1-4).

They say that we can think three times as fast as we hear, so as Nathan spins his tale, David's mind is humming. He's drawn into the narrative. While some suggest that the prophet's story was artless and simple,[3] in reality it was subtle in its approach. Nathan's good—real good! He chose a plot and evocative words that would elicit instinctive feelings—including imagery that the rich man raped the daughter-like treasure of the poor man.[4] It was an emotionally charged tale of cynicism, selfishness, exploitation, destruction, and greed.[5]

Evidently David perched on the edge of his chair, thinking that Nathan was talking about something that had recently happened in the city of Jerusalem.[6] The story did its work. The king's response is immediate, indignant, and on target. The callous cruelty in the story enraged him, and, as a righteous judge, he passed a death sentence on the rich man: "'As surely as the Lord lives,' he vowed, 'any man who would do such a thing deserves to die! He must repay four lambs to the poor man for the one he stole and for having no pity'" (verses 5, 6, NLT).

Then Nathan pounces, shifting from storytelling to interpretation—and confrontation! "You are the man!" (verse 7, NKJV). Before David could say a word, Nathan went on to name his sins and describe their consequences: "The Lord, the God of Israel, says, 'I anointed you king of Israel and saved you from the power of Saul. I gave you his house and his wives and the kingdoms of Israel and Judah. And if that had not been enough, I would have given you much, much more. Why, then, have you despised the word of the Lord and done this horrible deed? For you have murdered Uriah and stolen his wife. From this time on, the sword will be a constant threat to your family, because you have despised me by taking Uriah's wife to be your own. Because of what you have done, I, the Lord, will cause your own household to rebel against you. I will give your wives to another man, and he will go to bed with them in public view. You did it secretly, but I will do this to you openly in the sight of all Israel'" (verses 7-12, NLT).

David's mind must have reeled in shocked disbelief as Nathan's words plunged like a knife into his heart. Suddenly he saw himself for what he was—an adulterer, a liar, a hypocrite, a thief, and a murderer. A wretched man. He was the man who deserved to die. His anger turned to grief and remorse as meekness and shame replaced his fiery outburst.

"I have sinned against the Lord," David finally confessed.

"Yes," Nathan replied, "but the Lord has forgiven you, and you won't die for this sin" (verse 13, NLT).

As David listened to his pastor preach a sermon about somebody else he got all worked up about someone else's sin and someone else's plight. And then . . . it's him. His sins. His guilt. His plight. As Peterson writes: "This is the gospel focus: *you* are the man; *you* are the woman. The gospel is never about somebody else; it's always about you, about me."[7]

The Telltale Heart

At first thought Nathan's gripping story was no "chicken soup for the soul." It had nothing heartwarming about it. Or soothing or therapeutic. On the contrary, it went straight for the jugular confrontation that brought David to his knees in gut-wrenching confession. Not the kind of story most of us want to hear.

Perhaps you have heard of Edgar Allan Poe's haunting story "The Tell-Tale Heart"? The main character has committed a gruesome murder. Unable to escape the haunting guilt of his deed, he begins to hear the heartbeat of the victim he has buried under the floorboards of his living room. A cold sweat covers him as the beat-beat-beat-beat goes on, relentlessly growing louder—louder—*louder!* Ultimately it becomes clear that the pounding that drove the man insane was not from the dismembered corpse underneath the floorboards, but in his own chest.[8] So it is with an unforgiven conscience.

David was no stranger to the emotional and physical symptoms that accompany an unforgiven conscience and how it can drive you insane and drain spiritual passion. He appeared to be moving on with his life as if nothing had happened, but how do you suppose his sin affected his relationship with the Lord? Had he simply picked up with God at the same place he had been before? Hardly! Most of us have had seasons of unrepentance when we outwardly attempted to go on with life as if we had not sinned against God. However, our unwillingness to repent has internal effects. The king had become increasingly more physically ill and emotionally distraught the longer he refused to come to terms with the enormity of his guilt. Listen to his own words:

> "Oh, what joy for those whose rebellion is forgiven,
> whose sin is put out of sight!
> Yes, what joy for those whose record the Lord has cleared of sin,
> whose lives are lived in complete honesty!
> When I refused to confess my sin,
> I was weak and miserable,
> and I groaned all day long.
> Day and night your hand of discipline was heavy on me.
> My strength evaporated like water in the summer heat. . . .
> Finally, I confessed all my sins to you
> and stopped trying to hide them.
> I said to myself,
> 'I will confess my rebellion to the Lord.'
> And you forgave me!
> All my guilt is gone" (Ps. 32:1-5, NLT).

"When I lived in the true guilt of my soul, I could not stay silent down inside," David admits. "As a matter of fact, I groaned all day long." You know what that means? He felt the heavy hand of God on him. It was like a running fever. Unable to handle the pressures of work, the stress made him sick, and he ran out of energy. "My sin is ever before me," he wrote (Ps. 51:3). David could live a lie, but he couldn't escape the truth. His conscience may have been invisible, but it certainly wasn't inactive. Sleepless nights exhausted him. In his mind he could see his sin written across the ceiling of his room as he tossed and turned in bed. During the days it was emblazoned on the walls. Wherever he went, whoever he saw, his guilt kept whispering in his ears. That's what sin does to you. Taking your joy away is always part of the wages that sin inevitably demands.

Oscar Wilde's novel *The Picture of Dorian Gray* depicts the personal consequences of moral compromise through a powerful allegory. Having sat for a portrait of himself, the dashing young Dorian Gray regrets that he will age and change while the picture stays the same. He wants to stay forever as young and charming as the portrait. If only the situation could be reversed, he sighs. "Let me stay young and let the picture age." Gray gets his wish. He remains a handsome narcissistic (self-loving, egotistic) young socialite while the portrait in his attic begins to grow older.

Soon the portrait starts to bear the consequences of the real Gray's self-loving behavior. When he makes a cruel comment, the mouth on the portrait twists into a cruel grin. As he nurses hatred toward a rival, the eyes on the portrait narrow in rage. Finally, when he murders a man, the hands on the portrait drip with blood. Every time Gray chooses self, the portrait gets older while Gray stays young and healthy. At the end of the book Gray despises the portrait so much that he slashes it with a knife. When a servant comes up to the attic to check on his master, he finds that the portrait has vanished and Dorian Gray is lying on the floor with a knife through his heart. The painting had visibly represented his true self, and when he finally faced it he couldn't handle it. So he killed himself.[9] As bizarre as Wilde's story might be, I couldn't help thinking about what David's attic portrait looked like. Even more so, what would it be like to face my true self?

It surprised many Americans when Katherine Ann Power suddenly reappeared in 1993 and surrendered herself to the FBI after 23 years on the run. The tragic 1970 Boston bank heist, which led to police officer William Schroeder being mercilessly submachine-gunned in the back, sent Power on a long odyssey of internal turmoil. Through the years she assumed a different identity and whole new life: that of Alice Metzinger.

To some, Kathy Power had become something of a mythic figure—the one the police couldn't catch. But she finally was caught—not by the FBI, but by herself. By her conscience. Inside she had the haunting memory of a crime that would not let go of her. Struggling with her secrets, she became so emotionally and psychologically worn down that she could no longer go on; she knew that she had no choice but to do something about it. After months of intense therapy she finally decided to come clean with it. Power's husband told *Time* that "she wanted her life back. She wanted her truth back. She wants to be whole." Katherine herself said, "I know that I must answer this accusation from the past in order to live with full authenticity in the present."[10] This is what David experienced.

If you are harboring some secret wrong, don't expect to enjoy freedom from guilt. An unspoken axiom threads its way through Scripture: secret sin cannot coexist with inner peace. Peace returns only when we fully confess and forsake our sins. Nothing is more grinding than an unforgiven conscience.[11]

Grace Awakening

So Nathan's story was "chicken soup for the soul" after all. It engendered a "grace awakening" that brought relief to David's tortured soul. In mere moments—with just one masterful story with its penetrating interpretation and candid application—the king recovered his awareness of God and sin. "And in that double awareness of God and sin, David prayed the prayer that we call Psalm 51."[12]

> "Have mercy on me, O God,
>   because of your unfailing love.
> Because of your great compassion,
>   blot out the stain of my sins.
> Wash me clean from my guilt.
>   Purify me from my sin.
>
> For I recognize my shameful deeds—
>   they haunt me day and night.
> Against you, and you alone, have I sinned;
>   I have done what is evil in your sight.
> You will be proved right in what you say,
>   and your judgment against me is just.
>
> For I was born a sinner—
>   yes, from the moment my mother conceived me.
> But you desire honesty from the heart,
>   so you can teach me to be wise in my inmost being.
>
> Purify me from my sins, and I will be clean;

wash me, and I will be whiter than snow.
Oh, give me back my joy again;
you have broken me—now let me rejoice.
Don't keep looking at my sins.
Remove the stain of my guilt.
Create in me a clean heart, O God.
Renew a right spirit within me.
Do not banish me from your presence,
and don't take your Holy Spirit from me.
Restore to me again the joy of your salvation,
and make me willing to obey you.
Then I will teach your ways to sinners,
and they will return to you.
Forgive me for shedding blood, O God who saves;
then I will joyfully sing of your forgiveness.
Unseal my lips, O Lord,
that I may praise you.
You would not be pleased with sacrifices,
or I would bring them.
If I brought you a burnt offering,
you would not accept it.
The sacrifice you want is a broken spirit.
A broken and repentant heart, O God,
you will not despise" (Ps. 51:1-17, NLT).

Psalm 51 captures David's wholehearted repentance. In abject spiritual poverty he cast himself on the mercy of the Lord for the forgiveness and restoration he desperately needed. Life for him would be a relentless prison of guilt and shame unless he experienced God's forgiveness. Under the power of Nathan's story-preaching, the king saw his sin and realized that beyond exploiting and demeaning Bathsheba or murdering Uriah, he had sinned against God. Had David not rebelled against the Lord's Word, the two people would not have been murdered or abused.

Grace and Consequences

David's confession came without denial, rationalization, or excuse. The Lord's forgiveness was equally direct and unrestrained—and also without cost. Great mercy also accompanied that forgiveness. "The Lord has forgiven you," Nathan says, "and you won't die for this sin" (2 Sam. 12:13, NLT). Isn't that amazing? No sooner had David confessed than Nathan assured Him of the Lord's forgiveness. "David received immediate forgiveness, immediate cleansing, immediate restoration, and fellowship"[13] Sometimes that's hard for us to grasp—that we can be forgiven so quickly, cleansed so soon, and restored so instantly. It's awesome and always amazing.

But while David received immediate forgiveness, immediate cleansing, and immediate restoration and fellowship, there also followed unbelievably persistent suffering as a consequence of his sin. While the Lord forgave David and granted him the unmerited gift of life, he did not remove all consequences resulting from his sin. "From this time on," God announced through Nathan, "the sword will be a constant threat to your family, because you have despised me by taking Uriah's wife to be your own. Because of what you have done, I, the Lord, will cause your own household to rebel against you. I will give your wives to another man, and he will go to bed with them in public view. You did it secretly, but I will do this to you openly in the sight of all Israel" (verses 10-12, NLT).

Swindoll says it well: "All sins are forgivable, when confessed and forsaken, but some sins carry tremendous ramifications . . . the awful, sometimes lingering consequences."[14] The consequences for David included family turmoil and tragedy, rape and revenge, and an uncontrollable son who betrayed him and actually drove his own father from the throne. Talk about the consequences! In the short term his newborn son died after being seriously ill for seven days (verses 15-18). It was the child that the king had tried to pawn off on Uriah. But now, after being born at great shame, the king treasures him. David wills him life with all his power, fasting and praying and laying all night on the bare ground. But the innocent little boy perishes.[15]

In the aftermath of this heart-wrenching loss, though, David bathed, put on lotions, and changed his clothes. Then he went into the tabernacle and worshiped the Lord (verse 20), now "awakened to what is really important in life, and he was rebuked for his sin."[16] As he accepted the reality of consequences, he chose to receive them, however painful, with a worshipful heart. After all, God had forgiven him. The prophet had said so. But the consequences hurt so bad. How could he ever even want to dance again?

One of the biggest struggles we have is to keep our sense of forgiveness and the reality of consequences separate. The painful and relentless results of our sins tend to keep the sins fresh in our imagination. When that happens, it's hard to feel forgiven. But David shows us that we can not only feel forgiven; we can worship. Like him, we can accept even the consequences of sin, however painful, with a worshipful heart. After all, we are forgiven when we repent and confess, no matter what happens. Scripture says so: "If we confess our sins, He is faithful and just to forgive us our sins and to cleanse us from all unrighteousness" (1 John 1:9, NKJV).

What is really awesome about this story is that God matched consequences with grace. As the pain unfolded, so did God's gracious blessings. David would have tangible things to remind him that God was with still with him. Bathsheba became pregnant again and gave birth to a son. Recognizing it as a sign of the Lord's goodness to them, they named him Solomon—meaning "the man of peace" (something they must have experienced together in God). Scripture tells us that "the Lord loved the child and sent word through Nathan . . . that his name should be Jedidiah—'beloved of the Lord'—because the Lord loved him" (2 Sam. 12:24, 25, NLT).

Brueggemann suggests that "the placement of Solomon's birth in the narrative is stunning. Solomon is born so close to the sordidness, still within the echo of the prophetic lawsuit. Nonetheless, life begins again for this family. This God has an amazing capacity to work more life at the border of death, to act in promise-keeping ways (cf. 2 Sam. 7:12) just when the promise seems exhausted. The account of David and Bathsheba is a tale of alienation and judgment; in its midst, however, are gestures of grace made by Yahweh. This birth is marked by Yahweh's love, not anger (cf. Ps. 103:9-14)."[17]

Then there was his marriage. Although David and Bathsheba's relationship began sinfully, she became *the woman* in his life.[18] His other wives disappear from the Bible narrative after the introduction of Bathsheba. She was his companion the rest of his life.

By the way, Bathsheba, too, suffered the consequences of adultery. She endured days of anguish over her pregnancy before Uriah died. Her and David's first son's illness and death was hard on both her and the king. They knew they had caused it. As parents they were under great strain. Bathsheba shared Nathan's rebuke and repented along with David.[19] Because of his wise handling of such a ticklish matter, Nathan endeared himself to both David and Bathsheba, and long remained associated with them.[20] Bathsheba's close alliance with the prophet from then on shows genuine repentance. Her greatest influence came through the birth of her son Solomon. Nathan, incidentally, shared in his training.

God was mindful of public blessings as well. Now Joab brings David back to the real world with an urgent summons to come finish the siege of Rabbah, "otherwise I will take the city, and it will be named after me" (2 Sam. 12:28, NIV).[21] Through Joab God permits David a public success when he surely needed it to stop the gossip at court.[22] It would also affirm his moral, spiritual, and political leadership. So David goes out to battle, overwhelms the enemy, and takes much plunder, including a crown of gold set with beautiful gems.

Although David has fallen, the Lord has awakened him and even blessed him. In the end, Nathan's masterful story was "chicken soup for the soul" after all. God was simply keeping His promise: "If they violate My statutes and do not keep My commandments, then I will visit their transgression with the rod and their iniquity with stripes. But I will not break off My lovingkindness from him, nor deal falsely in My faithfulness" (Ps. 89:31-33, NASB).

It's All About You

"The gospel is never about somebody else," Peterson says, "it's always about you, about me. . . . It's always about actual persons, actual pain, actual trouble, actual sin: you, me; who you are and what you've done; who I am and what I've done."[23] Nathan speaks to every one of us: "You are the man!" "You are the woman!"

Like David, you may need to recover an awareness of God and of sin. And like Israel's king, you may be harboring some sin—keeping hidden a few secret regions of wrong. They make you miserable and tortured, draining the desire to dance right out of you. Your passion for God seems like lead, because secret sin cannot coexist with inner peace. Peace returns only when you have fully confessed and forsaken your sins. Nothing is more grinding than an unforgiven conscience.

As with David, perhaps it's time to hear the words of Nathan, "You! You are the man!" and confess, making things right with God. God singles out this sin as the one great element of displeasure that He had toward David's life: "For David had done what was right in the eyes of the Lord and had not failed to keep any of the Lord's commands all the days of his life—except in the case of Uriah the Hittite" (1 Kings 15:5, NIV). Through God's grace the king returned to a life of obedience and the peace and joy that such obedience brings. That's what God wants for you. Perhaps this very story could be God's intended "chicken soup" for your soul.

"We have a finite number of ways to sin," Peterson adds. "God has an infinite number of ways to forgive. . . . Sinning doesn't take much imagination. But forgiveness and salvation? That's a different story: every time it happens, it's fresh, original, catching us by surprise. Sin isn't creative work, and the more we're around it, the duller it seems. Salvation, in contrast, is 'new every morning' (Lam. 3:23)."[24] Is it time for you to take hold of it?

David declares:

> "Oh, what joy for those whose rebellion is forgiven,
>   whose sin is put out of sight!
> Yes, what joy for those whose record the Lord has cleared of sin,
>   whose lives are lived in complete honesty!
> When I refused to confess my sin,
>   I was weak and miserable,
>   and I groaned all day long.
> Day and night your hand of discipline was heavy on me.
>   My strength evaporated like water in the summer heat. . . .
> Finally, I confessed all my sins to you
>   and stopped trying to hide them.
> I said to myself,
>   'I will confess my rebellion to the Lord.'
> And you forgave me!
>   All my guilt is gone" (Ps. 32:1-5, NLT).

Ellen White tells us that "this passage in David's history is full of significance to the repenting sinner. It is one of the most forcible illustrations given us of the struggles and temptations of humanity, and of genuine repentance toward God and faith in our Lord Jesus Christ. Through all the ages it has proved a source of encouragement to souls that, having fallen into sin, were struggling under the burden of their guilt. Thousands of the children of God, who have been betrayed into sin, when ready to give up to despair have remembered how David's sincere repentance and confession were accepted by God, notwithstanding, he suffered for his transgression; and they also have taken courage to repent and try again to walk in the way of God's commandments. Whoever under the reproof of God will humble the soul with confession and repentance, as did David, may be sure that there is hope for him. Whoever will in faith accept God's promises, will find pardon. The Lord will never cast away one truly repentant soul."[25]

No relief can compare to repentance. "The first word of the gospel is not 'love.' It is not even 'grace.' The first word of the gospel is 'repent.' From Matthew through the Revelation, repentance is an urgent and indispensable theme that is kept at the very forefront of the gospel message."[26] A gift of God, repentance is not a single act, but an ongoing and continual attitude. It is not merely turning from what you have done, but from what you are. And it is open rather than secret and leads to a godly sorrow that produces actions consistent with that repentance. "Yes," Jesus told His disciples, "it was written long ago that the Messiah must suffer and die and rise again from the dead on the third day. With my authority, take this message of repentance to all the nations, beginning in Jerusalem: 'There is forgiveness of sins for all who turn to me'" (Luke 24:45-47, NLT).

As a repentant sinner who has experienced the misery of broken fellowship with God and reveled in the freshness of His forgiving grace, I would like to conclude this chapter with these powerful words about God:

> "Who is a God like you,
> who pardons sin and forgives the transgression
> of the remnant of his inheritance?
> You do not stay angry forever
> but delight to show mercy.

You will again have compassion on us;
you will tread our sins underfoot
and hurl all our iniquities into the depths of the sea"
(Micah 7:18, 19, NIV).

When David repented, he asked for mercy. God graciously granted his request. He will do the same for you.

---

[1] *Chicken Soup for the Soul: 101 Stories to Open the Heart and Rekindle the Spirit* ed. Jack Canfield and Mark Victor Hansen (Deerfield Beach, Fla.: Health Communications, Inc., 1993).

[2] E. H. Peterson, *Leap Over a Wall,* p. 184.

[3] *Ibid.*

[4] W. Brueggemann, *First and Second Samuel,* p. 280; R. Polzin, *David and the Deuteronomist,* pp. 120-122.

[5] Brueggemann, p. 280.

[6] C. R. Swindoll, *David: A Man of Passion and Destiny,* p. 201.

[7] Peterson, p. 185.

[8] Edgar Allan Poe, *Poetry and Tales* (New York, N.Y.: Literary Classics of the United States, 1984), pp. 555-559.

[9] See Oscar Wilde, *The Picture of Dorian Gray;* cited in Philip Yancey, *Rumors of Another World: What on Earth Are We Missing?* (Grand Rapids: Zondervan, 2003), p. 153.

[10] *Time,* Oct. 4, 1993.

[11] Charles R. Swindoll, *Living Beyond the Daily Grind: Book I* (Dallas: Word Publishing, 1988), p. 113.

[12] Peterson, p. 188.

[13] Theodore H. Epp, *A Man After the Heart of God,* p. 152.

[14] Swindoll, *David: A Man of Passion and Destiny,* p. 207.

[15] The child's death did not mean that God was unjust or unloving. On the contrary, it indicated that the divine word spoken by Nathan was trustworthy. See R. D. Bergen, *1, 2 Samuel,* p. 376.

[16] K. Kaynor, *When God Chooses,* p. 239.

[17] Brueggemann, p. 284.

[18] Kaynor, p. 240.

[19] *Ibid.,* p. 241.

[20] *Ibid.,* p. 235.

[21] A. Thompson, *Samuel: From the Danger of Chaos to the Danger of Power,* p. 230.

[22] Brueggemann, p. 284.

[23] Peterson, p. 185.

[24] *Ibid.,* p. 190.

[25] E. G. White, *Patriarchs and Prophets,* p. 726.

[26] Richard Owen Roberts, *Repentance: The First Word of the Gospel* (Wheaton, Ill.: Crossway Books, 2002), p. 23.

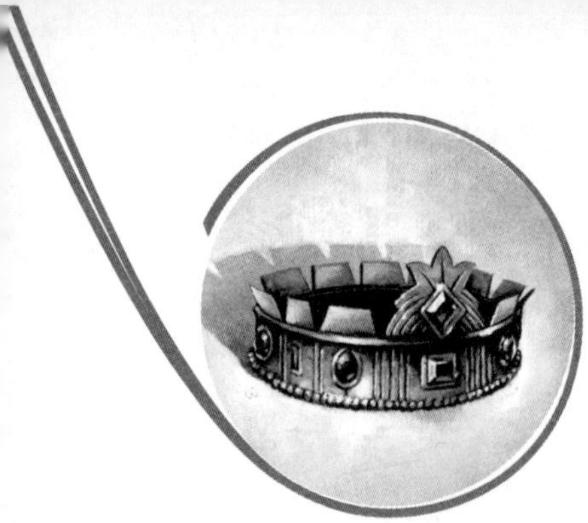

10

THE ARROW THAT FLIES

2 Samuel 13

Kahlil Gibran in his intriguing poem "On Parenting" compares parents with bows and children with arrows.[1] God loves those parents who will be stable bows in the hands of God and send their children on the right path. In other words, the moral and spiritual stability of parents makes a crucial difference in whether or not children reach the life target God has envisioned for them.

But David proved to be an unstable bow! His affair with Bathsheba and his murder of Uriah had a devastating impact on his family. Just as Nathan had predicted: " 'Now, therefore, the sword will never depart from your house, because you despised me and took the wife of Uriah the Hittite to be your own.' This is what the Lord says: 'Out of your own household I am going to bring calamity upon you. Before your very eyes I will take your wives and give them to one who is close to you, and he will lie with your wives in broad daylight. You did it in secret, but I will do this thing in broad daylight before all Israel' " (2 Sam. 12:10-12, NIV).

The rape of Tamar and the subsequent murder of Amnon by Absalom is a *family* story. It depicts the power that parents and children have to influence family (and society) for either good or evil. Some very important themes come into focus with regard to what Gibran calls "stable bows" and "living arrows."

Learning What They Live

The story gets to the point quickly. David's firstborn son, Amnon, found himself attracted to his beautiful half sister Tamar, the full-blood sister of David's third son, Absalom. It was a disgraceful, disgusting kind of love—incestuous lust. Amnon became so obsessed with his sister Tamar that he literally got sick. Because she was a virgin, it seemed impossible for him to get to her. Kings carefully protected their virgin daughters! Besides, what he had in mind violated social mores. Seeing his haggard appearance, Amnon's slimy cousin Jonadab asked what was wrong. After Amnon shared what he wanted to do with Tamar, Jonadab helped him scheme a plan. On the cousin's advice, Amnon pretended to be physically ill. When his father David came by to see him, he asked if his sister Tamar could take care of him.

Finally alone with Tamar, passion swept Amnon beyond reason. "Come to bed with me, my darling sister," he said, grabbing her.

"'No, my brother!' she cried. 'Don't be foolish! Don't do this to me! You know what a serious crime it is to do such a thing in Israel. Where could I go in my shame? And you would be called one of the greatest fools in Israel. Please, just speak to the king about it, and he will let you marry me.' But Amnon wouldn't listen to her, and since he was stronger than she was, he raped her" (2 Sam. 13:12-14, NLT).

Unreasonable and impatient, Amnon took what he wanted. Those who have experienced the trauma of rape know the injury doesn't end with the event. The actions and reactions of others multiply the pain. In this case Amnon quickly added to the hurt. His passion suddenly turned to hate.

"Then Amnon hated her with intense hatred. In fact, he hated her more than he had loved her. Amnon said to her, 'Get up and get out!'

"'No!' she said to him. 'Sending me away would be a greater wrong than what you have already done to me.'

"But he refused to listen to her. He called his personal servant and said, 'Get this woman out of here and bolt the door after her.' So his servant put her out and bolted the door after her. She was wearing a richly ornamented robe, for this was the kind of garment the virgin daughters of the king wore. Tamar put ashes on her head and tore the ornamented robe she was wearing. She put her hand on her head and went away, weeping aloud as she went" (verses 15-19, NIV).

What he had been calling love was just a passing desire, now completely spent. He felt no lingering attraction for Tamar, no desire for continued intimacy, nothing that we might remotely call love. At the moment he wanted her only to leave. "Get out of here!" he snarled. In embarrassment and disgrace Tamar tore the long beautiful robe that the king's daughters customarily wore as a sign of their purity and put ashes on her head. Then with her face in her hands, she left, weeping loudly.

The tragic irony of Tamar's dress touches my heart. The richly ornamented robe was her cloak of dignity and honor. She now tore the fabric of her robe as surely as Amnon had ripped the fabric of her honor. I am acutely aware that some who read these words have been victims of rape. I want to approach this subject with tenderness and reverence. It's something I, especially as a male, cannot even begin to comprehend. But I can make a few things clear. We can assign appropriate responsibility here. All blame for the rape belongs to the perpetrator—Amnon. That is true in every rape. Strangely but tragically, when we consider the roles of Amnon, Absalom, and David in Tamar's life, she fell victim to all three men surrounding this event. Both Absalom and David also reacted inappropriately toward Tamar and the crime she suffered. When Absalom learned of the rape, he was outraged and determined to avenge his sister's honor (verses 20, 22). His advice to Tamar, though, was to keep the incident a secret and pretend that nothing had happened. While the shame was crushing her to pieces, he minimized the significance of the terrible crime against her, even though he did invite her to live with him the rest of her life. In the end she was left desolate—like the living dead.

News of Amnon's behavior made David angry as well. In fact, he was furious (verse 21). But that's all—furious! The king didn't do anything concrete about it. He just fumed. Can you imagine how Tamar felt right then about the fact that her father didn't do a thing about it? The unfolding drama essentially sidelines Tamar. We don't hear about her anymore. But I believe that as she mourned before God—completely innocent, her life and future ruined forever—God was faithful. He did not look away for an instant. Someday He will replace her tattered robe and cover her with finest white linen, and she will stand before Him once again the virgin daughter of a king.[2] In the end, too, God will deal appropriately with the apparently unrepentant Amnon.

David's apparent inactivity hardened Absalom in his resolve to take vengeance on Amnon. Revenge smoldered in his mind for two years. Justice for Amnon need not be swift, but it must be sure. Waiting for the right time, Absalom plotted coolly and carefully. When everything was in place, he brutally murdered Amnon during a family party, then fled to his mother's home country of Geshur, where he stayed for three years because he feared his father (verses 23-38). As Brueggemann notes: "The narrative makes its point. Vengeance is accomplished. Absalom has avenged Tamar. [He] may have been too aggressive and brutal, but one can understand why he acts as he does. . . .This is not a wild, undisciplined killing."[3] Interestingly, events have opened the way for Absalom to ascend to the throne.[4]

On both counts David showed himself incapable of acting. He didn't do anything about Tamar's rape or Amnon's murder. The king let both crimes slide. Why didn't he take control of his family tragedy? I believe Satan may have been working on David, just as he does on us when we really blow it. His own sexual sin and premeditated murder had left him paralyzed. It blinded him to Tamar's need to find release for the fire of hurt and shame that burned in her. His sense of guilt kept him from serving justice on Amnon for his crime and from avenging his daughter. And it paralyzed him from holding Absalom accountable as well. Who was he to speak out and do anything when he was guilty of similar crimes? Satan uses sin and failure so effectively against us that even after sincere repentance we often remain completely disabled. He whispers all sorts of things in our ears. "How can you go to church after what you've done? How can you expect obedience from your children? Who are you to talk, you hypocrite!"

Ellen White tells us that following his sin with Bathsheba, "there was a great change in David himself. He was broken in spirit by the consciousness of his sin and its far-reaching results. He felt humbled in the eyes of his subjects. His influence was weakened. Hitherto his prosperity had been attributed to his conscientious obedience to the commandments of the Lord. But now his subjects, having a knowledge of his sin, would be led to sin more freely. His authority in his own household, his claim to respect and obedience from his sons, was weakened. A sense of his guilt kept him silent when he should have condemned sin; it made his arm feeble to execute justice in his house. His evil example exerted its influence upon his sons, and God would not interpose to prevent the result. He would permit things to take their natural course, and thus David was severely chastised."[5]

No longer did David hold the moral high ground or serve as a paragon of moral and spiritual influence. His sin produced a harvest of heartache. We can imagine the confusing messages his children received as they grew up. They had siblings, half siblings, and siblings born to concubines. All of them belonged to a household saturated with sexual excesses and lacking any example of parental restraint. We can't and must not excuse Amnon, but we can certainly understand the context in which his character developed. Amnon had watched his father take one wife after another in a nation that frowned upon polygamy. As far as Amnon could see, his father never wanted anything he did not ultimately get. It is interesting that, in our first introduction to them, Scripture describes both Bathsheba and Tamar as beautiful (2 Sam. 11:2; 13:1). Like father, like son. The apple doesn't fall far from the tree. As had been the case with his father, Amnon saw something beautiful and determined to have it. The son was manifesting the same kind of unbridled passion that his father had expressed with Bathsheba. He was the kind of guy who always got what he wanted. And Absalom? He grew up in the same environment of excess and power and murder. As with David's murder of Uriah, Absalom's murder of his half brother was premeditated. Dad got things done through murder. So why not follow his example?

David's failure to control his own sexual desires rendered him unfit to lead his sons to a way of purity. His calculated murder made him incapable of helping his sons to respect life. The king's sons followed him and exceeded him in their moral failure. "The sins of one generation imprint the next generation," Bergen observes. "Each sin not only fosters more sin, it also fashions it by providing precedents for others to follow."[6] Ellen White agreed. "As a rule, children inherit the dispositions and tendencies of their parents, and imitate their example; so that the sins of the parents are practiced by the children from generation to generation."[7] And so with godliness and moral integrity.

Children mirror our moral and spiritual values. This incident in David's life makes me think about all the ways we model such values as materialism, critical attitudes, violence, impatience, lust, racial bias, gender biases, integrity, and attitudes toward leadership, church, and worship. Our children observe such things and draw contrasts between our profession and our life. They long for authenticity, consistency, and integrity, but when they don't find it or sense it, they become jaded about spiritual things and often choose evil for themselves. Should we compromise, they are likely to follow and even go further.

If we blow it as a parent, spouse, servant, employee, or leader, we should fall before God in complete repentance and ask Him what we must do to cooperate with restoration. Then we should comply in utmost obedience to His Word. "Restoration does not mean you can no longer stand for the truth because you fell. Restoration means you must stand!"[8] While we can never change the past we can learn from our mistakes. We can tell others what we have discovered in them. Based on our painful experience, we can describe the emotional and physical symptoms resulting from an unforgiven conscience and how they drain spiritual passion and make us want to sit it out rather than dance. With powerful conviction we can testify to the painful consequences of sin and warn how our own sin hurts so many other lives. Above all, we can confess openly, be honest and candid, and point to a God who forgives and restores. By becoming zealous in our life and household and work we can with God on our side influence the present. Swallowing our pride, in God's strength we can take the lead. David could have done so, but he didn't. He chose to sit it out.

Like Father, Like Son?

Moral and spiritual disposition is ultimately a matter of personal choice. Scripture vividly describes Tamar's protest while Amnon raped her. She resisted, both verbally and physically. Her first word of response to her half brother's sinful request was "No!" "'No, my brother!' she cried. 'Don't be foolish! Don't do this to me! You know what a serious crime it is to do such a thing in Israel. Where could I go in my shame? And you would be called one of the greatest of fools in Israel. Please, just speak to the king about it, and he will let you marry me'" (2 Sam. 13:12, 13, NLT).

Tamar sought to appeal to Amnon's conscience and lead him to think about the lasting impact his actions would have on both of their lives. His theft of her virginity would place on her personal disgrace that she would never be able to get rid of. It would ruin Amnon's reputation as well, causing him to be thought of as one of the fools (Nabals) of Israel. Finally, Tamar urged Amnon to delay—not permanently forgo—his sexual gratification. If sexual intimacy with her was his objective, he still might have it. In fact, it could be his without the taint of disgrace or ruined reputation if he would first "speak to the king" and obtain permission to marry her.

"What an amazingly self-sacrificing attitude on Tamar's part; she is poised and has excellent clarity of mind despite the fact that she is being raped."[9] Unfortunately, Amnon was beyond the influence of any moral, religious, or rational considerations. Instead, he overpowered her and gratified himself.

Even after she'd been raped, Tamar suggested a way they might still preserve some of their dignity. The Torah required a man to marry a virgin he had seduced or raped (Ex. 22:16; Deut. 22:28, 29). Tamar reminded Amnon of that statute when he told her to get out. "'No, no!' Tamar cried. 'To reject me now is a greater wrong than what you have already done'" (2 Sam. 13:16, NLT).

But the morally reckless Amnon once again refused to listen to her. "Throw this woman out, and lock the door behind her!" he ordered his personal servant (verse 17, NLT).

With that, Tamar found herself confronted with one last ethical dilemma. Would she keep quiet, hoping that she wouldn't get pregnant, that no one would ever know that she had lost her purity, that she might still be marriageable? Tamar was a highly visible person in the court (verse 18). She had been wearing the distinctive dress of a royal virgin daughter when Amnon raped her. Now she consciously tore that ornamental robe as a visible sign of her loss of purity and change of status (verse 19). Thus she made a public gesture of humiliation, which also served to indict her half brother.

Amnon may have wished, as did his father, to have his wrong covered over and hidden from public notice. Tamar, however, would not comply with such a cover-up. "Because she has now made the scandalous matter visible, the other characters in the narrative must respond. They must deal with the new situation which Tamar, by her shame, has made visible."[10] "The torn robe, the ashes, and the loud weeping were all part of her public testimony that she had been violated and would confirm her innocence if a pregnancy were to follow."[11]

From the beginning the narrator contrasts Amnon's lack of character with Tamar's virtue. While he was upset because she was a virgin, and it seemed impossible for him to do anything to her, the narrator implicitly portrays Tamar as a person of the Torah who, as an unmarried woman, determined to retain her virginity (see Deut. 22:13-21). In the weeks before Amnon arranged to be alone with Tamar—while he was looking lustfully at her—a moral struggle took place in his mind. It was a time in which he knew himself to be confronted with the will of God—sexual purity. The intensity of his struggle shows that he was not "all bad,"since it left him torn between what he wanted and what he knew to be right.

Amnon's first mistake was in dwelling on such thoughts. He lived with them in the realm of his imagination until they absorbed him completely. His second mistake was making an intimate friend of Jonadab.[12] Finally, under the pressure of sexual passion, he changed. Through all Amnon's undisciplined and irrational behavior, Tamar has both a sense of moral propriety and a sense of her own best interests as well as what was best for Amnon. They were two young people from the same family. What made the difference? In the end it was character and choice, not their father or his sins.

Moral disposition is a personal decision. We can follow the moral dysfunction of our parents and extend it toward more evil. Or we can choose to rise above it and be different. Some see their parents' failures and proceed to fail in the same areas, going even further in some form of moral compromise or rebellion than even their parents had. Their parents' mistakes provide the rationale and license for their own moral compromise. But other children see their parents' failures and determine to be different. Learning and growing from their parent's mistakes, they rise above the evil and compromises they see within the home. It comes down to disposition and attitude—our internal value system, our understanding of fallen human nature, and how we choose morally.

All of us are children and have chosen to respond one way or another to our parents' strengths or weaknesses. Amnon and Absalom reacted to David's failures with their own sins, but Tamar chose the path of moral excellence. She maintained her dignity even while society would cast her off as used merchandise.

The painful reality is that some of us adults have not risen above the sins and mistakes of our fathers and mothers. We have let their hidden sins or glaring failures shape our attitude about God, the church, biblical standards, and our own behavior. Even how we train or restrain or hold accountable our own children. The problem is not with our parents as much as it is with ourselves. While the bow may be unstable, the arrow can also be crooked. It's a personal decision.

Grace for Hurting Parents

A 4-year-old girl was at the pediatrician's office for a checkup. As the doctor looked into her ears with an otoscope, he asked, "Do you think I'll find Big Bird in here?" The little girl did not answer.

Next the doctor took a tongue depressor and looked down her throat. "Do you think I'll find the Cookie Monster down there?" he questioned. Again, the little girl remained silent.

Then the doctor put a stethoscope to her chest. As he listened to her heart beat, he inquired, "Do you think I'll hear Barney in here?"

"Oh, no!" the little girl replied. "Jesus is in my heart. Barney's on my underpants."[13]

The greatest desire of any Christian parent is for their child to have Jesus in their heart and know it with a spontaneous innocence. But that's not so easy, as most of us know. Our hearts are not so naturally inclined. As we read David's story we realize his involvement in this whole dysfunctional affair. He was experiencing the painful chain reaction of sin in his own family. And yet his sons were responsible for their sinful choices. They could not blame what they did on their father's failures.[14]

The sword shall never depart from his house. But I thought David was forgiven, we say. He was. Nathan said so. But the consequences were still there. As we have already learned, what is really awesome about David's story is that God matched consequences with grace. Although the pain continued to unfold, so did His gracious presence and blessings. They were tangible things to remind David that God was with still with Him. Again, one of the biggest struggles we have is to keep our sense of forgiveness and the reality of consequences separate, especially when it has to do with our children and how their behavior mirrors or reacts to our own dysfunctional behavior. When that happens, it's hard to feel forgiven. But as we learned in our previous chapter, David shows us that not only can we feel forgiven; we can worship. Like him, we can accept the reality of consequences, and chose to receive them, however painful, with a worshipful heart. But unlike him, we must rise up in God's power and be the moral compass the Lord calls us to be in our home and marriage, church and workplace.

"Grace does not take away the consequences of sin."[15] It "means that God, in forgiving you, gives you the strength to endure the consequences."[16] Also, grace indicates that God is at work in the lives of those we influence—our children—even when we have not been all that good of an example. God continued to work on Amnon's heart during the two years leading up to his death.[17] And we will learn how He was at work in Absalom's life as well. We are not alone in our parenting. God is always at work to forgive, to heal, and to save.

Speaking to a generation headed for exile, whose children bore the brunt of their parents' failures and sins, God assured His people Israel that "the children born during your bereavement will yet say in your hearing, 'This place is too small for us; give us more space to live in.' Then you will say in your heart, 'Who bore me these? I was bereaved and barren; I was exiled and rejected. Who brought these up? I was left all alone, but these—where have they come from?' This is what the Sovereign Lord says: 'See, I will beckon to the Gentiles, I will lift up my banner to the peoples; they will bring your sons in their arms and carry your daughters on their shoulders. Kings will be your foster fathers, and their queens your nursing mothers. . . . Then you will know that I am the Lord; those who hope in me will not be disappointed.' Can plunder be taken from warriors, or captives rescued from the fierce? But this is what the Lord says: 'Yes, captives will be taken from warriors, and plunder retrieved from the fierce; I will contend with those who contend with you, and your children I will save'" (Isa. 49:20-25, NIV).

As parents, what kind of moral and spiritual influence are we exerting on our children?

And as children ourselves, how are we responding to the moral failures of our parents?

There is grace . . . if our parents have failed us.

There is grace . . . if we have failed our children.

There is grace . . . if we have failed as children.

If we have failed in some way, God promises to forgive and empower us to a new level of moral spiritual influence. Or if we see the failures of our parents, God calls us to be forgiving while choosing the higher ground.

It's never too late. I remember how an elderly gentleman by the name of Eldon Collier woke up out of his years of spiritual malaise and decided to become a stable bow just a couple months before he died. Nearly two years later I baptized two of his sons and a longtime family friend who had been part of his life since a teenager.

When I was a boy my parents shot competition archery. In fact, it was a family thing. I saw some incredible shooting in my days: the flames of candles snuffed out at 25 yards, and spinning silver dollars struck after being tossed in the air. It didn't take long to know the value of a stable, well-balanced bow, or the necessity of a straight-shafted arrow with good fletching (feathers) and an unbroken nock (where you fit the bowstring). It's best to have both, a balanced bow and a straight arrow. But one can learn to compensate if the arrow is crooked or the bow unstable. Stable parental bows are gifts of grace, as are straight children arrows of grace. God wants both, and He enables both. It's our choice . . . the only way we'll ever dance.

---

[1] Kahlil Gibran, "On Parenting," in *Chicken Soup for the Soul,* p. 119.

[2] B. Moore, *A Heart Like His,* p. 201.

[3] W. Brueggemann, *First and Second Samuel,* p. 290.

[4] *Ibid.,* pp. 289, 290.

[5] E. G. White, *Patriarchs and Prophets,* p. 723.

[6] R. D. Bergen, *1, 2 Samuel,* p. 379.

[7] White, p. 118.

[8] Moore, p. 204.

[9] K. Kaynor, *When God Chooses,* p. 247.

[10] Brueggemann, p. 288.

[11] A. Thompson, *Samuel: From the Danger of Chaos to the Danger of Power,* p. 244.

[12] H. Rolston, *Personalities Around David,* pp. 117, 118.

[13] "Barney," in *A 3rd Serving of Chicken Soup for the Soul,* ed. Jack Canfield and Mark Victor Hansen (Deerfield Beach, Fla.: Health Communications, Inc., 1996), p. 81.

[14] Rolston, p. 115.

[15] C. R. Swindoll, *David: A Man of Passion and Destiny,* p. 213.

[16] *Ibid.,* p. 211.

[17] "Notwithstanding [Amnon's] great sin, God had borne long with him. For two years he had been granted opportunity for repentance; but he continued in sin, and with his guilt upon him, he was cut down by death, to await the awful tribunal of the judgment" (White, *Patriarchs and Prophets,* p. 727).

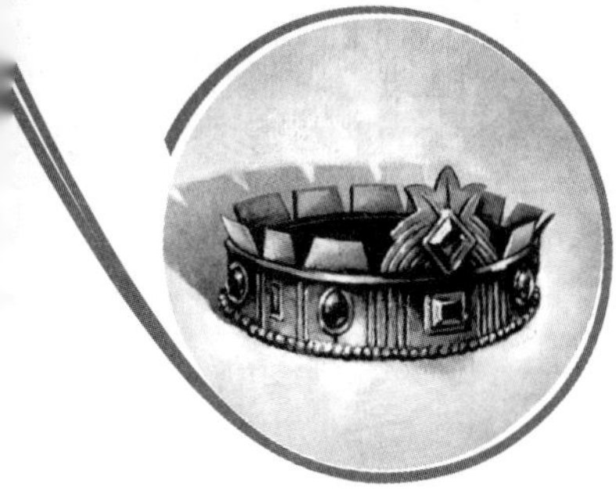

11

WHY DON'T YOU BRING BACK YOURS?

2 Samuel 14:1-33

One of Ernest Hemingway's short stories tells of a Spanish father who decided to reconcile with his son who had run away to Madrid. Now remorseful, the father took out an ad in the *El Liberal* newspaper: "PACO, MEET ME AT HOTEL MONTANA NOON TUESDAY. ALL IS FORGIVEN. PAPA." Paco is a common name in Spain, and when the father went to the square he found 800 young men waiting for their fathers.[1]

Hemingway knew about the pain families can inflict upon themselves. His religiously devout parents detested his libertine life, and after a time his mother refused to allow him in her presence. One year for his birthday she mailed him a cake along with the gun his father had used to kill himself. Another year she wrote him a letter explaining that a mother's life is like a bank. "Every child that is born to her enters the world with a large prosperous bank account, seemingly inexhaustible." The child, she continued, makes withdrawals but no deposits during all the early years. Later, when the child grows up, it is his responsibility to replenish the supply he has drawn down. Hemingway's mother then proceeded to spell out all the specific ways in which Ernest should be making deposits, including obeying God and his Savior Jesus Christ. Hemingway never got over his hatred of his mother or her Savior.[2]

Absalom, too, waited for a word of forgiveness from his father—an invitation to come home and be accepted and reconciled. Three years is a long time for a son to remain in exile (2 Sam. 13:38).[3] During that kind of time a lot of bitterness can multiply in a person's heart. That's the nature of bitterness—it never stays in its cage. Absalom wanted to come home and once more be in Dad's good graces. To everyone else David might be king, but to Absalom he was Dad. Their separation was a family matter. No doubt there was no simple resolution to his predicament. Despite all his desire to return home, he was still a murderer, killer of the crown prince. And while David longed to see him (2 Sam. 13:39; 14:1), he was in a bind. Justice must be done! The murderer must be punished. Could David dare be lenient toward his son while the whole nation looked on?

His predicament reminds me of FBI agent John Cook, who turned in his own son for murder. He had received a call from the Georgia Bureau of Investigation about a gruesome slaying that had taken place some time before. The agency wanted to talk with his son. Cook later learned from his son that he not only knew about the crime; he had been there. And did it! For years Cook had lived by the FBI's motto: "Fidelity, Bravery, Integrity." Now those same words gave him no option. As a man of the law, he knew what he had to do—yet as a father it was something he dreaded. It hurt and left him as if paralyzed. In the end Cook wound up not only turning his son in for the murder, but testifying against him in court.[4] What else could he do?

Scripture tells us that with Amnon dead and Absalom missing, David was grief-stricken. He mourned Amnon and longed for Absalom (2 Sam. 13:39; 14:1). Yet remember that while David became furious over Amnon's sin, he still did nothing. He had the appropriate feelings but inappropriate actions. Once again the king feels the right thing and does the wrong the thing.

Drama in Real Life

Joab sensed that David wanted his son home and knew that Absalom wanted to return. After a while he grew weary of seeing David mope around and do nothing. Enduring the king's irresponsibility toward Absalom for as long as he could, Joab finally devised a plan to get David's attention. Finding a woman from Tekoa who would not be intimidated by the king, he coached her with what to say (2 Sam. 14:1-3).[5] It was a piece of drama. The woman of Tekoa was the actress, Joab the writer and producer. She would play a role requiring consummate skill. Costumed as someone in mourning, she would present herself as a woman who had spent many days grieving for the dead. Prostrating herself before the king, she begged for his help. When David asked, "What's the trouble?" she unfolded a make-believe (but thoroughly credible) slice of life.

"'I am a widow,' she replied. 'My two sons had a fight out in the field. And since no one was there to stop it, one of them was killed. Now the rest of the family is demanding, "Let us have your son. We will execute him for murdering his brother. He doesn't deserve to inherit his family's property." But if I do that, I will have no one left, and my husband's name and family will disappear from the face of the earth'" (verses 5-7, NLT).

The woman speaks in the persuasive, pathos-filled voice of a mother. As Brueggemann observes: "The one who has killed is still her son. His violent act has not changed that elemental relationship. The woman seeks her son, not as a killer but as her son. He is all she has, and she wants him home. She yearns for her son and wants, beyond fear and vengeance of the family, to have her son, her only son, restored to her. The anguish and yearning of the mother are powerful and thick."[6]

Since he was a person of deep feeling, David found his sympathies aroused on the woman's behalf. After hearing her story, he dismissed her, promising that a ruling would soon be forthcoming (verse 8). In other words, he would have to think about it. The case before David was more ticklish than we might realize at first. It pitted the punishment of a murderer against the strong Hebrew concern that a man's family not die out. People considered the extinction of a name a great public disgrace. If the punishment were carried out, it would bring the woman's line to an end and make her childless, which would also impoverish her because the clan would claim all her possessions.[7]

But the intrepid woman continued to press the issue. She wouldn't let go, nor would she leave, but demanded a ruling from the king. "Please swear to me by the Lord your God that you won't let anyone take vengeance against my son. I want no more bloodshed" (verse 11, NLT).

By insisting on a ruling, she was maneuvering David toward a principle that could serve as a basis for the return of Absalom. As the woman appealed to his fatherly heart, the king finally guaranteed the son's safety at the expense of justice.

"As the Lord lives, not one hair of your son shall fall to the ground," he said (verse 11, NKJV).

David settled the legal dispute and expected the woman to depart, but she still lingered. "Please, let me ask one more thing of you!" she said.

"Go ahead," he replied. "Speak."

"Why don't you do as much for all the people of God as you have promised to do for me?" she said.[8] "You have convicted yourself in making this decision, because you have refused to bring home your own banished son. All of us must die eventually. Our lives are like water spilled out on the ground, which cannot be gathered up again. That is why God tries to bring us back when we have been separated from him. He does not sweep away the lives of those he cares about—and neither should you!" (verses 13, 14, NLT).

In effect she was saying, "Since you have been merciful to me and my son, why don't you apply the same principle to yourself and bring home your son Absalom. . . . It is true that God plays no favorites and renders justice, but He finds ways to restore His banished. Why don't you bring back *yours?*"[9]

Brueggemann capsules it succinctly: "The wise woman wants to free David from two mistaken notions, mistakes that come from his rage, resentment, and pride. David has fallen into a trap of thinking that something more must be done for Amnon; the woman counters that Amnon has only died as we all must, and that reality should not control David's life. Second, David seems to think there is virtue in keeping a grudge alive; the woman counters with the assertion that real virtue is not in keeping the banished one away but in bringing him home."[10] Amnon is gone and must be relinquished, but David has a chance for a saving act toward Absalom. "Death may be irreversible, but God's disciplinary dealings with his creatures are far from irreversible."[11]

Awestruck, the king realized that here was a new approach to his problem. He had not seen it in this way before. What David could not recognize in his own family he saw clearly in the woman's hypothetical family. "It is human nature that we all tend to apply judgment more wisely to others than to ourselves."[12] No doubt the king thought that what he was doing was good for Absalom. But underneath it there was a refusal to forgive, a withholding of grace, a denial of mercy.[13] At bottom, "the rejection of Absalom was a steady, determined refusal to share with his son what God had so abundantly shared with him. Day by day he hardened in this denial of love."[14] Retribution would keep Absalom away from his father forever, but such uncaring retribution is not what life is about. Rather, it is about breaking the cycle of fear and resentment and welcoming him home.[15]

David's three sins bring incredible pain, death, and near ruin in his family—adultery, murder, and refusal to forgive. The woman of Tekoa implies that true wisdom consists in moving beyond vengeance to forgiveness.

A Matter of Face

Composing himself, David pierced the facade of the whole charade. "Did Joab put you up to this?" he asked. "Yes," she replied, "Joab was behind the whole thing." After dismissing the woman, David summoned his nephew and commander of the army. "All right, go and bring back the young man Absalom," he said. Overjoyed, Joab "fell with his face to the ground . . . , and he blessed the king" (verse 22, NIV). As he joyfully hastened to Geshur, he no doubt pictured the emotional but wonderful reunion of father and son. But when he brought Absalom back to Jerusalem and prepared for the glorious reunion, David met them with the shocking comment, "'Absalom may go to his own house, but he must never come into my presence.' So Absalom did not see the king" (verse 24, NLT). The son's restoration was only partial. While allowed back in Jerusalem, he would not have the privilege of seeing Dad!

"He must never come into my presence. I don't want to see his face, and I don't want him to see mine." Can you imagine such a reaction from David?

Often the king's heart and actions revealed to us a picture of Christ. But when it came to his parenting, he showed just the opposite. How very much like ourselves David proved to be when it involved family. I am very grateful that God will not call us to the heavenly Jerusalem and say, "They must not see My face." I have waited all my life to see His beautiful face. And He promises me that I will: all "will see His face, and His name will be written on their foreheads" (Rev. 22:4, NASB). Should I not be the same with my own: "not to turn away from [my] own flesh and blood" (Isa. 58:7, NIV)?

David did not respond like the father of the prodigal son in Christ's parable did—the waiting father who daily searched the horizon for his wandering son to return home. That father, who represents our heavenly Father, caught a glimpse of his son in the distance and "ran to his son, threw his arms around him and kissed him" (Luke 15:20, NIV).

Some things in life are do-overs. God sometimes gives us a second chance at getting something right. Other things never come back around.[16] The chance for David and Absalom to be genuinely reunited in their hearts would not occur again. By the time David finally received Absalom, his son's heart was forever cold.

Thus David's pardon of Absalom was impersonal, his forgiveness a mere judicial act, not a fatherly embrace. He let Absalom return to his own city and gave him a place to live, but he didn't greet him by name or permit him in his presence—not so much as a look. David held on to his bitterness about Amnon's murder. His stance was probably a result of mixed political pressures and personal feelings, but whatever the ingredients, Absalom experienced rejection by his father.[17] Sin fed on sin. The rape of Tamar led to the murder of Amnon, which resulted in the hard-heartedness of David. Absalom responded to Amnon's sin by sinning. Then David reacted to Absalom's sin by sinning himself. Absalom got rid of Amnon by killing him. David disposed of Absalom by shunning him.[18]

Have you ever noticed what children will do to get their parent's attention? Absalom proved an extreme example. For two years he never saw his father's face (2 Sam. 14:28). During that period the son stewed in his banishment. He was home—but not really. This was no life, just to be permitted to exist. He wanted acceptance, a personal word of forgiveness. And he especially wanted his father's love. The king's son needed more than food and drink for survival—he had to have grace and mercy in order to live fully. At first he was glad to be back, but gradually he realized that he required far more than a piece of royal legislation in his favor—he needed a father.[19]

As Smedes so cogently observes: "When grace comes to us graciously, it heals. When grace is offered ungraciously, it shames. You can tell that grace is gracious if it makes you feel better for having it, feel lighter, and, when it comes down to it, feel like the worthy human being you are. . . . A grace that makes us feel worse for having it is an ungracious grace and therefore not really grace at all. If grace heals our shame, it must be a grace that tells us we are worthy to have it."[20] "Grace graciously given honors our worth as it overlooks our undeserving."[21]

Absalom found himself put into an impossible holding pattern. Being back home actually left him feeling worse—in fact, shamed. His in-limbo situation was intolerable. So he started going out of his way to be heard. He summoned Joab to send him to David, but the commander-in-chief refused to come. So Absalom told his servants, "Joab's field is next to mine, and he has barley there. Go and set it on fire" (verse 30, NIV). This time Joab delivered Absalom's message: "I want to see the king's face, and if I am guilty of anything, let him put me to death" (verse 32, NIV). Absalom's strategy successfully gained the audience with Dad that he wanted. David had one last chance. Sadly, he blew it again! Absalom bowed down with his face to the ground, and David kissed his son.

Sometimes I wish Scripture told us more. I would like more detail about their forced reunion. Perhaps Scripture doesn't reveal more about it because there was nothing more to tell. Nothing else happened. The scene had all the right ingredients: Absalom bowing down, the king kissing his son. But something important seems missing—the heart. The actions of David and his son reflect custom, not emotion. Fearing his son would do something more than set Joab's field on fire, David summoned Absalom to appease him, not accept him. Absalom sought his father's face to force David to look him in the eye and connect, be reconciled, not to beg forgiveness as the prodigal did.[22]

Both David and Absalom shared the blame for their separation, but the father did nothing to bring about reconciliation. Shouldn't it be the parent's initiative? God is never in the wrong when He and one of His children are separated, yet He goes out of His way to bring His banished ones home—so that none of us will ever need remain estranged from Him.

Reconciliation between a father and son is slow, painful, and costly. It cannot be rushed. But who would have expected two more years of waiting? But just as reconciliation cannot be rushed, so it also cannot be put off forever. We must never underestimate the significance of timing when it comes to mending. Sometimes we may never get another chance.

One commentator observes: "There is no way we can know how the history of his relationship with Absalom would have been different had

David punished Amnon for violating Tamar. There is a timing to life. Once the moment has passed when something could have been done, we do not get it back. What happened to Absalom is a powerful argument for dealing with problems in a family at the time they arise and not letting them slide until it's too late."[23] Absalom gave up hope of intimacy with his father and determined to take things into his own hands. It was the seeds of his later rebellion. "Energetic, ambitious, and unprincipled, shut out by his exile from participation in the affairs of the kingdom, [Absalom] soon gave himself up to dangerous scheming."[24]

When you are a parent, alienation and grace are shockingly personal. But what should you do? Banishing, shutting out, shunning, snubbing, evading, ostracizing, and blacklisting are so much a part of our ways of relating when our child has done something wrong.

Why Don't You Bring Back Yours?

This episode begins with Absalom in exile and ends with his experiencing the kiss of forgiveness from his father (verses 1, 33). We know from the comment of 2 Samuel 14:1 and the later grief of David (2 Sam. 18:33-19:4) that David cares passionately and intensely for him. But he has not always treated his son lovingly. The scene in which David and Absalom see each other for the first time in five years is tense and moving. If this were the end of the story, it would make a wonderful illustration of forgiveness and reconciliation. Subsequent events, however, indicate that whatever may have been in David's heart at the time he received his son back, Absalom never recovered from the way his father had treated him, and he used his new status to undermine David.[25]

The woman of Tekoa confronted the king with his broken relationship with Absalom. While God plays no favorites and renders justice, He always finds a way to restore His banished ones. Jesus told the story of the prodigal son and his "waiting father." Even though the son had done a terrible thing, the father never quit looking for a way to forgive him and restore him to full sonship. He kept watching down the road, longing to see that familiar face. When the son did finally come, the father ran to greet and embrace him, welcoming him home with a huge banquet (Luke 15:11-32). Peterson asks: "What if David had been that father? What if

Absalom had been allowed to sit with his father, tell the story of his affection for Tamar, his anger at Amnon, his disappointment that his father had not intervened, and the purgatory of his exile? David would once more have had a son; Absalom would once again have had a father."[26]

Are you struggling to know how to parent and heal broken relationships with your children? Whom have you drawn a circle around and ostracized, perhaps haven't spoken to in years? A child? A sibling? A spouse? A parent?

"So open your hearts to one another as Christ has opened his heart to you, and God will be glorified" (Rom. 15:7, Phillips).

"Let there be no more resentment, no more anger or temper, no more violent self-assertiveness, no more slander and no more malicious remarks. Be kind to one another; be understanding. Be as ready to forgive others as God for Christ's sake has forgiven you" (Eph. 4:31, 32, Phillips).

"And parents, never drive your children to resentment but bring them up with correction and advice inspired by the Lord" (Eph. 6:4, New Jerusalem).

"You should each be converted anew and transformed into the divine likeness. You would better err, if you err at all, on the side of mercy and forbearance than that of intolerance."[27]

"Every true teacher will feel that should he err at all, it is better to err on the side of mercy than on the side of severity.[28]

The parents of a young girl growing up on a cherry orchard farm just above Traverse City, Michgan, were a bit old-fashioned and tended to overreact to her nose ring, the music she listened to, and the length of her skirts. After they had grounded her a few times, she began to seethe inside. "I hate you!" she screamed at her father when he knocked on the door of her room after an argument, and that night she acted on a plan she had mentally rehearsed scores of times. She ran away.

The girl had visited Detroit only once before, on a bus trip with her church youth group to watch the Tigers baseball team play. Because newspapers in Traverse City reported in lurid detail the gangs, the drugs, and the violence in downtown Detroit, she concluded that it would be probably the last place her parents would look for her. California, maybe, or Florida, but not Detroit.

On her second day in Detroit she met a man who drove the biggest car she'd ever seen. He offered her a ride, bought her lunch, and arranged a place for her to stay. Then he gave her some pill that made her feel better than she'd ever felt before. She had been right all along, she decided—her parents had been keeping her from all the fun.

The good life continued for a month, two months, a year. The man with the big car—she called him "Boss"—taught her a few things that men like. Since she was underage, they paid a premium for her. She lived in a penthouse and ordered room service whenever she wanted. Occasionally she thought about her parents back home, but their lives now seemed so boring and provincial that she could hardly believe that she had grown up there.

She had a brief scare when she spotted her picture printed on the back of a milk carton with the headline "Have you seen this child?" But by now she had blond hair, and with all the makeup and body-piercing jewelry she wore, nobody would mistake her for a child. Besides, most of her friends were runaways, and nobody in Detroit squealed.

After a year the first sallow sign of illness appeared, and it amazed her how fast the Boss turned mean. "These days we can't mess around," he growled, and before she knew it she was out on the street without a penny to her name. Although she still turned a couple of tricks a night, they didn't pay much, and all the money went to support her habit. When winter blew in, she found herself sleeping on metal grates outside the big department stores. But "sleeping" was the wrong word—a teenage girl at night in downtown Detroit could never relax her guard. Dark bands circled her eyes. Her cough worsened.

One night as she lay awake, listening for footsteps, all of a sudden everything about her life looked different. No longer did she feel like a woman of the world; instead she felt like a little girl, lost in a cold and frightening city. She began to whimper. Her pockets were empty, and she was hungry. Even worse, she needed a fix. Pulling her legs tight underneath her, she shivered under the newspapers she'd piled atop her coat. Something jolted a synapse of memory, and a single image filled her mind: of May in Traverse City, when a million cherry trees bloom at once, with her golden retriever dashing through the rows and rows of blossoming trees in pursuit of a tennis ball.

God, why did I leave? she thought to herself, and pain stabbed at her heart. *My dog back home eats better than I do now.* As she started sobbing, she knew in a flash that more than anything else in the world she wanted to go home.

Three times she phoned home, but each time she got only the answering machine. The first two times she hung up without leaving a message, but the third time she said, "Dad, Mom, it's me. I was wondering about maybe coming home. I'm catching a bus up your way, and it'll get there about midnight tomorrow. If you're not there, well, I guess I'll stay on the bus until it hits Canada."

It takes about seven hours for a bus to make all the stops between Detroit and Traverse City, and during that time she realized the flaws in her plan. What if her parents had been out of town and missed the message? Shouldn't she have waited another day or so until she could talk to them? And even if they had been home, they had probably written her off as dead long ago. She should have given them some time to overcome the shock.

Her thoughts bounced back and forth between those worries and the speech she had been preparing for her father. "Dad, I'm sorry. I know I was wrong. It's not your fault—it's all mine. Dad, can you forgive me?" She repeated the words again and again, her throat tightening even as she rehearsed them. After all, she hadn't apologized to anyone in years.

The bus had been driving with lights on since Bay City. Tiny snowflakes hit the pavement. She'd forgotten how dark it got at night out here. A deer darted across the road, and the bus swerved. Every so often she caught a glimpse of a billboard in the headlights or a sign posting the mileage to Traverse City.

When the bus finally rolled into the station, its air brakes hissing in protest, the driver announced in a crackly voice over the microphone, "Fifteen minutes, folks. That's all we have here." Fifteen minutes to decide her life. Checking herself in a compact mirror, she smoothed her hair and licked the lipstick off her teeth. Glancing at the tobacco stains on her fingertips, she briefly wondered if her parents would notice—if they showed up at all.

Not knowing what to expect, she walked into the terminal. But not one of the thousand scenes that had played out in her mind prepared her for what she saw. There, in the concrete-walls-and-plastic-chairs bus terminal in Traverse City, Michigan, stood a group of 40 brothers and sisters and great-aunts and uncles and cousins—and a grandmother—and a great-grandmother to boot. They were all wearing goofy party hats and blowing noisemakers, and taped across the entire wall of the terminal was a computer-generated banner that read "Welcome Home!"

Out of the crowd of well-wishers stepped her dad. Staring out through the tears quivering in her eyes like hot mercury, she began the memorized speech: "Dad. I'm sorry. I know . . ."

"Hush, child," he interrupted her. "We've got no time for that. No time for apologies. You'll be late for the party. A banquet is waiting for you at home."[29]

It's the only way to dance like the king of heaven. A dance that King David could not bring himself to do. But you and I can. "Why don't you bring back yours?" Let's bring our banished home and be like God.

---

[1] Ernest Hemingway, "The Capital of the World," *The Complete Short Stories of Ernest Hemingway* (New York: Charles Scribner's Sons, 1987), p. 29.

[2] See James R. Mellow, *Hemingway: A Life Without Consequences* (New York: Houghton-Mifflin Company, 1992), pp. 116-125, 374-376; P. Yancey, *What's So Amazing About Grace?* p. 38.

[3] Having avenged his sister by killing Amnon, Absalom fled to Geshur, the homeland of his mother, Maacah.

[4] Charles Hurt, "I Turned In My Son," *Reader's Digest,* December 2000, pp. 66-72.

[5] Scripture does not give Joab's reasons for interceding, but there are several possibilities: (1) the king's attitude toward Absalom was softening (2 Sam. 14:1); (2) Joab likely admired the handsome Absalom, who obviously had a strong and attractive personality (see 2 Sam. 14:25-27; Scripture pictures Absalom as a person with property and family and a strong following among the people); (3) being a power-oriented person, Joab would have been concerned about the potential instability created by an aging king without a clearly designated successor. See K. L. Chafin, *1, 2 Samuel,* p. 323.

[6] W. Brueggemann, *First and Second Samuel,* p. 292.

[7] K. Kaynor, *When God Chooses,* p. 256.

[8] "By failing to restore Absalom to the court of Jerusalem, David was acting 'against' the interests of 'the people of God'—for if, as it appears from the text, Absalom was the heir-apparent to the throne, then keeping Absalom in exile threatened the fledgling dynasty of David, and thus a continuation of quality leadership for Israel" (R. D. Bergen, *1, 2 Samuel,* p. 391).

[9] Kaynor, p. 256.

[10] Brueggemann, p. 294.

[11] Robert P. Gordon, *I & II Samuel* (Grand Rapids: Zondervan Publishing House, 1986), p. 268.

[12] Chafin, p. 324.

[13] "The Tekoite woman's strange request to David that he spare the remnant of her father's house despite her subsequent proclamation of the guilt of her father's house is not more paradoxical than David subsequently returning the supposed heir of his house to Jerusalem in spite of Absalom's guilt; or than God's graciously sparing Jerusalem despite David's proclamation of his guilt and that of his father's house in 2 Samuel 24; or, for that

matter, than God's openly calling David his servant in 2 Kings 19:34 and promising to preserve David's father's house, despite the king's grievous sin in 2 Samuel 11 and his open admission in 2 Samuel 24 that both he and his father's house were guilty" (R. Polzin, *David and the Deuteronomist,* p. 147).

[14] E. H. Peterson, *Leap Over a Wall,* p. 197.

[15] Brueggemann, p. 295.

[16] B. Moore, *A Heart Like His,* p. 207.

[17] Peterson, p. 196.

[18] *Ibid.*

[19] *Ibid.*

[20] L. B. Smedes, *Shame and Grace,* p. 119.

[21] *Ibid.*, p. 120.

[22] Moore, p. 208.

[23] Chafin, p. 319.

[24] White, *Patriarchs and Prophets,* p. 728.

[25] Chafin, p. 327. See also Kaynor, p. 257.

[26] Peterson, p. 197.

[27] Ellen G. White, *Testimonies for the Church* (Mountain View, Calif.: Pacific Press Pub. Assn., 1948), vol. 4, p. 65.

[28] White, *Education* (Mountain View, Calif.: Pacific Press Pub. Assn., 1903), p. 294. "There are souls who err, and who feel their shame and their folly. They are hungry for words of encouragement. They look upon their mistakes and errors until they are almost driven to desperation. Instead of lifting up the finger, instead of speaking vanity, instead of reproving and condemning and taking away the last ray of hope that the Sun of Righteousness sheds into their hearts, let your words fall as healing balm upon the bruised soul. Be not like desolating hail that beats down and destroys the tender hope springing up in the hearts. Leave not the hungry, starving soul in his helplessness to perish because you fail to speak words of tenderness and encouragement" (White, in *Review and Herald,* Aug. 20, 1895).

[29] As told by P. Yancey in *What's So Amazing About Grace?* pp. 49-51.

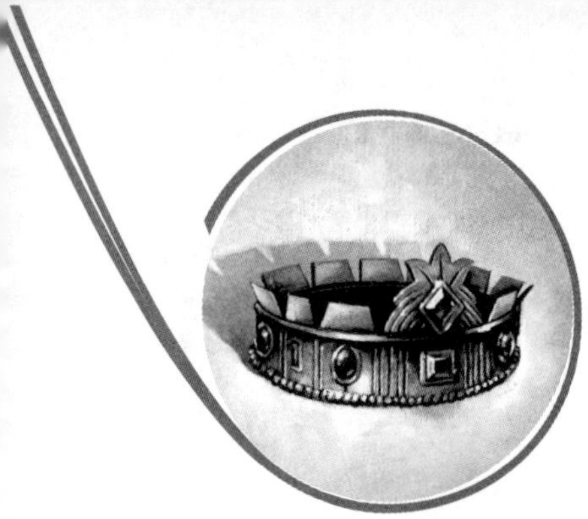

12

WHO WILL TELL THE KING?

2 Samuel 18:31-33

O my son Absalom,
my son, my son Absalom!
Would I had died instead of you,
O Absalom, my son, my son!" (2 Sam. 18:33, NASB).

These have got to be among the saddest, most heartrending words ever spoken. Words wrenched out of David's gut when he learned that his son had perished in the forest of Ephraim.[1] It happened before he had a chance to clear up several unresolved conflicts between himself and his son. Before they could sit down and come to terms with their differences. The news of Absalom's death hit him square in the face, and his world caved in around him. We see David's sorrow, and we hear his anguish in one of the most poignant scenes in all of Scripture.[2]

Every parent can intuit David's agony.[3] My wife, Kathie, has a saying she repeats regularly as our four sons mimic shooting each other while playing civil war, cowboys, or special forces, or when they watch that occasional war video. "Who will tell their mother?" she asks in alarm. We first heard her impassioned dismay when as a family we watched the four-plus-hour video *Gettysburg*—one of the most accurate, honorable depictions of the events, battles, and personal struggles of valor on both sides of the Civil War. Thousands die as the three-day turning-point battle at Gettysburg explodes on the screen in all its horror and heroism.

"Who will tell their mother?" we heard her exclaim again and again.

To Kathie, death is personal, individual, never just a piece of news or something to watch impassively on video. The concept of masses of people dying is incomprehensible—it is individuals who die. Always it is the sons of loving mothers who would feel the full emotional reality of their son's loss and understand the shocking permanence of death. That's the imagery *Saving Private Ryan* plays on as, based on a true story, it unfolds the reality of a mother receiving simultaneously the news of the loss of three sons in separate battles and the potential of losing a fourth.

"Who will tell their mother?" my wife asks, knowing the pain such violent death engenders, even though it is something that she never wants to experience. No mother does, for that matter. Nor does any father.

Who will tell the king? Joab wondered, now that Absalom was dead and the rebellion he led had collapsed. Ringing in his ears was David's last request as the troops passed in review before him en route to the battle. "Be gentle with the young man Absalom for my sake," he whispered in the ear of each of his three commanders, Joab, Abishai, and Ittai the Gittite (2 Sam. 18:5, NIV). Scripture notes that everyone heard those instructions (verse 5). It was common knowledge among the troops that David was struggling with his emotions. In the process he put his loyal people in an impossible situation. They were going into battle against the king's son, who was seeking the king's life (and subsequently most of theirs). And the king just told them all to be nice to Absalom.[4] Although his commanders had no choice but to win, yet they must "deal gently" with Absalom. How does one pull that one off? The last sound in their ears was David's lingering plea: "Deal gently." Not harshly, not cruelly, not with vengeance.[5]

Now with Absalom dead (contrary to David's wishes), Joab confronted the dilemma of how to break the news, especially since it was he who had killed Absalom—and against orders. Furthermore, that death was not accidental but deliberate. Ahimaaz, son of Zadok, volunteered. "Let me run and take the news to the king that the Lord has delivered him from the hand of his enemies," he proposed (verse 19, NIV). Young and loyal to David, he wanted to be the first to deliver the welcome news that the king could safely return home. But Joab said no. The son of Zadok the priest,

Ahimaaz was a close associate of Joab's. One does not send the son of another ranking cabinet officer on such a high-risk mission.[6] The mission was dangerous, because "the king's son is dead" (verse 20, NIV). Joab remembered well David's treatment of previous messengers who had announced the death of his adversaries. David had killed those who had brought news of both Saul's and Ish-bosheth's deaths (2 Sam. 1:4-16; 4:8-12). Joab feared that the old king might do the same again—to Ahimaaz. So Joab sent a Cushite—a non-Israelite figure who likely was unaware of David's past history—to be the official runner. But Ahimaaz insisted on going so much so that Joab finally let him run, only to have the priest's son overtake the Cushite and sprint into David's view first.

The exchange between Joab and Ahimaaz and then the watchmen reporting to David on the incoming runners builds the suspense of the story. Everything focused on David's reception of the news. The king eagerly and anxiously waited for the outcome of the battle as he sat at the city gate. Watchmen had climbed to the roof of the gateway by the wall. With each call from the watchman, David found a way to interpret the news as positive. A single runner meant good news, he told the watchman (2 Sam. 18:25). Since both of the messengers were running alone, he suggested, each must be bringing good news (verse 26). Then, when Ahimaaz got close enough to be identified, David declared him to be a good man and hence a bearer of good news (verse 27).

Ahimaaz arrived first and blurted out, "All is well!" Then he bowed down with praise on his lips to God, saying, "Blessed be the Lord your God, who has handed over the rebels who dared to stand against you" (verse 28, NLT). But David pressed Ahimaaz with the only question that mattered. "What about young Absalom?" the king demanded. "Is he all right?" (verse 29, NLT). That was all that really counted to this father!

Realizing David's anxiety (and remembering Joab's caution), Ahimaaz avoided telling the king the truth. His failure to give David a definitive answer only added to the king's anxiety. With growing concern, the king ordered Ahimaaz to step aside. When the Cushite finally arrived, he asked the same question, and this time got the painful answer: "May all your enemies, both now and in the future, be as that young man is!" (verse 32, NLT).

The dreaded news had come, leaving David crushed. Unrestrained sorrow gushed out of him like a torrent of water as he fled upstairs, sobbing. "And as he went, he cried, 'O my son Absalom! My son, my son Absalom! If only I could have died instead of you! O Absalom, my son, my son'" (verse 33, NLT).

Everyone could hear David weeping. The triumphal returning troops caught wind of his wails and slipped back into the city "as men steal in who are ashamed when they flee from battle" (2 Sam. 19:3, NIV).

Hurting Parents

Let's step back a bit. After nearly five years of separation King David and his son Absalom had finally seen each other face to face. But as we have already learned, their reunion was too little too late. Their meeting did nothing but fuel Absalom's lingering bitterness. Reuniting and reconciliation can be two different things. Many previously separated couples have returned to each other to live under the same roof for the sake of the children, finances, religious convictions, or the family business. They may spend the rest of their lives together without healing or without dealing with the problems. It can happen in church, at work, in the community, and between siblings or other family members. Reuniting is one thing; reconciliation is quite another.

His meeting with his father had disappointed Absalom. He possibly suffered from the same thing many adults suffer from today. When Absalom was a child, his father had been his hero. David had plenty of shortcomings, but the boy could not see them until one day an emotional bombshell hit home—exploding in the bedroom of Amnon. Although people got angry, no one cleaned up the mess. Lives continued to be torn by the shrapnel that no one even tried to remove. Suddenly Dad no longer lived up to Absalom's expectations. The son wanted justice, but the father didn't deliver. Later he wanted reconciliation, but Dad didn't even want to see his face. His frustration and anger deepened further when after forcing the issue it led only to his ceremonial bowing down before the king and a father's perfunctory kiss on the cheek. He determined that his father would pay for what he had done.

Absalom tried everything he knew—good and bad—to get his father's attention. Since he could not get to David through his home, he decided to get back at him through the throne.[7] So Absalom began a deliberate campaign to win the hearts of the people. Each morning he impressively arrived at the city gate with a chariot and an entourage of men and horses. When anyone entered the city with a complaint, Absalom would pull them aside and listen, telling them that if he were appointed judge they would get justice. He became quite a politician as well as a patient and diligent schemer. For four years he continued to work through each step of his plan, waiting for the right moment to overthrow the father he now hated.

Let's do a little calculating. Absalom spent two years waiting for his father to punish Amnon for raping Tamar. Nothing. Next he endured three years in hiding after taking matters into his own hands and killing his brother. Still Dad did nothing. Then he passed two more years in Jerusalem before Dad received him. Again, nothing. Now Absalom expends four more years working his devious plan of vengeance against his father. Unforgiveness, bitterness, and retaliation stole 11 years of his life. Eleven years is a long time for anyone to seethe and harbor bitterness. Has anger or bitterness robbed you of years of your life? God tells us to forgive those who hurt us, but He never qualifies the command by saying forgive only when someone asks for our forgiveness. He simply says forgive (Luke 6:37). That's what Jesus did when He cried, "Father, forgive them, for they do not know what they are doing" (Luke 23:34, NIV).

It appears that David never asked for forgiveness from Absalom. Nor did he take the initiative or his rightful place of authority over family matters and events. Although his father made plenty of mistakes, Absalom did not have to follow suit. He could have called on the mercy of God and forgiven his father for failing him—even if his father never admitted how wrongly he had handled his family or treated him as a son. If Absalom had done so, then God would have held David responsible, and the son would have been free to dance again. Instead, Absalom locked himself in the prison of bitterness and let the darkness of his soul erode his character.

So often we resist forgiveness, saying, "It's too hard. And if I do, I'll be letting them off the hook. They must pay." But the fact of the matter is that "forgiveness may be excruciating for a moment, but anger and bitterness are excruciating for a lifetime."[8] Learning to forgive those who hurt us, even if they take no responsibility for or fully understand the implications of their actions, will save us from the kind of misery that ultimately destroyed Absalom.

Finally, after waiting and scheming for four years, Absalom went to Hebron and set his bid for the throne in motion. When David heard of the rebellion, the warrior king did a remarkable thing—he packed up, abandoned Jerusalem, and ran (2 Sam. 15:14, 15). He found himself right in the middle of a cycle of self-appointed failure. Stricken with grief and dressed for mourning, he and his followers trudged up the Mount of Olives toward wilderness hiding—the kind of place David had always employed to his advantage when running from Saul. Near the forest of Ephraim Absalom drew up to fight his father. David reluctantly sent his army to meet the forces of Absalom. Up till now they had been locked in an emotional match—two opponents torn between love and hate. Now one of them would go down forever. Absalom would never come home again!

Jesus told the story of the waiting father who never quit searching for a way to forgive his prodigal son and restore him to full sonship. He kept looking down the road with his binoculars, longing to see that familiar face rise on the horizon. But what of the father who's son does not come home? There is no reconciliation, no restored sonship or party, only unending regret and sorrow.

With Absalom David experienced in the very depths of his being the full measure of rejection, alienation, and rebellion. It immersed him in an experience of betrayal and ruin. He tasted the bitterness and took in the full reality of sin-sourced suffering.[9] His heart wrenched with the reality of a son who was gone forever. As memories of his failed past swamped him and guilt assaulted him, he couldn't get past his grief. David found himself caught in an emotional vortex that paralyzed him.

David felt defeated about Absalom. Many parents have had child-raising experiences that led to strained relationships and alienation. Death has then come without change of heart or resolution. Such parents stare eternity in the face without their son or daughter. Keith Kaynor notes that "parents create an equal when an infant is conceived. A child is his parent's equal in power of choice, potential, and having a sinful nature."[10] Our children ultimately are responsible for their own choices and behavior, but in the process they can bring incredible pain because of their rebellion against us. Hurting parents also suffer because of their own sins and failures. They ache because their actions, reactions, and nonactions reverberate in the lives of their children. But hurting parents agonize, too, because of choices, attitudes, actions, and reactions their children are fully responsible for. As Peterson writes, "it's hard to rank events, but this might very well be the most integrated human/divine thing David ever did—face, taste, and experience to the depths this complex tangle of love and hate, righteousness and sin, good and evil that came to a head in Absalom."[11]

God also knows the agony of David's heart-wrenching pain. The Lord Himself is a hurting parent. Unlike David and the rest of us, though, He is the perfect parent—holy, merciful, compassionate, welcoming, forgiving, and just. When God made us in His image, He extended us incredible potential through the power of choice. Holmes Rolston characterizes Absalom as a "rebellious son of an undisciplined father."[12] While David was partially to blame for Absalom's choices, God is not so responsible for ours. But He hurts just the same! "When Israel was a child," God recalls sorrowfully, "I loved him as a son, and I called my son out of Egypt. But the more I called to him, the more he rebelled, offering sacrifices to the images of Baal and burning incense to idols. It was I who taught Israel how to walk, leading him along by the hand. But he doesn't know or even care that it was I who took care of him. I led Israel along with my ropes of kindness and love. I lifted the yoke from his neck, and I myself stooped to feed him. . . . Oh, how can I give you up, Israel? How can I let you go? How can I destroy you like Admah and Zeboiim? My heart is torn within me, and my compassion overflows. No, I will not punish you as much as my burning anger tells me to. I will not completely destroy Israel, for I am God and not a mere mortal. I am the Holy One living among you, and I will not come to destroy" (Hosea 11:1-9, NLT).

Peter writes that "the Lord isn't really being slow about his promise to return, as some people think. No, he is being patient for your sake. He does not want anyone to perish, so he is giving more time for everyone to repent" (2 Peter 3:9, NLT).

"As surely as I live, declares the Sovereign Lord, I take no pleasure in the death of the wicked, but rather that they turn from their ways and live. Turn! Turn from your evil ways! Why will you die, O house of Israel?" (Eze. 33:11, NIV).

Can you feel the heart of God in these passages? He is a hurting parent knowing full well the painful and eternal consequences of human choices. The great controversy is replete with the reality of the eternal loss of those who are not reconciled with the Father. How will God feel? How will He respond? Does Scripture paint the picture of brutal, heartless anger and cold, calculated justice? Hardly. Dealing with sinners who refuse reconciliation and forgiveness will always be God's strange act (Isa. 28:21). Often I wonder what it will really be like to be among the redeemed during the millennium. So much gut-wrenching sorrow will pour out of human hearts during that divinely ordained era of final reconciliation of people and nations. Will not God sorrow along with every hurting parent at the eternal loss of a beloved son, daughter, or grandchild? My heart shudders even to try to envision the unimaginable moment at the close of the millennium when parents within the city look out upon those who will be consumed forever, knowing that their actions, reactions, and inaction played a part in the ultimate choices made by those they loved. Will not the great heart of God bow down in incomprehensible sorrow here too?

David was tasting with God the bitterness of sin-sourced suffering and loss. "Deal kindly with . . . " "Would I had died instead of you." Such words invite us to stand in awe. The worst rejection of his life precipitated an expression of the most wonderful love.[13] In doing so I believe David anticipated the cross and the sufferings of God for the lost.

Between Heaven and Earth

The battle with Absalom took place in the forest of Ephraim, and it was a brutal scene. Without explaining why, Scripture says that "the forest claimed more lives that day than the sword" (2 Sam. 18:8, NIV). By choosing a forest as a battlefield, David hoped to minimize the value of Absalom's numerical advantage. The king's forces used the terrain to maximum advantage. The larger inexperienced rebel army fled in wild confusion as his three seasoned commanders fragmented the opposition, spreading Absalom's troops "over the whole countryside" (verse 8, NIV), thus preventing them from making a united stand. In the confusion, whoever didn't die by the sword perished miserably in the tangled vegetation of the forest.

Absalom's end came when his head (not his hair) got caught in the forked branches of a low-hanging oak tree (verse 9). His mule kept on going, leaving the prince suspended in midair. Evidently, Absalom had run into some of David's men and veered into a thicket of trees to escape. Now trying to dislodge himself, his long thick locks of hair entangled around the forked branches. One of David's pursuing soldiers discovered the prince's predicament. "I saw Absalom dangling in a tree," he told Joab. The commander-in-chief mocked the soldier who reported Absalom's predicament but refused to touch the king's son. "'What?' Joab demanded. 'You saw him there and didn't kill him? I would have rewarded you with ten pieces of silver and a hero's belt!' 'I wouldn't do it for a thousand pieces of silver,' the man replied. 'We all heard the king say to you and Abishai and Ittai, "For my sake, please don't harm young Absalom." And if I had betrayed the king by killing his son—and the king would certainly find out who did it—you yourself would be the first to abandon me'" (verses 10-13, NLT).

Ever quick to kill, Joab didn't hesitate. Taking three javelins, he thrust them into Absalom, stabbing Absalom's swinging body viciously. Then his 10 armor bearers moved in for the kill and slashed away mercilessly (verses 9-15). Afterward Joab and his men buried Absalom's mangled corpse right there in the forest under a heap of stones.

The imagery of Absalom, a rebel dying while hanging on a tree, gives pause for thought to anyone acquainted with Scripture. Deuteronomy 21:23 explicitly states that a person "who is hung on a tree is under God's curse" (NIV).[14] The form of Absalom's burial was also laden with symbolic value. Being thrown into a big pit in the forest and covered with a large heap of rocks was an act of contempt. Joab and his men denied Absalom the honor of being laid to rest in the family tomb. In essence they excluded him from the Promised Land, since the burial site was east of the Jordan River. His rebellion caused him to remain outside the Promised Land forever.[15]

While still alive Absalom literally hung in midair—"between heaven and earth"—suggesting more than his physical condition. Absalom was "suspended between life and death, between the sentence of a rebel and the value of a son, between the severity of the king and the yearning of the father."[16] The moment, though, could not last forever. Absalom, the king's son, must either live or die.

Scripture draws a stark picture for us of one of humanity's finest specimens ("no one in Israel was as handsome as Absalom. From head to foot, he was the perfect specimen of a man" [2 Sam. 14:25, NLT]) hanging from a tree with three javelins thrust into his body, and then buried under a pile of stone somewhere in a forest. Absalom had the massive armies of Israel fighting to protect him, and he was personally equipped with a fast means of escape not afforded other soldiers—a mule. Nevertheless, in spite of such advantages, "Absalom could not escape God's judgement."[17] Getting caught by his marvelous hair in the tree seemingly happened "by chance." No one planned it. But it was as though a great, ominous darkness surrounded him, and he was helpless in the face of it.

The imagery here of judgment and eternal loss is powerful. We find something here for everyone of us to ponder solemnly. The rebellion of Absalom mirrors what's at the heart of the great controversy.

Another Son, Another Tree

"O my son Absalom,
my son, my son Absalom!
Would I had died instead of you,
O Absalom, my son, my son!" (2 Sam. 18:33, NASB).

"David's cry is an anguished review of all that could have been and was not," Bruggemman writes.[18] Thompson asserts that, for a Christian, David's anguished cry "immediately calls to mind the picture of One who did die in the place of His wayward children. And the swirling emotions of familial ties presents us with a rich potential for exploring the mind and heart of God. What does it mean for God to clothe Himself in human flesh so that the Father dies in the Son—and thus God dies on our behalf and in our place?"[19] he asks.

David could not die for Absalom, but God can do what a human being cannot. As the woman of Tekoa said, "God devises ways to bring his banished back" And so in His wonderful plan "one day another Son of David would hang from another tree, but in such a way as to transform the curse into a blessing."[20] God Himself has taken on human flesh, hanging from a tree in order to become "a curse for us." "Christ redeemed us from the curse of the law by becoming a curse for us, for it is written:

'Cursed is everyone who is hung on a tree.' He redeemed us in order that the blessing given to Abraham might come to the Gentiles through Christ Jesus, so that by faith we might receive the promise of the Spirit" (Gal. 3:13, 14, NIV).

Jesus hung on a tree and was covered by a stone outside the gate. Thus God has provided a sacrifice so that sinners might live.

In this lament "David's story most clearly anticipates and most nearly approximates the gospel story, the story of Jesus that now extends into our stories."[21] David's grief for Absalom can help us to understand the cost to God the Father when He sent His Son to the cross to make atonement for human sin.[22]

When we read a story like this we cannot help asking, "How in the world do we keep sin from simply leaving a sobbing father over the city gate and a pile of stones over a beautiful body somewhere in the forest? There has to be a better way. God had to come and die in our place. And He had to live again. Or we are all forever under a pile of stones somewhere in the forest. The story of David and Absalom is not the answer. But it is the question. And in the question we begin to sense that answer that is our hope."[23]

"Would that I had died in your stead!" The fact is that God has. Our hurting Parent is hurt even more deeply for us. What should we do about these wonderful realities? We can accept God's death in our behalf and thus do not need to die for our own sin. And we can feel a sense of the predicament of the lost. Each one of us can then connect with the heart of God by way of intercession ("deal kindly with the young man") and self-sacrifice ("would that I had died instead of you"). This is what the gospel is all about—hurting parents and the hurting Parent who alone helps. "Praise the Lord, the God of Israel, because he has visited his people and redeemed them. He has sent us a mighty Savior from the royal line of his servant David, just as he promised through his holy prophets long ago. Now we will be saved" (Luke 1:68-71, NLT). "Because of God's tender mercy, the light from heaven is about to break upon us, to give light to those who sit in darkness and in the shadow of death, and to guide us to the path of peace" (verses 78, 79, NLT).

"Would that I had died in your stead!" "I did die for you," Jesus says. "I did die for you!" And so the hurting Father waits. What will it be, a prodigal who returns . . . or the one who stays away forever? "Who will tell the King?" What will you tell Him?

---

[1]E. H. Peterson, *Leap Over a Wall,* p. 193.

[2]C. R. Swindoll, *David: A Man of Passion and Desitny,* p. 248. As Rolston writes: "The biblical narrative of Absalom's rebellion, with its climax in the grief of David for his son, is one of the great stories of literature. It is difficult to find in either ancient or modern literature a more masterful piece of writing than this portion of Second Samuel" (H. Rolston, *Personalities Around David,* p. 121).

[3]K. Kaynor, *When God Chooses,* p. 291.

[4]A. Thompson, *Samuel,* p. 267.

[5]"In that moment the narrator perhaps wants us to remember with David that Saul went berserk when he found his own son against him (1 Sam. 20:30-33)" (W. Brueggemann, *First and Second Samuel,* p. 317).

[6]*Ibid.*, p. 321.

[7]B. Moore, *A Heart Like His,* p. 212.

[8]*Ibid.*, p. 213.

[9]Peterson, p. 194.

[10]Kaynor, p. 294.

[11]Peterson, p. 194.

[12]Rolston, *Personalities Around David,* p. 121.

[13]Peterson, p. 203.

[14]Bergen notes that "the words used by the soldier to report Absalom's condition are of great theological and thematic significance: 'Absalom was hanging [יְלְתֹּ:בָה] in an oak tree.' The word translated 'hanging' here is used only once in the Torah (Deut. 21:23) to declare that 'anyone who is *hung* [יְלְדָאת] on a tree is under God's curse'" (R. D. Bergen, *1, 2 Samuel,* p. 421).

[15]Bergen, p. 422.

[16]Brueggemann, p. 319.

[17]Bergen, p. 421.

[18]Brueggemann, p. 323.

[19]Thompson, pp. 270, 271.

[20]*Ibid.*, p. 268.

[21]Peterson, p. 204.

[22]Rolston, p. 125.

[23]Thompson, p. 271.

13

CELEBRATING VICTORY

2 Samuel 19-23

David's grief over Absalom consumed him. As the troops heard of the king's intense sorrow over his son, it turned the joy of that day's victory into paralyzing sadness. They crept back into the city as though they had been beaten in battle. The king had run upstairs to his room over the gateway, where he buried his face in his hands and couldn't stop weeping, "O my son Absalom! O Absalom, my son, my son!" Once again Joab stepped in. Going to David's room, he jerked him back to reality: "We saved your life today and the lives of your sons, your daughters, and your wives and concubines. Yet you act like this, making us feel ashamed, as though we had done something wrong. You seem to love those who hate you and hate those who love you. You have made it clear today that we mean nothing to you. If Absalom had lived and all of us had died, you would be pleased. Now go out there and congratulate the troops, for I swear by the Lord that if you don't, not a single one of them will remain here tonight. Then you will be worse off than you have ever been" (2 Sam. 19:4-7, NLT).

It was blunt and to the point. But what else should we expect from Joab? At this pivotal moment he had the best interest of his soldiers in mind rather than the emotional well-being of a mourning father. That day he had seen many lives snatched in battle. Absalom was just one more casualty to the battle-hardened warrior. But we can assume, too, that his resistance to David's grief betrayed his own guilt for having disobeyed David's order to spare his son's life. He was the one who had scolded the soldier who first found Absalom for not killing him, then thrust three javelins into his swinging body and let his bodyguard go at him. As it had been a calculated military decision while Absalom remained suspended between heaven and earth, so his counsel now. The fate of the kingdom hung in the balance. This was no time for mourning or to lick wounds. How David responded to the returning troops would determine whether or not his kingdom would hold together. His heart might be broken, but he was still king of Israel and had a job to do.

Though gripped by grief, David listened. He knew Joab's advice was right. Realizing that his army had fought for him, he must not let them return in shame. Suppressing his grief, he returned to the business of the kingdom, setting at the city gate to greet them in person as they filed by. It was a pivotal moment: "So the king went out and sat at the city gate, and as the news spread throughout the city that he was there, everyone went to him" (verse 8, NLT). The gate of the city was where the kings or the leaders appeared to give audience, to judge, to counsel, to meet with the people. So when David went to the gate, the people knew he was back in leadership.

Divided loyalties, however, still threatened to leave God's chosen nation in an upheaval. "Meanwhile, the Israelites who supported Absalom had fled to their homes. And throughout the tribes of Israel there was much discussion and argument going on" (verses 8, 9, NLT). Everywhere people were talking, arguing, wondering what to do. Is David still king? Should we take him back? Will he take revenge on us? "The king saved us from our enemies, the Philistines," they said to one another, "but Absalom chased him out of the country. Now Absalom, whom we anointed to rule over us, is dead. Let's ask David to come back and be our king again" (verses 9, 10, NLT). But not everyone thought that was a good idea. The leaders down in Judah weren't so sure. They were "holding out" (verse 11, NLT), considering other options. David realized the tribes of Israel were in a quandary because they had alienated their king and pledged allegiance to a now-dead individual. He responded by appealing to his own tribe, Judah, suggesting they lead the way for Israel in restoring the throne to Israel's rightful king (verses 11-14). In the process he promised some leadership changes. Most significantly, Amasa—who had been Absalom's general—would replace Joab.

Apparently David's victory combined with his fair treatment of the defeated won the hearts of the people of Judah. So they escorted David back across the Jordan to Jerusalem. On the way back David had several challenging encounters that showed his intention to bring reconciliation and healing. When Shimei, the Benjamite who had cursed and thrown rocks at him and his men as they retreated from Jerusalem, now came begging forgiveness, Abishai asked permission to kill him. "He cursed the Lord's anointed. He kicked you when you were down. Kick him back, and kick him hard. Finish him off—he's a loser." But David said there had been enough killing (verses 15-22). It was a hard moment of choice. He could be offended and resentful and take revenge on the man—or not. Instead, he chose to model a spirit of forgiveness.

The king ended another rivalry as quickly and as simply as possible when he took both Mephibosheth's and Ziba's word about whether or not Miphibosheth had allied himself with Absalom. Rather than spending the time chasing down the truth of the matter, David ordered the property he had once given to Miphibosheth now divided equally with Ziba (verses 24-30). Interestingly, Mephibosheth's integrity emerged as he responded in effect, "Let Ziba have everything as long as I have you back safely." It was a priceless moment of reconciliation, another example of David's forgiving spirit that could break the cycle of hurt.

A thousand men from Judah had hurried to David to help in every way they could and worked hard to ferry the king's household back over the Jordan River (verses 15-18). Unfortunately they complicated a tense situation when they commented that they had transported David because he was their kinsman. "But the men of Israel complained to the king that the men of Judah had gotten to do most of the work in helping him cross the Jordan. 'Why not?' the men of Judah replied. 'The king is one of our own tribe. Why should this make you angry? We have charged him nothing. And he hasn't fed us or even given us gifts!' 'But there are ten tribes in Israel,' the others replied. 'So we have ten times as much right to the king as you do. Why did you treat us with such contempt? Remember, we were the first to speak of bringing him back to be our king again.' The argument continued back and forth, and the men of Judah were very harsh in their replies" (verses 41-43, NLT).

Thus David crossed the Jordan with an entourage escorting him back to his throne, and before he could dry off his feet, his people were fighting among themselves. They were like children arguing over toys, space, companions, and even over work to be done, not because they necessarily wanted it but because of what someone else might get or do. How typical and human. It happens when leaders haven't established the kind of unifying administration their people need. Moral compromise not only keeps us from dancing—it affects how others dance as well, setting off a whole chain reaction. Some of the most difficult interpersonal experiences emerge in the backwash of sin. Hurting parents don't have the emotional resources or moral high ground to keep their family from infighting. Neither do kings. While David regained his kingdom, the tragic conflict and crisis took its toll on its interpersonal fabric. God's holy nation would not officially split into a northern kingdom (Israel) and a southern kingdom (Judah) until after Solomon's death, but the tribe of Judah already functioned in many ways as a separate people.

Return of the Giants

When people begin to bicker, they provide opportunity for troublemakers. Thus David found that reclaiming a kingdom was no small matter. Having to take his throne back rather than receive it from cheerful givers, he needed to reestablish his respect and authority as a leader. The politics and inevitable battles must have seemed insurmountable. It wasn't long until he was faced with civil war again as the disgruntled leader Sheba sounded a trumpet and urged the Israelites to a rebellion against him: "'We have nothing to do with David. We want no part of this son of Jesse. Come on, you men of Israel, let's all go home!' So the men of Israel deserted David and followed Sheba. But the men of Judah stayed with their king and escorted him from the Jordan River to Jerusalem" (2 Sam. 20:1, 2, NLT). Sheba's call in effect was a summons to political separatism, thus undermining David's claim to sovereignty and threatening the union of the southern and northern tribes.[1]

David sent Amasa, the new commanding general, to gather the army of Judah. But it took the new military leader longer than the three days allotted him. To the king's amazement, Amasa failed to show up at the appointed time as he continued to seek more men after David's deadline passed. He thought superior numbers would ensure victory, even though it had been the fatal flaw in Absalom's tactics. In the process he was willing to sacrifice speed and the element of surprise. Did he realize that waiting for more men had been the reason Absalom failed? The difference between Ahithophel's and Hushai's counsel had centered on this factor. Ahithophel had urged a quick kill of David, even if it meant going with fewer men. Hushai had argued that a larger force would surely triumph, but it would require time. Now Amasa repeated the same strategy that had previously proved disastrous.[2]

When Amasa failed to show up on time, David sent his veterans, his "mighty men," and his bodyguard under the direction of Abishai. "That troublemaker Sheba is going to hurt us more than Absalom did," he told Abishai. "Quick, take my troops and chase after him before he gets into a fortified city where we can't reach him" (verse 6, NLT). So Abishai and Joab set out after Sheba with an elite guard from Joab's army and the king's own bodyguard. As they arrived at the great stone in Gibeon, Amasa met them, coming from the opposite direction. Joab wore his uniform with a dagger strapped to his belt. As he stepped forward to greet Amasa, he secretly slipped the dagger from its sheath. "How are you, my cousin?" Joab said and took him by the beard as if to give him the customary kiss of greeting, only to stab him and leave him to bleed to death in the road (verses 8-10). The biblical account is gruesome: "Amasa didn't notice the dagger in his left hand, and Joab stabbed him in the stomach with it so that his insides gushed out onto the ground. Joab did not need to strike again, and Amasa soon died. Joab and his brother Abishai left him lying there and continued after Sheba" (verse 10, NLT). David should have known that Joab wasn't about to clean out his desk and resign peaceably when replaced by Amasa.

Although Joab meant to cause Amasa's death, he didn't intend to create a traffic jam. "One of Joab's young officers shouted to Amasa's troops, 'If you are for Joab and David, come and follow Joab.' But Amasa lay in his blood in the middle of the road, and Joab's officer saw that a crowd was gathering around to stare at him. So he pulled him off the road into a field and threw a cloak over him. With Amasa's body out of the way, everyone went on with Joab to capture Sheba" (verses 11-13, NLT). The army pursued the insurgent to the city called Abel-beth-maacah. There Joab laid siege to it and prepared to break down the wall. As his men began preparations for demolishing the city, a wise woman willing to become more than a spectator to imminent disaster called to the general from the wall, claiming that the city was "peaceful and faithful in Israel" (verse 19, NIV). Just give me Sheba, Joab responded, and he would withdraw (verse 21). The woman promised the rebel's head. After she consulted with her fellow citizens, they soon tossed Sheba's head over the wall, and Joab lifted the siege. The civil war was over. Brueggemann makes an interesting aside here: "The wisdom of the woman and the well-being of the city stand together. Wise words override ruthless policy. At the end, not only the woman and the city are saved; something of David's dignity and self-respect are also rescued from Joab's mad, obedient intent."[3] She displayed the kind of intelligent peacefulness and faithfulness that a bitterly divided nation needed at that crucial moment. Interestingly, as in previous situations in Israel's history, a woman's daring initiative resolved a significant crisis (cf. Judges 4:17-21; 9:52-54; 1 Sam. 25:14-35).

But David was not yet safe and secure. One last enemy arose before David could take a breath and finally proclaim victory. The Philistines were at it again. Once more they invaded Israel (2 Sam. 21:15), taking advantage of David's loss of respect and authority as Israel's leader and of the nation's divided loyalties. Whenever we're busy with jealousy and getting even, old enemies will rear their head. They will take advantage of every opportunity—our weaknesses, failures, disunity, and preoccupation with self and pettiness.

The appearance of the Philistines again at this point in David's story is almost ironic. It depicts a weakened and vulnerable David.[4] As they invaded his kingdom once again, he went out to fight. Rather than directing his troops from a distance as he had become accustomed to doing, he placed himself in the midst of the fray. Perhaps he sought to demonstrate to his people that he was still in charge and could be the trusted leader who would vanquish Israel's real enemies. That he could be truly kinglike again in the eyes of his people. After all, war has a way of diverting attention from pettier things, bringing unity among otherwise fractured people. A nation at war will rally around leaders who communicate resolve, purpose, and initiative. Besting the Philistines again would strengthen David's position. So he joined in the fray, but soon found himself in trouble.

When the Philistines became aware that Israel's king was on the battlefield, they focused their efforts on eliminating him.[5] As a result, David became weak and "exhausted" but unable to retreat from the conflict (verse 15, NIV). Ishbi-benob, one of Goliath's relatives, was on the battlefield that day too. Like Goliath, he dwarfed all those around him. Scripture tells us that his bronze spearhead weighed more than seven pounds and that he sported a sharp new sword. As David wilted, Ishbi-benob moved in for the kill—almost succeeding. Somehow he managed to corner Israel's ruler and was about to kill him, but Abishai son of Zeruiah came to the king's rescue and slew the giant Philistine (verse 17). It's an amazing episode in the unfolding story of David's fortunes following Absalom's death. Here the king is not strong, vigorous, or capable, but rather weak, exhausted, and vulnerable. His powers have diminished significantly. It's hard to imagine that David even previously knew about exhaustion in battle! The word for "exhausted" in Hebrew means to "fly away like a bird, faint, flee away" (cf. Hosea 9:11; Ps. 55:6, 7). It implies an overwhelming desire to run and to hide physically, emotionally, and psychologically.

I can imagine that when the Philistines once more began to spread themselves through the land of Israel, David at first despaired. It was the unwelcomed sight of an old enemy. *Why now?* he must have wondered to himself. *This just complicates the problems I have putting my life and my kingdom and my people back together.* Few things make us want to flee more than the prospect of refighting an old battle.[6] The moment that old enemy reappears, we want to give up. Satan always chooses just the right time to haunt us through an old enemy. When we haven't had enough rest, when things have been emotional and turbulent, when we've been swinging from one extreme to another, when like David we're struggling to regain our footing after some major crisis that has led to divided loyalties and infighting—that's when the enemy strikes. But like David, many of us go out to battle anyway—only soon to become weak and exhausted. Were it not for the intervention of others, we'd go down.

That brings me to a parallel theme running through these episodes recounting David's struggle to put his kingdom back together. From the tribal infighting to constant threats of civil war to the invasion by an old enemy, we see continued victory. But now it comes through someone else.[7] No doubt, David would have liked to put everything back together again on his own so the people would be in awe over his great strength. He would be their hero again. Unlike before, God graciously makes him dependent on someone else. In the end, facing an old enemy, he is weak, exhausted, and vulnerable. Were it not for Abishai, David wouldn't have survived. God purposely brought victory to him through the courage and strength and support of others—including the likes of Joab. David was bound to disappoint the people again, just as he already had. As a result, the Lord wanted His people to look to Him, not David. The king had come to believe that nothing could overtake him. But he was wrong. So God humbled David and made him depend on others for his life—and in the end, depend fully on God once more. None of us will escape this important life lesson. To gain it, God will teach us dependency by allowing us to become exhausted and forcing us to receive help from others and—most of all—from Him.

After nearly losing him in battle, David's men declared, "You are not going out to battle again! Why should we risk snuffing out the light of Israel?" (2 Sam. 21:17, NLT). It must have been an affirming moment. His band of brothers in arms regard David's leadership as valuable to the nation as a steady light source would be on a dark night. His very person embodies what is precious and life-giving (cf. 2 Sam. 18:3).

Another battle took place against the Philistines at Gob. As they fought, Sibbecai from Hushah killed Saph, another descendant of the giants. In yet another battle at Gob, Elhanan son of Jair from Bethlehem slew the brother of Goliath of Gath. The handle of the giant's spear was as thick as a weaver's beam! A battle with the Philistines at Gath involved a huge man with six fingers on each hand and six toes on each foot—a descendant of the giants—who defied and taunted Israel. But Jonathan, the son of David's brother Shimeah, destroyed him. Although all were descended from the giants of Gath, David and his warriors defeated them (2 Sam. 21:16-22).

In the end Israel finally crushed the old enemy again, giants and all. After all the ups and downs of his journey back to the throne, David could finally rest as his nation's king. Like a steady source of light on a dark night, his leadership was valuable to his people. But it had been a terrible journey. His personal and family failures had put him on display for all Israel to gawk at, leaving him crushed, humiliated, and vulnerable. His son was dead, and he had a general that he couldn't control. It had involved so much shedding of blood. The kingdom was on the verge of breaking apart into northern and southern factions. Who had the energy to rise and bind the nation's wounds? Yet Israel expected David to do so. One of the heaviest burdens of leadership is that initiative always rests on the leader. No matter how defeated, embarrassed, or down a leader might be, the "follower types" sit back and wait to be led.[8]

Singing to the Lord

Long before David was a king he had been a singer. Now, after all his ups and downs we find him singing again—dancing like a king in his heart before God. Second Samuel 22:1 tells us: "David sang this song to the Lord after the Lord had rescued him from all his enemies and from Saul (NLT)."[9] It celebrates the victory that God sovereignly and majestically won for him. Think about what motivated David to sing such words. Nothing he ever prayed or sang or said gathers more of his life together in one place than does this psalm.[10] Some of the most awesome and creative imagery and celebration of God likewise appears here—365 words of Hebrew poetry displaying the richest vocabulary.[11] The passage is one of the oldest major poems in the Old Testament.[12] While Psalm 18 contains an almost identical set of verses to those found here in 2 Samuel 22, it was intended for hymnic use in public worship. Here, however, we find a deeply personal reality, as the psalm reveals the religious core of Israel's most revered king.[13] It shows his passion for God and why it never wavered in spite of major failure and crisis.

"The One who delivered David from his enemies [including his own self] was no distant deity. He was the object of the psalmist's deepest emotions, the One with whom he shared authentic relationship."[14] David deeply loved God. His strongest instinct was to relate his life to God. By comparison, nothing else mattered at all.[15] Now, after all he had been through, that long enduring passion breaks through again.

"The Lord is my rock, my fortress,
and my savior;
my God is my rock, in whom I find protection.
He is my shield, the strength of my salvation, and my stronghold,
my high tower, my savior, the one who saves me from violence.
I will call on the Lord, who is worthy of praise,
for he saves me from my enemies.
The waves of death surrounded me;
the floods of destruction swept over me.
The grave wrapped its ropes around me;
death itself stared me in the face.
But in my distress I cried out to the Lord;
yes, I called to my God for help.
He heard me from his sanctuary;
my cry reached his ears.
Then the earth quaked and trembled;
the foundations of the heavens shook;
they quaked because of his anger.
Smoke poured from his nostrils;
fierce flames leaped from his mouth;
glowing coals flamed forth from him.
He opened the heavens and came down;
dark storm clouds were beneath his feet.
Mounted on a mighty angel, he flew,
soaring on the wings of the wind.
He shrouded himself in darkness,
veiling his approach with dense rain clouds.
A great brightness shone before him,
and bolts of lightning blazed forth.
The Lord thundered from heaven;
the Most High gave a mighty shout.
He shot his arrows and scattered his enemies;
his lightning flashed, and they were confused.
Then at the command of the Lord,

at the blast of his breath,
the bottom of the sea could be seen,
and the foundations of the earth were laid bare.
He reached down from heaven and rescued me;
he drew me out of deep waters.
He delivered me from my powerful enemies,
from those who hated me and were too strong for me.
They attacked me at a moment when I was weakest,
but the Lord upheld me.
He led me to a place of safety;
he rescued me because he delights in me.
The Lord rewarded me for doing right;
he compensated me because of my innocence.
For I have kept the ways of the Lord;
I have not turned from my God to follow evil.
For all his laws are constantly before me;
I have never abandoned his principles.
I am blameless before God;
I have kept myself from sin.
The Lord rewarded me for doing right,
because of my innocence in his sight.
To the faithful you show yourself faithful;
to those with integrity you show integrity.
To the pure you show yourself pure,
but to the wicked you show yourself hostile.
You rescue those who are humble,
but your eyes are on the proud to humiliate them.
O Lord, you are my light;
yes, Lord, you light up my darkness.
In your strength I can crush an army;
with my God I can scale any wall.
As for God, his way is perfect.
All the Lord's promises prove true.
He is a shield for all who look to him for protection.
For who is God except the Lord?
Who but our God is a solid rock?

God is my strong fortress;
  he has made my way safe.
He makes me as surefooted as a deer,
  leading me safely along the mountain heights.
He prepares me for battle;
  he strengthens me to draw a bow of bronze.
You have given me the shield of your salvation;
  your help has made me great.
You have made a wide path for my feet
  to keep them from slipping.
I chased my enemies and destroyed them;
  I did not stop until they were conquered.
I consumed them; I struck them down
  so they could not get up;
  they fell beneath my feet.
You have armed me with strength for the battle;
  you have subdued my enemies under my feet.
You made them turn and run;
  I have destroyed all who hated me.
They called for help, but no one came
  to rescue them.
  They cried to the Lord,
  but he refused to answer them.
I ground them as fine as the dust of the earth;
  I swept them into the gutter like dirt.
You gave me victory over my accusers.
  You preserved me as the ruler over nations;
  people I don't even know now serve me.
Foreigners cringe before me;
  as soon as they hear of me, they submit.
They all lose their courage
  and come trembling from their strongholds.
The Lord lives! Blessed be my rock!
  May God, the rock of my salvation, be exalted! End
He is the God who pays back those who harm me;
  he subdues the nations under me

> and rescues me from my enemies.
> You hold me safe beyond the reach of my enemies;
> you save me from violent opponents.
> For this, O Lord, I will praise you among the nations;
> I will sing joyfully to your name.
> You give great victories to your king;
> you show unfailing love to your anointed,
> to David and all his descendants forever"
> (2 Sam. 22:2-51, NLT).

Can you catch David's pervasive awareness of God? How immersed he is in the Lord? How he basks in the reflected glory of God's favor? How his contrasts between the realities of flesh and blood and the glories of divinity stand out with striking clarity?[16]

Notice the profusion of metaphors and how much David characterizes his life by God's mercy, grace, and love. He finds himself unknown yet named and known, unequipped yet triumphant, undeserving yet forgiven. Unworthy, he yet recovers his kingship.[17] Although he stumbles, he still manages to dance. As Peterson observes: "David's story is a gospel story, God doing for David what David could never do for himself. A sinner saved."[18] His language of superlative, exaggeration, and hyperbole is that of believers when they celebrate God's goodness—a world that was very dark until God intervened with a burst of glorious light.[19]

If this psalm compels us to see anything, it is that God is a personal deity that we can call our own. He is my strength when I am weak, my rock when I am slipping, my deliverer when I am trapped. The Lord is my refuge when I am pursued and my shield when I am exposed. Only such a God has a way of keeping my soul dancing.

It Was Never Really Gone

The kinds of things David experienced in the wake of his affair with Bathsheba had a way of making him want to sit it out rather than dance. It's a reality of life. Sin drains spiritual passion, and family dysfunction saps the life out of it. So does the loss of one's respect and authority of leadership and the hard struggle to regain it. The quarreling, infighting, revenge, bitterness, violence, and jockeying for power on the part of those around us, as well as the reappearance of old enemies, likewise absorb our spiritual energy. During such times it's hard to sustain spiritual and emotional equilibrium enough to keep dancing with any honor. An incredible series of events tucked in the middle of this long journey gives us a window into David's heart at a time when it would have been easier to sit it out than dance.

They happened during his escape from Jerusalem. In the hastily arranged flight the Levites brought the ark of the covenant of God (2 Sam. 15:24). "At the sight of the ark joy and hope for a brief moment thrilled David's heart."[20] "The presence of that sacred symbol was to them a pledge of deliverance and ultimate victory. It would inspire the people with courage to rally to the king. Its absence from Jerusalem would bring terror to the adherents of Absalom."[21] But other thoughts soon filled David's spiritually sensitive heart and made him unwilling to make the ark a "lucky rabbit's foot." Recognizing the hand of God in the events unfolding against him, he sensed that no personal interests, only the glory of God and the good of his people were to be uppermost in the unfolding events—no matter what happened to him.[22] So he commanded Zadok the priest, "Carry the ark of God back into the city. If I find favor in the eyes of the Lord, he will bring me back and let me see both it and his dwelling place. But if he says, 'I have no pleasure in you,' behold, here I am, let him do to me what seems good to him" (verses 25, 26, ESV). I marvel at his statement. David casts himself completely upon the favor and will of God. He has no desire to manipulate the Lord, but is prepared to entrust himself to God's good way and to take the outcome willed for him. It's a glimpse of spiritual passion amid incredible personal turmoil and uncertainty.

Stricken with grief and dressed for mourning, David and his loyal followers trudged up the Mount of Olives. There, as he approached the summit, an amazing thing happened: "David prayed" (verse 31, NIV). Somewhere on that mountain David got down on his knees and prayed that God would confound the wisdom of Absalom's counselor, Ahithophel (see Psalm 55, especially verses 12-14, 20, 21).[23] But David had even deeper things on his heart. Psalm 3 expresses the feelings that raged within him.[24]

"O Lord, I have so many enemies;
so many are against me.
So many are saying,
'God will never rescue him!'
But you, O Lord, are a shield around me,
my glory, and the one who lifts my head high.
I cried out to the Lord,
and he answered me from his holy mountain.
I lay down and slept.
I woke up in safety,
for the Lord was watching over me.
I am not afraid of ten thousand enemies
who surround me on every side.
Arise, O Lord!
Rescue me, my God!
Slap all my enemies in the face!
Shatter the teeth of the wicked!
Victory comes from you, O Lord.
May your blessings rest on your people"
(Ps. 3:1-8, NLT).

While Psalm 3 reminds of David's personal grief, it reveals the larger questions pressing on David: the rising tide of disloyalty (verses 1, 6; cf. 2 Sam. 15:13), the rumor that God had withdrawn from him (verse 2; cf. 2 Sam. 15:26), and the precarious state of his people (verse 8).[25] Some of the people thought that their king had gone beyond the possibility of forgiveness. David knew that and felt that he had no right to hope that God would help him. And yet, he prayed, claiming God as his shield. The Lord would be the one who lifted his head. So passionate was David's prayer that afterward he could lay down and sleep because he believed the Lord was watching over him. The king was on his knees again, recovering the life of prayer that had been integral to his life.

Along the way toward the crossing of the Jordan David encountered the profane, violent Shimei. It happened near Bahurim, where a ridge paralleled the route of retreat for a considerable distance.[26] Shimei walked along the ridge, showering rocks and insults on David, his officers, and his warriors: "'Get out of here, you murderer, you scoundrel!' he shouted at David. 'The Lord is paying you back for murdering Saul and his family. You stole his throne, and now the Lord has given it to your son Absalom. At last you will taste some of your own medicine, you murderer!'" (2 Sam. 16:7, 8, NLT). The man was the kind of person who kicks you while you're on your face, down and out. You're at your lowest, and along comes Shimei to hit you below the belt. And when you squirm, he comes back with another blow. During David's prosperity Shimei had not shown by word or act that he was not a loyal subject. But now he reveals his true character. Whereas before he had honored David on his throne, now he cursed him in his humiliation. While the stones struck the king, I have a feeling that the words hurt even more. Shemei's actions were wrong, but David feared that what he said might be right.

"Why should this dead dog curse my lord the king?" Abishai finally retorted. "Let me go over and cut off his head!"

"No!" David replied. "What am I going to do with you sons of Zeruiah! If the Lord has told him to curse me, who am I to stop him? . . . My own son is trying to kill me. Shouldn't this relative of Saul have even more reason to do so? Leave him alone and let him curse, for the Lord has told him to do it. And perhaps the Lord will see that I am being wronged and will bless me because of these curses" (verses 9-12, NLT).

"So David and his men continued on, and Shimei kept pace with them . . . , cursing as he went and throwing stones at David and tossing dust in the air" (verse 13).

Through all his ups and downs, victories and failures, we've never seen David dance through this kind of humiliation. "Many a wrongdoer has excused his own sin by pointing to David's fall, but how few there are who manifest David's penitence and humility. How few would bear reproof and retribution with the patience and fortitude that he manifested."[27]

Here is passion for God at its best. Ellen White reflects on its eloquence:

"This chapter in his experience, when, under cruelest wrong and insult, he shows himself to be humble, unselfish, generous, and submissive, is one of the noblest in his whole experience. Never was the ruler of Israel more truly great in the sight of heaven than at this hour of his deepest outward humiliation.

"Had God permitted David to go on unrebuked in sin, and while transgressing the divine precepts, to remain in peace and prosperity upon his throne, the skeptic and infidel might have had some excuse for citing the history of David as a reproach to the religion of the Bible. But in the experience through which He caused David to pass, the Lord shows that He cannot tolerate or excuse sin. And David's history enables us to see also the great ends which God has in view in His dealings with sin; it enables us to trace, even through darkest judgments, the working out of His purposes of mercy and beneficence. He caused David to pass under the rod, but He did not destroy him; the furnace is to purify, but not to consume. The Lord says, 'If they break my statutes, and keep not my commandments; then will I visit their transgression with the rod, and their iniquity with stripes. Nevertheless my loving-kindness will I not utterly take from him, nor suffer my faithfulness to fail' (Ps. 89:31-33)."[28]

Thus, as Peterson suggests, during the sufferings of this period David recovered his humility. He got back in touch with himself and resumed his prayer life. In the process he got in personal touch again with his personal God. And he regained compassion—his extraordinary capacity to love and forgive. In the end he was more human, praying, and loving.[29] Truly dancing like a king.

---

[1] W. Brueggemann, *First and Second Samuel,* p. 330.

[2] K. Kaynor, *When God Chooses,* pp. 301, 302.

[3] Brueggemann, p. 332.

[4] A. Thompson, *Samuel,* p. 289.

[5] R. D. Bergen, *1, 2 Samuel,* p. 448.

[6] B. Moore, *A Heart Like His,* p. 237.

[7] *Ibid.*

[8] Kaynor, p. 304.

[9] The book of 2 Samuel is not the only place in which we find David's words. Psalm 18 contains an almost identical set of verses to those found in 2 Samuel 22.

[10] E. H. Peterson, *Leap Over a Wall,* p. 205.

[11] Bergen, p. 450.

[12] *Ibid.,* p. 451.

[13] *Ibid.*

[14] Moore, p. 243.

[15] Philip Yancey, *Reaching for the Invisible God* (Grand Rapids: Zondervan Corporation, 2000), p. 192.

[16] A. Thompson, p. 291.

[17] Peterson, p. 211.

[18] *Ibid.*

[19] Thompson, pp. 290, 291.

[20] E. G. White, *Patriarchs and Prophets,* p. 732.

[21] *Ibid.*

[22] *Ibid.*

[23] Many scholars see Psalm 55 as including Ahithophel among the conspirators with Absalom (Peterson, pp. 200, 201; Kaynor, p. 279).

[24] It is the first psalm to bear a title and is linked with David's flight from Absalom as recounted in 2 Samuel 15:13ff. Moore suggests that David prayed this prayer while on the Mount of Olives (Moore, pp. 214, 215), while Kaynor places it the morning after crossing the Jordan River (Kaynor, p. 279).

[25] Derek Kidner, *Psalms 1-72* (Leicester, Eng.: InterVarsity Press, 1973), p. 53.

[26] Kaynor, p. 278.

[27] White, p. 737.

[28] *Ibid.*, p. 738.

[29] Peterson, pp. 198-204.

14

WAS IT NOT I . . . ?

1 Chronicles 21–22:1; 2 Samuel 24

Nothing captivates me more than watching a string of dominoes fall in fluid succession. As a boy I used to line them up, each carefully spaced from the other. Sometimes I would have them turn corners or make designs. Then I'd tip that first one over and . . . *click click, click, click, click, click,* they'd all go. There's a trick to it, of course. And it's always frustrating when one isn't balanced quite right and falls before its time.

Part of Japan's 2001 New Year's celebration included a large domino exhibition. Those who had set it up used literally millions of dominoes to create artistic scenes and all kinds of contraptions on the floors of a Tokyo convention center. They included a castle, where a line of dominoes went all the way up and down the parapet walls, setting off cannons that fired missiles in the air as they fell. One large mosaic featured panda bears eating bamboo in a lush green forest. When the dominoes began to fall, you could see sunlight ripple across the forest landscape. It was incredible—same bears, same bamboo, and same landscape, but different lighting. Each domino had been hand-painted to look one way standing up and another way after it fell. It's amazing how one falling domino can produce such a creative chain reaction of visual beauty and delight.

The devil craftily applied the domino effect when he prompted David to have a count taken of Israel's eligible fighting men. "Satan rose up against Israel and caused David to take a census of the Israelites. David gave these orders to Joab and his commanders: 'Take a census of all the people in the land—from Beersheba in the south to Dan in the north—and bring me the totals so I may know how many there are.' But Joab replied, 'May the Lord increase the number of his people a hundred times over! But why, my lord, do you want to do this? Are they not all your servants? Why must you cause Israel to sin?'" (1 Chron. 21:1-3, NLT).

The target was not just David but the nation as a whole as Satan "rose up against Israel." He understood the principle well. One falling domino creates a chain reaction. When it comes to moral and spiritual things, the first and best domino to have fall is always any group's leader. The devil does not waste time on the circumference of life but goes right to the heart of it. It is the leaders, the parents, the ministers, the ones chosen by God to be spiritual/moral undershepherds who become the target of his attack. Why? When a spiritual leader wanders from the things of God, the consequences are often devastating and always far-reaching. Leadership is the ability of one person to influence others.[1] Godly leaders have a divine calling to move people on to God's agenda—to lead people from where they are to where God wants them to be.[2] But when men and women who claim to model the message of Christ defect from that purpose and message, either by their actions or the statements that fall from their lips, they leave a destructive wound in the body of Christ.[3]

So Satan moved against Israel's leader in order to get to the nation itself. Israel found itself put on trial through its king and a moral link that involved the whole nation.[4] While David bore the brunt of the test, the people were on trial by proxy—at bottom they had an attitude similar to David's.[5]

A census is essentially amoral—neither good nor bad in itself. But in this case Satan tempted David to count his fighting men. The idea appealed to his pride and self-sufficiency.[6] God had blessed Israel for nearly four decades, even during the distraction of Absalom's revolt and its subsequent unrest. Now things had settled down again. The last of the Philistine giants were gone. It was a great time to be an Israelite. But the people had slipped spiritually as pride and self-confidence had increased. They had begun measuring themselves by their standing among other nations.[7] In keeping with such a spirit, David now wanted to know how strong his nation was militarily. "With a view to extending his conquests among foreign nations, [he] determined to increase his army by requiring military service from all who were of proper age."[8] It was a sign that he was beginning to emphasize his military force. But the strength of Israel's army meant nothing if God was not with the nation to give it the victory. David didn't need to number the people. Counting the children of Israel was a matter of pride. And it would further foster the already too great self-confidence of both king and people. Thus the spirit in which the people initiated and received the census was wrong.[9]

We've learned that David was both a complex and sensitive man. When he got the census numbers from Joab, he began to study the report: 1 million men in Israel and 470,000 men in Judah. Not bad! As he read the report, though, suddenly it didn't seem all that important anymore. And the question began to haunt him, *Why have I done this thing?* The longer he thought about it, the louder the answer pulsated in his brain: *The only reason is my own pride.* The Samuel version of this account tells us that "after he had taken the census, David's conscience began to bother him. And he said to the Lord, 'I have sinned greatly and shouldn't have taken the census. Please forgive me, Lord, for doing this foolish thing'" (2 Sam. 24:10, NLT).

Turning once again to 1 Chronicles, we get more details. "God was very displeased with the census, and he punished Israel for it" (1 Chron. 21:7, NLT). The Lord's response was quick and hair-raising. Through the prophet Gad God gave David a choice of judgments: three years of famine, three months of military defeat by invading armies, or three days of devastating plague in the land (verses 9-12). Suddenly David had a choice to make. He must decide on the consequences of pride. Any one of the three options was dreadful. The bottom line, though, was that it was the people of Israel who would be punished. There would be a chain reaction extending out to others because of his sin, because his leadership had galvanized their shared attitudes. Many dominoes would fall—literally.

"I am in deep distress," the king exclaimed. The tremendous guilt he felt down inside and the nature of the choice he had to make were almost more than he could bear.

"Let me fall into the hands of the Lord," he finally told Gad, "for his mercy is very great; but do not let me fall into the hands of men" (verse 13, NIV).

So the Lord sent a plague upon Israel, and 70,000 Israelite men died as a result (verse 14). It's the kind of thing that makes you wonder about God. Seventy thousand grieving families suffered from David's compromise with pride. Oh, how the dominoes fall! Ironically, when the king wanted to know how many soldiers were at his command, God promptly removed 70,000 from the national arsenal through the plague.[10] It showed that if the Lord desired, He could make those men as nothing. God was letting David, all Israel, and the whole world know that no individual or nation has any reason to boast in their strength. In a moment they can be taken, as were those 70,000 who died of the pestilence in Israel.[11]

The experience taught David three things about sin. First, he learned that it inevitably brings a sense of guilt. The king's heart troubled him after he had numbered the people (2 Sam. 24:10). His conscience took a real beating. The Hebrew word used here means to be attacked, to be assaulted. Scripture often uses it to refer to a destroyed city.[12]

Second, David again faced the reality that sin inevitably carries punishment or consequences with it.[13] You can't get around the fact that sin has its effects and aftermath. Once more David experienced its ugliness, its devastation, and its horror. Most of the time we can't choose what those consequences are. Scripture tells us that the ultimate wages of sin is death. In the meantime there are a host of temporal results of sin.

Third, David found that nobody can sin alone.[14] "One does not sin without making waves and causing a wake."[15] It's even more so for leaders. The entire nation suffered divine displeasure because of the sin of one individual. We can only imagine the agony in the king's heart as he realized that 70,000 Israelite men had already perished.

"Was it not I," he asked (1 Chron. 21:17, NKJV). "Was it not I who commanded the people to be numbered? I am the one who has sinned and done evil indeed; but these sheep, what have they done? Let Your hand, I pray, O Lord my God, be against me and my father's house, but not against Your people that they should be plagued" (verse 17, NKJV).

It's a sobering reality that nobody sins to himself. So often those who are most affected are the very ones we would desire at all cost to escape the consequences of our failures.[16]

When I read this passage, I hear God telling me that I need to be a "census taker." No, I don't mean counting the number of members I have in my church or how many come to worship. Or how many have been baptized this year. Nor how many faithfully return tithe and liberally support the church's operating budget. Rather, I need to discover whom I am affecting with my attitudes and behaviors rather than counting what I have, what I am, or what I've accomplished. Every one of us needs to be in touch with the domino effect. We must ask ourselves, What instance in my life can I recall in which my sin has caused or is causing others to suffer? We need to take measure of our influence, to determine how our motives, attitudes, and decisions affect the well-being of others. Above all, we must come to realize that attitude sins can be extremely costly.

Drama at the Threshing Floor

Something about this story, though, especially troubles me. Satan always seeks to make us believe that God is unfair or unkind. Surely whacking 70,000 people because of one person's pride seems out of balance. It doesn't present the kind of God that you can love—only fear, literally. No matter the leadership issues we just affirmed, God's response still haunts us. Thinking people wonder about it all. Satan likes to use difficult-to-understand stories such as this tragic episode to confuse and unsettle our confidence in God and His Word. But 1 Chronicles 21 (and 2 Samuel 24) gives us an opportunity to go deeper. As we do so, we must remember that we do not always have all the facts of a given story, nor do we usually have the explanations for certain events and acts of God.

When Scripture records an event or judgment of God that seems cruel or unfair, we need to do two things. First, recognize that we may not have all the information or understanding of a given story. We have no idea the depth of evil God may have seen in human hearts that necessitated such serious judgment. As a result we must acknowledge that His ways are higher than our own (Isa. 55:8-11) and that He always sees and works faithfully, honestly, and redemptively (Rom. 8:28). Second, we must affirm what we do know about God. Anytime we find ourselves overwhelmed by what we do not know or understand about Him, we can consider what we do know. In the process it can calm our heart and mind so that we can walk in faith.[17] This incident allows us to practice these skills so that we can deal with similar difficulties in future study.

The mind-boggling thing about the story is how Satan was directly responsible for impressing David's mind with the thought of ordering a census. It shouldn't be surprising, though. The real battle for our lives occurs in the mind—deep within our inner private world of thoughts and feelings, motives and aspirations. That's where it happened with David. Satan nudged him in his private thoughts and said, "Why don't you number these people? Let's see how big the kingdom really is. Why not inventory how vast your land has become and in the process find out how large an army you can muster?"

But wait! Doesn't the 2 Samuel version of this episode tell us that God did it?

"Once again the anger of the Lord burned against Israel, and he caused David to harm them by taking a census. 'Go and count the people of Israel and Judah,' the Lord told him. So the king said to Joab, the commander of his army, 'Take a census of all the people in the land—from Dan in the north to Beersheba in the south—so that I may know how many people there are" (2 Sam. 24:1, 2, NLT).

Reading it, we would naturally wonder why God would ask David to do something and then kill 70,000 people as a result. We better understand such passages by comparing "parallel" accounts. So who enticed David to sin—God or Satan? As we confront something we find difficult to explain, we should first consider what we do know. How do the following passages help us?

"When tempted, no one should say, 'God is tempting me.' For God cannot be tempted by evil, nor does he tempt anyone; but each one is tempted when, by his own evil desire, he is dragged away and enticed" (James 1:13, 14, NIV).

"No temptation has seized you except what is common to man. And God is faithful; he will not let you be tempted beyond what you can bear. But when you are tempted, he will also provide a way out so that you can stand up under it" (1 Cor. 10:13, NIV).

From the two passages we know that God does not tempt us. He may allow us to face temptation to test, prove, or help us to grow; but He is definitely not the tempter. In each experience of temptation He always makes a way of escape.

I find it interesting how in the 1 Chronicles version of the narrative

Satan comes on the scene without warning. Bam! Right there at the beginning of the story. The name of Satan appears in only two other places in the Old Testament—Job and Zechariah (see Job 1:6-2:10; Zech. 3:1). In each case Satan works to accuse and to bring about evil. Interestingly, God both permits and limits the evil that he causes.[18] Only at the end of the New Testament does Scripture fully identify Satan as the dragon, the serpent, the devil, and the deceiver (Rev. 12:9; 20:2). So there's something unique about this story. It has things in it that we need to think carefully about. God allowed Satan to tempt David by giving him the idea of a military census, which even the king's military leader Joab recognized was contrary to faith in God. In light of 1 Corinthians 10:13, Joab's protest against it was David's "way out."[19]

But what about the punishment? Did it exceed the crime? If we are not careful to study the text, 70,000 men seemed to die as a result of the king's sin. Although his actions no doubt displeased God and caused judgment, Scripture clearly tells us that the anger of the Lord burned against *Israel* (2 Sam. 24:1). We've touched already on how the nation's growing pride and self- confidence lay behind God's response. In general, God promised blessing for obedience and cursing for disobedience (Deut. 28:1-24). We can be sure that His response here was consistent with that which He had warned about choosing a path independent from Him. But we have no idea, however, why 70,000 were singled out from other men of Israel. Was it just a round number or symbolic? Or were their lives in clearer rebellion against God? In the end we simply don't know.

In the heart of this difficult account of anger and judgment appears something vital we must not miss—God's mercy. The Lord is present in the episode in a most unique way unlike in any other incident in David's life. Here God sent an angel to destroy Jerusalem. The "sword of the Lord" in the hand of the angel (1 Chron. 21:12) cuts down people by the tens of thousands as the plague marches southward through the land toward the capital city. Then, as the angel reaches the old Jebusite threshing floor and Jerusalem itself is about to feel the brunt of divine punishment, the Lord Himself grieves at what has been happening and declares, "Enough! Withdraw your hand" (1 Chron. 21:15, [NIV]; 2 Sam. 24:16). Simultaneously, it seems, the angel becomes visible to human eyes, "standing between earth and heaven, and in his hand a drawn sword stretched out over Jerusalem" (1 Chron. 21:16, NRSV). David and the Israelite leaders see Him as well as Ornan and his sons at the threshing floor itself (verse 20).

Anchor that point in your mind: God grieved when the angel stretched out his hand to destroy Jerusalem. As we continue we will see the special significance of the threshing floor and the mercy God poured out at this place.

As the angel became visible to human eyes, David and the elders, clothed in sackcloth, fell facedown. The king said to God, "Was it not I who ordered the fighting men to be counted? I am the one who has sinned and done wrong. These are but sheep. What have they done? O Lord my God, let your hand fall upon me and my family, but do not let this plague remain on your people" (verse 17, NIV).

Then the angel of the Lord commanded Gad to tell David to build an altar to the Lord on the threshing floor of Ornan the Jebusite (verse 18). "So David obeyed the instructions the Lord had given him through Gad. Araunah, who was busy threshing wheat at the time, turned and saw the angel there. His four sons, who were with him, ran away and hid. When Araunah saw the king approaching, he left his threshing floor and bowed to the ground before David. David said to Araunah, 'Let me buy this threshing floor from you at its full price. Then I will build an altar to the Lord there, so that he will stop the plague.'

"'Take it, my lord, and use it as you wish,' Araunah said to David. 'Here are oxen for the burnt offerings, and you can use the threshing tools for wood to build a fire on the altar. And take the wheat for the grain offering. I will give it all to you.'

"But the king replied to Araunah, 'No, I insist on paying what it is worth. I cannot take what is yours and give it to the Lord. I will not offer a burnt offering that has cost me nothing!'

"So David gave Araunah six hundred pieces of gold in payment for the threshing floor. David built an altar there to the Lord and sacrificed burnt offerings and peace offerings. And when David prayed, the Lord answered him by sending fire from heaven to burn up the offering on the altar. Then the Lord spoke to the angel, who put the sword back into its sheath" (verses 19-27, NLT).

Did you catch those last couple verses? "David built an altar there to the Lord and sacrificed burnt offerings and peace offerings. And when

David prayed, the Lord answered him by sending fire from heaven to burn up the offering on the altar. Then the Lord spoke to the angel, who put the sword back into its sheath." References to fire descending onto an altar appear in only three other Old Testament passages (Lev. 9:24; 1 Kings 18:38; 2 Chron. 7:1; see also Judges 6:21). On each occasion the fire symbolized extraordinary pleasure from God toward His people.

When He so clearly manifested His presence and His acceptance of David's offering on the altar on Ornan's threshing floor, the king concluded that it was the place where Israel should erect the Temple and where the people were to come to offer sacrifices and worship God.[20] "This will be the location for the Temple of the Lord God and the place of the altar for Israel's burnt offerings!" he concluded (1 Chron. 22:1, NLT). Let's step back a moment and orient ourselves to this little piece of geography. Ornan's threshing floor was located on Mount Moriah, where Abraham had offered up Isaac (Gen. 22:1-14). And the Temple would later be built there: "So Solomon began to build the Temple of the Lord in Jerusalem on Mount Moriah, where the Lord had appeared to Solomon's father, King David. The Temple was built on the threshing floor of Araunah the Jebusite, the site that David had selected" (2 Chron. 3:1, NLT).

Mount Moriah has had a long association with sacrifice. Genesis 22:10-12 tells us that when Abraham reached out his hand to take the knife to slay his son, God intervened and stopped him. The Lord then presented a sacrifice in the young man's place. Consider the timing here with David. The king looked up and saw the angel of the Lord standing between heaven and earth, a sword in his hand that extended over Jerusalem (1 Chron. 21:16). When the angel stretched out its hand to destroy Jerusalem, the Lord felt sorrow because of the calamity and said to the angel, "Enough! Withdraw your hand." As with Abraham and Isaac, the moment God saw a blade intent on destroying life at this location, He intervened and accepted substitutionary sacrifices. That both these events happened at the same place and at the moment a knife or sword was being drawn is no accident.

This incredible story, then, of the Temple site's selection belongs here with David's decision to "fall into the hands of the Lord, for his mercy is very great" (1 Chron. 21:13, NLT), for the Temple symbolizes divine willingness to grant mercy.[21] It is a theme emphasized in Solomon's dedicatory prayer (2 Chron. 6:22-42) and God's response to it (2 Chron. 7:12-14). The purpose of the story is to move us from David's sin to the threshing-floor story to the building of the Temple, the central concern of Chronicles and the theme of our next chapter.

God's halting of the plague at Ornan's threshing floor provides one of the most dramatic scenes in the Old Testament.[22] Satan is here. God is here. Judgment is here. Mercy is here. And atonement is here. Wilcock observes that "as on those other occasions when the Old Testament reveals to us the doings of Satan, in the poetry of Job and the prophecy of Zechariah, we are taken behind the scenes, to be shown something of the workings of evil and of the way in which God overrules it for good."[23] The larger picture presented here brings the great controversy between Christ and Satan into view. In it we catch a glimpse of Satan's character and see our sin and its effects on others. The angel standing with drawn sword over Jerusalem, 70,000 already dead, forcefully portrays the reality of impending judgment because of sin. The compassionate and merciful character of God comes into focus as we hear David exclaim, "Let me fall into the hand of the Lord, for His mercies are very great" (1 Chron. 21:13, NKJV). We find substitutionary atonement through the sacrifice of burnt offerings, especially as the Lord accepts it with fire from heaven and averts judgment. Finally, we have the location of God's house—Mount Moriah—at which God's people can come to find reconciliation and forgiveness. For us today it is the heavenly sanctuary.

"Here shall be the house," David declares. Where? On a site at which, 800 years earlier, another sacrifice had been offered and another disaster averted. It is Mount Moriah, the place where Isaac once lay bound on an altar, as good as dead beneath the knife poised in his father's hand, and where in the nick of time God prevented the sacrifice and gave Abraham his son back from death by providing the lamb (Gen. 22:1ff.; Heb. 11:17-19).

But we must make a still more remarkable connection. "Here shall be the house." Where? On a hill above the City of David, at the northern end of which a thousand years later the ultimate sacrifice was offered and the ultimate plague finally halted. The place called Calvary lay beyond the city wall, outside the Temple site (Heb. 13:12), but the area was all Moriah. The place, and the events that happened there, twice as foreshadowings and the third as fulfillment, were God's gift to His people. The third time the sword was not stayed. No hand was asked to relax. Rather, divine justice and mercy converged in the death of Jesus. "God so loved the world, that he gave his only begotten Son, that whosoever believeth in him should not perish, but have everlasting life" (John 3:16).

The point of the passage is that while David deliberately yielded to temptation, God was able to turn it to good. Three times the king expressed his distress and deep contrition (1 Chron. 21:8, 13, 17). In the process the mercy of God came into full relief, and an altar emerged. When we sin, God can take that sin and its evil effects and transform them into something that will contribute to our redemption and His glory.

David knew by experience that the Lord would be more merciful than any of his enemies. If you want grace, fall into the hands of God. Redpath writes, "The answer of God to the cry of every heart today is fire from heaven."[24]

The same divine grace that triumphed over David's sins and led to the establishment of God's house remains His principal attribute available to human beings. Reaching out to draw and sustain the weak, God Himself always takes the lead in lifting up the fallen.[25]

"For the word of God is full of living power. It is sharper than the sharpest knife, cutting deep into our innermost thoughts and desires. It exposes us for what we really are. Nothing in all creation can hide from him. Everything is naked and exposed before his eyes. This is the God to whom we must explain all that we have done. That is why we have a great High Priest who has gone to heaven, Jesus the Son of God. Let us cling to him and never stop trusting him. This High Priest of ours understands our weaknesses, for he faced all of the same temptations we do, yet he did not sin. So let us come boldly to the throne of our gracious God. There we will receive his mercy, and we will find grace to help us when we need it" (Heb. 4:12-16, NLT).

Was It Not I?

As God ordered his angel to stop, David saw the being with a drawn sword in his hand extended over Jerusalem (1 Chron. 21:16). The angel paused to wait for a final decision from God as to whether to destroy Jerusalem or not. Seeing the angel, David asked for mercy a second time (verses 17, 18). This time his heart turned from concern for his own well-being to the interests of the nation. "Was it not I . . . ?" he confessed. David pleaded with God to treat the matter as his own personal offense. He then asked the Lord to show mercy to the nation and "offered himself as a substitute."[26] At that moment David reflected the passion of the Son of David who centuries later would present Himself as a substitute.

"Let me fall into the hand of the Lord, for His mercies are very great" (1 Chron. 21:13, NKJV).

"As surely as I live, says the Sovereign Lord, I take no pleasure in the death of wicked people. I only want them to turn from their wicked ways so they can live. Turn! Turn from your wickedness, O people of Israel! Why should you die?" (Eze. 33:11, NLT).

First Chronicles 21:27 is one of the most wonderful verses we could ever read. "Then the Lord spoke to the angel, and he put his sword back into its sheath" (NIV). Here is the peace that David experienced and enjoyed at the end of his long journey through life. His whole life as Israel's king was a *dance,* so to speak, between the fine moral and spiritual nuances of the issues and decisions he confronted as a king, a parent, a man of faith, and as a human being. Sometimes David danced well. Other times he flat out blew it. In all the ups and downs of his *royal years* with their leadership and family ethical opportunities and dilemmas he constantly needed God's undergirding mercy and substitutionary atonement—grace. He would have never ended well were it not for this sense of God's grace and how thoroughly he experienced it in his life. It's one reason I keep thumbing back to David's story of passion—because behind it all is God's passion to save us from the inevitable consequences of our sins. I learn that God is hardly surprised by my failure. After all, He knows me better than I know myself. I am more sinful than I could ever imagine—and also more loved by God. Oh, that you would experience the same sense of God's grace in your life in spite of who you are or what you've ever done.

---

[1]Henry and Richard Blackaby, *Spiritual Leadership: Moving People On to God's Agenda* (Nashville: Broadman & Holman Publishers, 2001), p. 17.

[2]*Ibid.,* pp. 19-21.

[3]C. R. Swindoll, *David: A Man of Passion and Destiny,* p. 272.

[4]T. H. Epp, *A Man After the Heart of God,* p. 191.

[5]K. Kaynor, *When God Chooses,* p. 312.

[6]Second Samuel 24 deals with the sin of pride in the nation of Israel and in David. The nature of the temptation sent to David shows this was the basic sin God was dealing with. See Kaynor, p. 311.

[7]E. G. White, *Patriarchs and Prophets,* pp. 746, 747.

[8]*Ibid.,* p. 747.

[9]"It was pride and ambition that prompted this action of the king. . . . This would tend . . . to foster the already too great self-confidence of both king and people" *(ibid.).*

[10]Kaynor, p. 315.

[11]Epp, p. 193.

[12]Swindoll, *David,* p. 275.

[13]A. Redpath, *The Making of a Man of God,* p. 242.

[14]*Ibid.*

[15]Swindoll, *David,* p. 277.

[16]Redpath, p. 242.

[17]B. Moore, *A Heart Like His,* pp. 244, 245.

[18]Michael Wilcock, *The Message of Chronicles* (Downers Grove, Ill.: InterVarsity Press, 1987), p. 90.

[19]Moore, p. 247.

[20]R. L. Pratt, *1 and 2 Chronicles,* pp. 169, 176.

[21]Marti J. Steussy, *David: Biblical Portraits of Power* (Columbia, S.C.: University of South Carolina Press, 1999), pp. 112, 113.

[22]Wilcock, p. 95.

[23]*Ibid.,* p. 91.

[24]Redpath, p. 241.

[25]Roddy Braun, *1 Chronicles* (Waco, Tex.: Word Books, Publisher, 1986), p. 218.

[26]Pratt, p. 174.

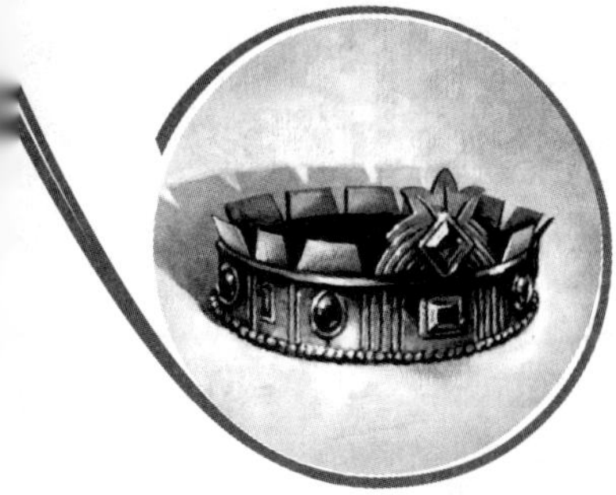

15

FRAGILE MOMENTS, NO ORDINARY FACES

I Chronicles 29:1-18

It was an old rundown auditorium on the outskirts of a decaying little city called Mineyviche in the middle of nowhere Ukraine. The last night of four weeks of evangelistic meetings in a predominantly Pentecostal and Russian Orthodox stronghold had finally arrived. I was there with my two oldest sons and a couple hundred adults and almost as many children. I had preached my last sermon, made the final call. Everywhere people were standing and tears flowing. Now I prayed and tried to say goodbye and leave.

Time suddenly became painfully real, each lingering second priceless and irretrievable. People started coming from what seemed everywhere to tell us what God had done in their lives and how my ministry had touched hearts. They wanted to express their love and gratitude by bringing flowers and gifts and making speeches. The city mayor, with tears, told how amazing it was to her and others in the community that anyone would invest so much in them. "Is this not like God?" she wondered out loud. After all, who were the people of Mineyviche to receive such a blessing?

My sons, too, tried to hold on to the fleeting moment. One of them stepped to the microphone to exhort the just baptized young people to remain faithful. They needed to fill their minds with the Word, pray, and help each other stay strong. His brother, not ever one to say much in public, haltingly told how much various people had come to mean to him. How he would carry them on his heart and memory forever.

We lingered, seeking to put off the inevitable—leaving—afraid to go out for fear what we had experienced together would never return. Would be lost forever.

Sometimes you experience things you never want to let go of. No one likes to have special moments come to an end, especially when they've been emotionally moving. Perhaps such occasions have welded hearts together in unity through some common purpose or shared experience or raised our level of spiritual awareness or commitment as we clearly felt the presence of God's Spirit. Every one of us has had times that we want to hold on to and keep alive as long as we can. And repeat if possible! But such experiences don't come very often. So when they do, we want desperately to preserve them. That's how King David felt when he and his people rose up to meet the challenge for the work of God in their generation.

Throughout his long reign as Israel's king his most cherished dream had been to build a new house for God. The thought that the Lord's house was only a portable tent, showing the wear and tear of time, particularly disturbed him. "Here I am living in this beautiful cedar palace," he told Nathan the prophet, "but the Ark of the Lord's covenant is out in a tent!" (1 Chron. 17:1, NLT). David saw the contrast between the tired-looking old structure and his own aesthetically pleasing modern home. "Building a temple was logical, in light of the needs created by the growth of the capital city. About 26,000 Levites and priests we're serving the religious life of the nation. Having a facility commensurate with the portion of religious personnel that served in Jerusalem made sense."[1] David longed for a more representative expression of the Lord's presence and work.

By now the king was an old man. Solomon already reigned on his throne. Sensing that he was nearing the end, David summoned Israel's leaders to talk about the priority of God's house in their lives. Standing in their presence, he reminded them of his own commitment to the long-dreamed project: "Using every resource at my command, I have gathered as much as I could for building the Temple of my God. Now there is enough gold, silver, bronze, iron, and wood, as well as great quantities of onyx, other precious stones, costly jewels, and all kinds of fine stone and marble. And now because of my devotion to the Temple of my God, I am giving all of my own private treasures of gold and silver to help in the construction. This is in addition to the building materials I have already collected for his holy Temple. I am donating more than 112 tons of gold from Ophir and over 262 tons of refined silver to be used for overlaying the walls of the buildings and for the other gold and silver work to be done by the craftsmen. Now then, who will follow my example? Who is willing to give offerings to the Lord today?" (1 Chron. 29:2-5, NLT).

David knew that dreams never become a reality on their own. They always have a practical side—in which very down-to-earth things such as detailed building plans, adequate financing, and preparations for construction come into view. On this occasion, God's people responded in willing commitment to make their dream for God's work and His house a reality: "Then the family leaders, the leaders of the tribes of Israel, the generals and captains of the army, and the king's administrative officers all gave willingly. For the construction of the Temple of God, they gave almost 188 tons of gold, 10,000 gold coins, about 375 tons of silver, about 675 tons of bronze, and about 3,750 tons of iron. They also contributed numerous precious stones, which were deposited in the treasury of the house of the Lord under the care of Jehiel, a descendant of Gershon. The people rejoiced over the offerings, for they had given freely and wholeheartedly to the Lord, and King David was filled with joy" (verses 6-9, NLT).

The people "rejoiced," and David was filled with "joy." It's the same Hebrew word in both cases—being glad or joyful with one's whole disposition, so much so that your eyes light up. The king literally "rejoiced with great joy" (KJV)—*sämah simhâ güdôlâ.* Once again he was *dancing like a king*. And so were the people.

More was taking place that day than the mere collecting of money for a grand building project. It was a spiritually defining moment for the people of Israel. David knew, though, that it was a fragile experience, one that needed thoughtful nurturing. If he could only help them to hold on to it forever. So we find David praying, "I have seen with joy how willingly your people who are here have given to you. O Lord, God of our fathers Abraham, Isaac and Israel, keep this desire in the hearts of your people forever, and keep their hearts loyal to you" (1 Chron. 29:17, 18, NIV).

"Keep this desire in the hearts of your people forever." Let this occasion of consecration not be for the moment only, but rather a lifelong pattern of thinking, a way of being. A habit of their hearts as long as they lived.

Filling the Hand

First Chronicles 29 is not a story about collecting money or huge building programs. It's about forming a heart habit of joyful commitment to God and His work—what dancing like a king is all about. That's why David asked the pressing question: "Who then is willing to consecrate himself this day to the Lord?" (verse 5, NASB). The expression translated "consecrate himself" means literally to "fill the hand." It is not something like the time I asked my son if he would share his chocolate-chip cookie with me. He broke off a tiny piece and handed it to me with a smile. "Filling the hand" means giving ourselves wholly to the Lord. Holding back nothing from Him, we release our very best for His work and glory. It has to do with motive and potential. As I write this I'm asking myself if I've ever come to God loaded down with all I have, all that I am.

Who is willing to fill their hand in total commitment to the Lord? David wonders. Consecration means to be devoted, committed—for God. That's what David said about himself when he stood up and shared from his heart his own personal testimony. He was telling everyone how he felt about God's work and what he was going to do to move it along. The king would support it not just for the moment but for as long as he lived. David was willing to be counted in, and he was willing to be counted on. The same was true for the various levels of Israel's leadership. They too, one by one, expressed their willingness to sustain the work and house of God (verse 6). Everyone came with a full hand. David's generosity was lavish and served as a catalyst for the magnanimity of the people (112 tons of gold from Ophir and more than 262 tons of refined silver is no small change!). Leaders will never see total commitment or openhanded giving from their people if they are not willing to take the lead.[2] Never underestimate the power of a positive example! David could not have motivated the leaders of Israel to give freely and wholeheartedly to the Lord unless he had so given himself.

Many today are simply not good at commitments of any kind. Commitment means responsibility, and responsibility sounds confining.

Being counted in and counted on demands a humble heart. Sometimes it means letting go of our individuality, our opinions, our priorities. Often we're afraid of making a commitment to God or His work because we're not sure we can deliver. But commitment means we're willing to stand up and be counted—and counted on. It's something thought through and consistent rather than *haphazard, whenever,* or *iffy*. True commitment implies habit and consistency. It begins with the dedication of our lives.

As a result, God's work became a priority. David declared that "because my affections are set on the house of my God, I have also given what gold and silver I personally own for the house of my God, over and above everything which I have already provided for the holy Temple" (verse 3, New Jerusalem). For him the Temple was "God's footstool" in a dying world (1 Chron. 28:2),[3] the place where God was actively at work leading and redeeming His people.

In his book *When Not to Build,* Ray Bowman outlines the dangers of church-building programs. Often when a growing congregation erects a new home, its focus unwittingly shifts from people to the physical structure itself. In time the major concern of the church switches to paying for the building—debt reduction. That can kill a church. Most of the time it will take a whole generation to recoup lost ministry and evangelism energy. With this in mind, Bowman posits "The Principle of Focus," suggesting that "a church should build only when it can do so without shifting its focus from ministering to people to building a building."[4] In principle, a growing church can plan and pay for a building program in such a way that the members never take their concentration off meeting the needs of people through caring ministries or evangelism.[5]

I believe that David understood the principle of focus, though he may not have called it such. But that's why he worked to move the ark and the Temple to Jerusalem. The Temple was where God was actively at work leading and redeeming His people. It was a place of ministry, reconciliation, atonement, encouragement, faith-building, worship, renewal, and decision. He didn't want such powerful things taking place in some out-of-the-way or inconveniently located spot. David wanted it there at Israel's capital. There it would focus on God, helping hurting people and offering hope, reconciliation, and redemption.

Naturally, consecration—filling the hand, being counted in and counted on—always touches our personal lives in some significant way. David says, "because my affections are set on the house of my God, I have also given what gold and silver I personally own." The Hebrew word translated "personal treasures" is *sügullâ*. A *sügullâ* was of special importance to ancient monarchs because it was a kind of personal security against times of political hardship or disaster. It was like money squirreled away in a Swiss bank. Today we would call it life savings or retirement—the treasure we channel into safeguarding our future. The king's gift was more than simply a gesture of great generosity. It amounted to his giving away part of his personal future security—his accumulated wealth. Clearly he understood the difference between accumulated wealth and earned income and that both were needed for advancing the Lord's mission. He wasn't going to pass everything on to Solomon or his other children as inheritance. The work of God was a priority in his thinking. How he distributed his assets was both a moral and spiritual matter, something not to be taken lightly.

As David gave what was personally his, the people overwhelmingly responded. Do you give that which is personal? Do your monetary gifts come from your heart, not just your checkbook? And does the contribution of your time flow from rejoicing, not resentment? God delights in the giving of your personal treasures—and your example motivates others!

We're talking here about more than money. Our devotion to God and His work should affect every aspect of our lives—time, talent, influence, skills, material resources, and accountability. A habit of commitment touches our personal life in significant and tangible ways. When we are consecrated—we're committed and come with a full hand. There is personal sacrifice.

Finally, consecration means that our hearts have become willing hearts. What's exciting to me is to see how the people responded to David's personal testimony and passionate appeal for the needs of God's house. Scripture tells us that all the leaders of Israel gave willingly, wholeheartedly, and with rejoicing (1 Chron. 29:9). It was a spiritually moving experience. They looked upon the approaching building program with anticipation and joy, as something positive and desirable. And it was an aggressive project, too! Anyone who gets into the detail of Solomon's Temple can only go away amazed at the creative architecture, the sheer size, and the mind-boggling expense. But God's people looked upon the entire project with anticipation and joy. As something positive and desirable because it was part of doing God's work. They were *willing* and *wanted* to see His mission on earth go forward. David prayed that the Lord would preserve the experience forever in their hearts. What was happening in their lives went beyond the building itself. Consecration means that our hearts have become willing hearts for God and that we will do our best for Him.

Let Your Face Light Up

When I think about this period in David's life, I am absolutely amazed. I can't help asking, How in the world could David and the leaders do what they did? Why did they commit themselves to God's house and work with such joy and generosity? It doesn't make sense to a casual observer. Even David realized it was a fragile, unusual experience. What made the difference? Were they more generous than we are, or did they have more money?

Members of the church I pastor told me that a friend had informed them that they didn't want to join our church.

"Why?" they asked.

"Because your church is filled with rich people."

"What makes you think that?" the church members asked with surprise—thinking about the very down-to-earth, mostly blue-collar people in the congregation they knew.

"Well, they have this multimillion-dollar building project, and they're paying cash for it!"

Are we rich? I wondered. *Or is it God who has the deep pockets?*

No, we don't release our best for God because we're rich. We "fill the hand" and step forward in commitment—being counted on and counted in—because we're overwhelmed by the sheer generosity and tremendous promise of God's provision. In David's thinking, our generosity is dependent on the gifts of God. We really don't have anything of our own. "O our God," he prayed, "we thank you and praise your glorious name! But who am I, and who are my people, that we could give anything to you? Everything we have has come from you, and we give you only what you have already given us! We are here for only a moment, visitors and strangers in the land as our ancestors were before us. Our days on earth are like a shadow, gone so soon without a trace. O Lord our God, even these materials that we have gathered to build a Temple to honor your holy name come from you! It all belongs to you!" (verses 13-16, NLT).

"Everything we have has come from you." "We give you only what you have already given us!" "Even these materials that we have gathered to build a Temple . . . come from you!" "It all belongs to you!" We possess much but own nothing, David says. If you own your own home, take a walk around your property to get a feel for the reality of this principle. Reflect on how long that dirt has been there and how long it will be there when you're gone. Then ask yourself if you really own it or whether you merely possess it for a time. You may have title to it, but that title reflects your right to possess it temporarily, not forever. Only God literally owns it for eternity. All that we have really belongs to Him.

My wife and I often dream of giving large gifts for the Lord's work. "If only we had the money, we would give it in a moment." A million. A hundred thousand. At least $10,000.

"Wouldn't it be wonderful to give like a rich person?" we would say with a hopeful smile. Ours, however, was just the usual economy of young church employee families with several children. We had no savings, no accumulated assets, only a checkbook balance hovering around $1.92. With a steady stream of bills and four children in Adventist schools.

The church we were pastoring was in a building program. Our family had already made a generous commitment from our earned income—a monthly amount for three years. It would be challenging to meet the pledge, but we had made it based on the promise that God would return enough for us to give while meeting our own needs as well—"God is able to give you more than you need, so that you will always have all you need for yourselves and more than enough for every good cause" (2 Cor. 9:8, TEV).

Then we remembered the violin under the bed. It had been my wife's since she was 12 years old. Years ago we had purchased a newer, better-sounding one, so the old one just lay there collecting dust.

"Let's sell it and give half to the building program," my wife suggested. Twice before, we had considered selling it for another, but we hadn't been satisfied with the $1,000 or $2,000 offered us. Now, however, $500 or

$1,000 would be a sizable addition to our commitment toward the new church building.

When we took the violin to a luthier (a dealer in violins, lutes, and other musical instruments) to sell he was skeptical. "I will not handle this instrument until we can verify what its label says it is," he said. So we shipped it to an international violin appraiser in another state and waited.

Two weeks later we lifted our hearts in wonder at God's providence. Our little under-the-bed violin was worth $45,000. We couldn't believe it. But it was true, and within a few months we sold it. God gave us the joy of giving $22,500 above what we had already promised, allowing us to taste the joy of giving like a rich person. It reminded us that when we give generously, God in return provides us enough for us to give again and again and to meet our own needs as well.

Our violin story doesn't end here, though. In order to avoid hefty sales tax on our half of the violin sale, we needed to invest again in other instruments as part of my wife's music business. So we bought a cello and another violin. That's where the other miracle happened. No, we didn't get a great deal on these two new instruments. Rather, we learned another precious lesson of God's gracious surprise and goodness. We had gone to the upscale and very high-brow Bein & Fushi luthier in downtown Chicago to sell our violin. So it was a logical place to begin looking for new instruments. While my wife, Kathie, played through a dozen or more violins one afternoon—testing sounds and tones and which violin she might want to take home to try out for a couple weeks—I wandered around looking at cellos, violas, violins, artwork, whatever. Noticing a unique twisting knot-bur on the back of one cello, I asked the salesperson how it affected the sound. I don't remember much about his answer as the man was soon showing me a delicate little violin with what appeared to be a crack running through its back. "It looks like a crack that's been glued," he said, "but it's a mineral trace in the wood."

"Does it affect the way it plays?" I wondered, turning the violin around in my hand and looking at its exquisite features from the top.

"No, it actually sounds very nice," he replied.

"What make is it? How old?" I asked, just killing time.

"It's a Stradivarius. One of his early ones. Worth about $2 million. Has absolutely beautiful tone."

Suddenly I found myself holding on to the violin more tightly. Two million dollars' worth of wood, right there in my hands. Years ago I had played violin, and like every violinist, I had heard of Strads and had dreamed of playing or even owning one. Never had I imagined that someday I would actually hold one in my hands.

"Say, could my wife just play this a little?" I asked sheepishly.

"Sure!"

So we went out into the posh showroom, where Kathie was fiddling away with lesser things.

"Hey, Kathie! Your husband has a violin here that he said he'd buy if you like it," he said to her with a sly smile.

"Yeah, right!" she said, taking it from my hand. Then she began to play. I watched the expression on her face as she was drawn into the instrument by the way it responded to her touch.

"Whoa! What's this?" she said in amazement, knowing the instrument she was playing was far superior to anything she had tried that day—or ever played in her life.

She played that Strad for the next half hour. At first it was too mind-boggling. All she could play were the simple haunting strains of "Amazing Grace." No fancy concerto or mind-boggling run of scales—just "Amazing Grace."

As we drove out of Chicago that afternoon we couldn't believe what had just happened. How many violinists—of all the millions in the world and through time—would ever have the privilege we just had? To see, hold, and play a real $2 million Stradivarius? Very few. But we had been part of that few. It was humbling. As we talked during the drive home we marveled at God's grace and how thoroughly dependent on Him we are. For like that high-dollar Strad that wasn't ours, but that we were allowed to play for a while, then had to return it to its real owner, our lives here on earth are really not our own. Nor is what we have in the dance of life ours. It's all borrowed, whether time, money, health, or opportunities—lent to us to play for a time. Only the real Owner keeps it forever.

According to David, we are like children who receive offering money from our parents on Sabbath morning so we will have something to give. The thrilling truth that captured his heart was that, in spite of our apparent nothingness, God gives—and He gives abundantly. Have we given anything? We have only given what was first given to us. And have we given heartily and with joy? If so, it's because we have simply given to the Giver Himself. The One who joyfully fills our lives with untold blessings. Consecration to God flows from a sense of His generosity and provision for our lives. The sheer generosity and tremendous promise of God's provision captures our imagination and the loyalty of our heart. And it's not just about money. We experience forgiveness, inner peace, and hope for the future and the coming resurrection. Such blessings swell up in our hearts to the place that we dedicate ourselves unreservedly to Him.

In addition, we "fill the hand" and step forward in consecration, because we've caught a glimpse of God's exalted majesty. David prayed: "Yours, O Lord, is the greatness, the power, the glory, the victory, and the majesty. Everything in the heavens and on earth is yours, O Lord, and this is your kingdom. We adore you as the one who is over all things. Riches and honor come from you alone, for you rule over everything. Power and might are in you hand, and it is at your discretion that people are made great and given strength" (1 Chron. 29:11, 12, NLT). In his powerful imagery we can almost see him struggling with all that God is in contrast to what we think we are and what we have in this decaying world. It leaves the king at a loss for words. Leslie Allen has noted that David's prayer "ransacks the theological dictionary" for terms expressing God's sovereign and boundless power and regal grandeur.[6] The king ascribes to God possession of everything in heaven and earth. He is the exalted head over all (verse 11). Wealth and honor come from Him, and in His hand is the power to exalt and give strength to all. All that we can, in our most exalted praises, attribute to God, He has unquestionable title to. Oh that we would grasp the greatness of the living God.

Passionate hearts and genuine praise are invariably contagious. David's overflow caused a tidal wave of praise among his people. When he summoned the whole assembly to praise the Lord their God, "they bowed low and fell prostrate before the Lord and the king" (verse 20, NIV). First Chronicles 29 reports one of Israel's most precious moments—a contagion of praise! David and his people found themselves overwhelmed with the privilege of giving.

Finally there comes the crucial contrast. "But who am I," David exclaims, "and who are my people, that we could give anything to you?

Everything we have has come from you, and we give you only what you have already given us!" (verse 14, NLT). The enormity of what they had been able to give represented the immensity of what they had received. The king's soul bows humbled as he contrasts the brevity of our little human life with the eternity of God. "We are here for only a moment, visitors and strangers in the land as our ancestors were before us. Our days on earth are like a shadow, gone so soon without a trace" (verse 15, NLT). David next speaks of persons without property and who therefore lack security and need protection. In our very nature we are only resident aliens and sojourners on earth. Our days flash by like a shadow. And even if we have wealth, it cannot alter the inevitability of death.

Every once in a while I'll walk by my wife while she's engaged in some task, and in the fraction of the moment that our eyes meet, she'll blurt out, "What?" It's because she sees a big grin on my face, something shining in my countenance. Instantly she thinks I'm up to something or that something juicy has happened that I'm keeping from her. Evidently, in her view, smiling isn't my ordinary expression, or at least the one I have just then is different enough for her to think something's up. "Nothing!" I'll usually say. "I'm just happy!" And my face can't hide that fact.

Charles Haddon Spurgeon, the famous English preacher, once said, "When you speak of heaven, let your face light up, let it be irradiated with heavenly glory, let your eyes shine with reflected glory. But when you speak of hell, well, then your ordinary face will do." David is telling us that when we ponder the Lord of heaven, His gifts to us, and His work for us on earth, our countenance will change, our faces will brighten, and our eyes will shine with reflected glory. And when we ponder ourselves—what we are and what we have in ourselves—our ordinary face should do just fine.

That's what's really behind these fragile moments of heartfelt, joyful support for building a better, more representative house for God. In the conscious presence of God David and the leaders of Israel felt their nothingness, their unworthiness to do anything at all for the Holy God of heaven. Yet the person of God and His cause gripped them. The Lord became so big in their minds that He took first place in their affections. In the process they lost their ordinary faces and lit up with heartfelt response to the King of kings and the Lord of lords. And they came with filled hands—of their lives, their time, their talents, and their monetary gifts. They were willing to be counted in and counted on for the Lord.

"Surely time stood still in David's mind as the people fell prostrate before the Lord and before their king. Close your eyes for a moment and picture the scene. . . . We've waited through more than 50 years of David's life to witness an entire kingdom in unity before God!"[7] While his legs may have trembled with illness and age, his heart blazed with emotion. The streets of the city were paved with praises, blanketed with the prostrate bodies of all who called the Lord their God.

The Lord invites each one of us to have this same kind of experience. Our consecration will be in proportion to our view of God, and our commitment in proportion to the love and wonder that swells our heart because of Him. His holy love is what prompts us to give with a full hand. It initiates the grateful dance.

Filling the hand has to do with motive and potential. We give with a full hand from what God has given us. It is always proportionate to whatever He has first given. Only we can know for sure—deep down inside—whether our hand is full when we give or we are only handing back to Him cookie crumbs.

The question this passage leaves us to answer is a pressing one: "Who then is willing to consecrate himself this day to the Lord?" (1 Chron. 29:5, NASB). Are you willing to come with a hand filled with love and intention, sharing whatever gifts you have been given or will be given to make the strengthening of God's work a reality?

And what about your face? Will your ordinary face be enough?

---

[1] See K. Kaynor, *When God Chooses*, pp. 202, 203.

[2] J. A. Thompson, *1, 2 Chronicles, The New American Commentary* (Broadman & Holman Publishers, 1994), vol. 9, p. 195.

[3] Depending on your reading of the text, either the ark of the Lord's covenant is the footstool envisioned here, or it is the Temple itself. Elsewhere Scripture uses the phrase "the footstool of our God" for the Temple. "Let us go into His dwelling place; let us worship at His footstool. Arise, O Lord, to Your resting place; You and the ark of Your strength" (Ps. 132:7, 8, NASB). "The close affinity of this verse to Ps. 132 gives it a polemic edge: it is the ark, and not the Temple, which is God's footstool; and the Temple itself is a place of rest, not for God but for the ark" (Sara Japhet, *I & II Chronicles* [London: SCM Press Ltd, 1993], p. 487. Whatever the passage means, the ark comes to rest in the Temple. They are inseparable.

[4] Ray Bowman with Eddy Hall, *When Not to Build: An Architect's Unconventional Wisdom for the Growing Church* (Grand Rapids: Baker Book House, 1992), p. 24.

[5] *Ibid.*, p. 33.

[6] L. C. Allen, *1, 2 Chronicles, The Communicator's Commentary* (Waco, Tex.: Word Books, Publisher, 1987), p. 191.

[7] B. Moore, *A Heart Like His*, p. 272.

16

THROUGH THE SHADOWLANDS

I Kings 1:1-5, 9-15

I knew him when he was bent over like a hunchback, his hands gnarled with arthritis, his chin sagging, and his eyes magnified through thick Coca-Cola bottlelike lenses. Grandpa Baasch was 97 years old. Age had worn everything down for him—like it will all of us. Some 70 years earlier, though, he had been a pipe-chomping, swaggering India Trade Company representative stationed in Burma with a dozen other turn-of-the-twentieth-century friends. My wife's family has a picture tucked into the family archives of a consciously posed gathering of "beautiful people." The men wore white suits, hair slicked, derby hats in hand. A few had status cigars jutting from their mouths. Women friends, with their parasols and hoops, had coyly interspersed among the haughty young businessmen. The photo exudes youthfulness, confidence, and the prospect of unlimited future success. It was the world of yuppiedom long before anyone ever invented the term.

The photograph is nothing like the memories I have of him: shrunken, physically enfeebled, shelved from active life—far different than the impressive, youthful scene that encapsulated, by worldly standards, the peak of his turn-of-the-century business career. By human standards, the near century of his life went on to follow that ominous big "bell curve" our human family knows so well, in which we go up, up, up to some elusive vantage point called the top, and then we slide down, down, down until life has stripped our dignity away and we can hardly function anymore.

But let me tell you what no photos can show. The Grandpa Baasch I knew, behind the wrinkles and humpback, was a spiritual giant whose faith and commitment to Jesus warmed the hearts of all those who knew him. That unprofessional hole-in-the-wall evangelistic series he attended decades earlier in Burma—on a dare by cynical friends out for a laugh—began a life of spiritual growth that never quit. His spiritual passion never peaked when the bell curve of his physical life began its decent. Here was a man who pioneered our work in Puerto Rico and established a college in Medellín, Colombia, South America. He was a pastor and union president and later taught religion at Southern Adventist University (getting his master's degree in his 60s). Then, in his 80s, he returned to South America to teach at the college he had helped start some 40 years earlier. Grandpa taught himself Hebrew during his 90s so he could keep pace with me while I was learning it at the seminary. And he did a better job at it than I! In fact, he read passages in both Greek and Hebrew until the day he died in 1981.

I can remember Grandpa Baasch's fervent prayers, his thoughtful words of wisdom and firm exhortation to faithfulness, and his penetrating questions. He'd bring young people in off the street and lead them to Christ. Age didn't matter. Grandpa Baasch had spiritual passion, power, and influence. I loved and respected him dearly. The night after he died, my wife, Kathie, and I lay in bed reflecting on his life and his influence for God. With moist eyes staring into the darkness, my mind imagined Grandpa's head being opened like a lid and all that he knew as well as his spiritual passion being transferred to me—like downloading software into my moral/spiritual/mental hard drive. "Why did I have to start at the bottom?" I wondered. "Why couldn't I begin right where he left off? I could do so much more if I had what he had—plus my youth."

I longed to have Grandpa's experience with God and his spiritual maturity. But that was impossible. I knew I had to grow on my own, experience God for myself, and develop my own spiritual passion. I must fill my mind with the Word and will of God the hard way—one day at a time through reading Scripture and through prayer, careful study, and personal discipline. But at least Grandpa Baasch had helped me understand some of what that meant. His life had been a gripping model to this young pastor of what Scripture means when it says that we should "be mature and full grown in the Lord, measuring up to the full stature of Christ" (Eph. 4:13, NLT).

In the end, David dies. No one's story is complete until death comes. To be human is to perish. By dying we attest to our humanity.[1] The record of David's final days is a pathetic picture of the aged king shivering under a pile of blankets.[2] "Now King David was very old, and no matter how many blankets covered him, he could not keep warm. So his advisers told him, 'We will find a young virgin who will wait on you and be your nurse. She will lie in your arms and keep you warm.' So they searched throughout the country for a beautiful girl, and they found Abishag from Shunem and brought her to the king. The girl was very beautiful, and she waited on the king and took care of him. But the king had no sexual relations with her" (1 Kings 1:1-4, NLT). It's an image of gray hair, poor circulation, and impotence. One of the most well-documented lives in history is hastening to an end.

Now 70 years old, David is no longer the vigorous, decisive leader of the past. Instead, he's the almost passive object of the actions and agendas of others. It's hard to relate the aged David with the one who had killed a lion and a bear, severed the head of an overgrown Philistine, and conquered nations. His sudden mortality almost shocks us. As he lay chilled beneath the weight of heavy blankets, we realize his humanity.

As this moment in his story, he is the subject of no active verbs. Things are done to David, not by David.[3] People can live a whole life for God doing mighty things but in the end have to lay everything down. They must let go of every human effort and achievement and allow others to take their place or care for them as they shiver. It takes a lot of grace to do it without bitterness, anger, cynicism, or loss of faith. David would do anything for God, but now he just can't. "I have all kinds of grand ideas of things to do, but no energy to do them with," my father told me the summer he died. "I find myself sleeping and sleeping. Nothing that I dream of doing gets done anymore." Enormous reading glasses magnified his eyes into dark pools of weariness and longing. His emaciated frame, once a picture of barrel-chested bravado, tipped precariously in the faded wing-backed chair. His mind was active, driven, but his body just wouldn't do anything anymore.

Undoubtedly, David's interest in life was flagging badly now. He was no longer capable of functioning as king much anymore. Others likely cared for the day-to-day affairs of state. We find his servants both making him comfortable and testing his potency. The remark that David didn't have sex with Abishag does not reflect his moral restraint but his terminal infirmity. He's impotent. His attendants linked David's sexual energy with his continued ability to lead. It was a widespread concept in the ancient world. They saw his physical impotence as symptomatic of his loss of control of public affairs. If not even the most beautiful young woman in the kingdom could stir David's blood, then he was certainly nearing the end. The king was losing his grip.[4] Surprisingly, the text makes no mention of senility, mental dullness, or depression—only shivering cold and impotence. David's mind is still sound, clear, and strong, as we will soon see.[5]

So What's in the Will?

David's frailty points up the pressing importance of determining who will be his heir. His impotency and physical limitations intensify the intrigue between rival political and religious factions. And it all took place right under David's nose within the palace precincts.

They say that no one sleeps when a lawyer reads a will. It can be high drama when there's big stakes involved. Everyone wants to know who's getting what and who's gonna be who. At this point, though, David had no will. The king hadn't officially stated his choice of a successor. And so the most powerful figures of his time became embroiled in behind-the-scenes jockeying—a dramatic power struggle for the throne. Would it be Adonijah, the eldest of David's surviving sons? Or Solomon? Somewhere along the way David had promised Bathsheba that Solomon would be the next to sit on the throne. And she later pleaded at David's bedside, "You are the man, my lord king, to whom all Israel looks, to tell them who is to succeed my lord the king" (1 Kings 1:20, New Jerusalem). Everyone was watching and wondering. The uncertainty over who would be David's successor sparked a family struggle. His highly discordant family was at it again, eventually enveloping an entire nation in their conflict.[6] One thing was certain: if there was to be a stable transfer of political power in the kingdom, David needed to act decisively on the vital matter.[7]

The biblical narrator portrays David as dying in the middle of a family squabble with no hint of either tribute or eulogy. Instead of dying in peace, with his children and wives gathered around him expressing love and gratitude, he finds himself embroiled in intrigue and deceit.[8] As we look on, we see people who apparently don't know how to behave in the presence of pending death.[9] Losing all sense of what it means to be a human being, they wind up seeking to secure their own position and safety.

First, we find David's servants treating his death as a problem to be solved (1 Kings 1:1- 4).[10] His circulation is sluggish and he gets cold, especially when he's trying to sleep. The servants do everything they know, which in this case is piling on more and more blankets. But it doesn't work. So they look for a miracle cure. Having heard stories of beautiful young virgins bringing old men to life again, they give it a try. Finding the most ravishing young woman, they make her David's private nurse and bedmate. As she snuggles up to him under the blankets, her naked body should warm David both physically and erotically. But it does not work. As Peterson observes, "each failure turns David into more of a problem that they must deal with. And the more death is dealt with them as a problem, the more David is a problem. The more problem, the less person."[11]

Next we learn how David's oldest living son, Adonijah, considers his father's imminent death as an opportunity to seize.[12] At 70 years David has already lived far longer than most people of his day. He was taking a long time to die. Adonijah, who was in line to succeed him to the throne, was tired of waiting. As news of David's deteriorating health and impotence spreads, he thought, *It won't be long now!* And so he did the logical and responsible thing—he took charge. First he got the wheels rolling by assuming the role of crown prince—prepared to assume national responsibilities and leadership when the moment came. "About that time David's son Adonijah, whose mother was Haggith, decided to make himself king in place of his aged father. So he provided himself with chariots and horses and recruited fifty men to run in front of him" (verse 5, NLT). After all, his father was no longer capable of functioning as ruler. The country needed vigorous and youthful leadership. Both Joab and Abiathar the priest threw their support to him. That he would be the next king seemed a foregone conclusion. But Adonijah did not count on Bathsheba warning David about his plan.

In the process of putting himself forward as crown prince Adonijah essentially treated his father as an obstruction to living out his personal destiny. His father was an obstacle. But David's death would finally allow Adonijah to be king. Hurry up and die, Dad!

Peterson again capsules it well: "Every life is a limitation on my life. Those closest to me limit me most. Children are a limitation; spouses are a limitation; parents are a limitation. These limitations aren't minor inconveniences; they're major and unavoidable conditions in the all-demanding exercise of being human. . . . It's quite inevitable that from time to time we fantasize an end to the limitations: death of the other as freedom for the sovereign self. But it never works out that way: honoring the limits, giving dignity to the death, is what deepens life. . . . . Ridding ourselves of inconvenient lives that seem to interfere with *our* living results not in more life for us, but less."[13]

That's what happened to Adonijah. By treating his father's death as an opportunity for a larger life for himself, the son precipitated his own death. And in failing to honor his father's death, he hastened his own. Shortly after Solomon's coronation Adonijah exposed himself as an opportunistic usurper when he asked to marry Abishag and wound up executed for treason (1 Kings 1:50-53; 2:13-25).[14] "Honoring the limits, giving dignity to death, is what deepens life."[15]

The third response to David's death that makes us stop and wonder is Bathsheba's. We would imagine her there with David every day, caring for his every need, perhaps reading David one of his own psalms and telling him how much she loved him. Maybe she did, but the image Scripture brings us is that it was Abishag who was tenderly nursing David. Instead, Bathsheba is caught up in a flurry of anxious activity trying to make sure that David keeps his promise to her that Solomon would be the next king.

"Then Nathan the prophet went to Bathsheba, Solomon's mother, and asked her, 'Did you realize that Haggith's son, Adonijah, has made himself king and that our lord David doesn't even know about it? If you want to save your own life and the life of your son Solomon, follow my counsel'" (1 Kings 1:11, 12, NLT).

After a long absence from Scripture, the prophet Nathan reenters the scene. Reading the political realities and grasping the implications, he warns Bathsheba about Adonijah's plans. Nathan knew she was the key to restoring decision-making strength to the king. He sent her to inform David of what was happening.

"So Bathsheba went into the king's bedroom. He was very old now, and Abishag was taking care of him. Bathsheba bowed low before him.

"'What can I do for you?' he asked her.

"She replied, 'My lord, you vowed to me by the Lord your God that my son Solomon would be the next king and would sit on your throne. But instead, Adonijah has become the new king, and you do not even know about it. He has sacrificed many oxen, fattened calves, and sheep, and he has invited all your sons and Abiathar the priest and Joab, the commander of the army. But he did not invite your servant Solomon. And now, my lord the king, all Israel is waiting for your decision as to who will become king after you. If you do not act, my son Solomon and I will be treated as criminals as soon as you are dead'" (verses 15-21, NLT).

Again, Peterson captures it well: "What brings Bathsheba to David's deathbed isn't his death as such but responsibilities connected with his death. David has been negligent in taking care of kingdom affairs; David hasn't made out his will. If David dies as is, things will be a mess."[16] Her response isn't wrong in its content as much as in its style and timing, for what Bathsheba does is quite necessary—for herself, her son, and the kingdom.[17] What can be wrong with that? After all, her life would be in danger if Adonijah became king. And David did promise her that Solomon would be Israel's next ruler (verses 13, 17). Supposedly God had even made it clear that her son would be David's successor.[18]

Nathan, who himself pays David a visit and affirms the political jockeying by Adonijah, Joab, and Abiathar, guides Bathsheba through it all. He underscores the urgency of David's doing something immediately (1 Kings 1:11-14; 22-27).[19] I remember the urgency when my best friend Stu Peters was dying. His lawyer had written up some papers assuring that Stu's business and personal things were in order. But as his sons read the fine print, they realized that the unscrupulous lawyer would get everything, the family nothing. The scene is still vivid in my mind: the dimmed hospital room, sons and son-in-law gathered around the bed, my friend hastily signing page after page of a different set of legal documents just hours before the brain cancer took away his ability to reason.

Behaving in the Presence of Death

We would like a better ending for David. His death had become a problem to be solved, an opportunity to be seized, a difficulty to be negotiated. It reminds us that in the presence of death we so often forget how to live and love. Sometimes we unwittingly desert the dying person. Death and dying often brings out the worst in many people.

I remember the feelings I had when I stepped into my sister's house and saw the large cast-iron cannon I played with as a boy. Having been my dad's since when he had been a kid, it had deep meaning to me. He had often told stories about it; then I had played with it as a boy. For a while it had even been in my room. As children so often do, I imagined that it would be mine someday. Now it was in my sister's entry. *How did she get it?* I wondered. *I can't remember her ever playing with it,* my surprised thoughts kept rolling. Then I stopped myself short, startled at myself and my jealousy or whatever it was. Right then and there, I decided to let it go. *It's OK!* I said to myself. I knew that in the course of time I would struggle with a flurry of feelings about all sorts of *meaningful* things. Somehow I would release them and hold anything I might have with a loose hand. *Besides,* I thought to myself, *I might have something that one of my sisters wished to have. Would I be quick to let her have it? Let it go?* I was determined not to let things and attachments to things jade the important relationships around me.

As a pastor I have watched children ridding themselves of the inconvenient lives of parents or selfishly burning up an inheritance at the expense of siblings. Some financially drain aging parents down to the point at which they worry whether they will have enough money to make it to death. Children may grasp for power, hold grudges, or refuse to grant or ask for forgiveness.

We behave so poorly in the presence of death. Looking back through the years, I realize that I have not always acted well.

Interestingly, while Abishag failed as a cure, she stays as a person.[20] The young woman appears to be the one bright spot in the darkness and chaos surrounding David's deathbed. Present only to serve, she's free of the ambitions or agendas that everyone else seems to have. As such, she is a quiet rebuke to how others in the story respond to the king's death. We have no record of anything she says, but her very silence places everyone else in dramatic contrast.[21] All through the scriptural account of David's dying and death, Abishag remains a silent and persistent witness to the dignity of death. Her name appears, unobtrusively and without comment, in the context of each attempt to deny or ignore or reduce the large, sacred, and human mystery of death. In a way, Abishag, without saying a word, has the last word.[22] She points to the reality that there are some who can be truly beautiful. While death brings out the worst in many people, it also brings out the very best in others.

And this I see too as a pastor—other people behaving well in the presence of death. Children will go out of their way to care for a parent till death, sometimes wearing themselves out in the stress and sacrifice of it all—physically, emotionally, financially. They will make promises that assure closure or facilitate some final wish. As with my mom, who repeatedly shared the gospel with my schizophrenic grandma, whom I tell about in *Faith on the Run,* and came away filled with awe, that even in the life of an often-confused granny—in whom demonic forces continued waging long and hard as the result of a history of spiritualism and connection with the occult—there could be a final surrender, hope in Jesus, peace deep down inside, a closing of life with dignity.

Abishag is an image of what it means to behave properly in the presence of death. David needed that kind of presence in his life in order to dance through his final moments.

A House in Order

Bathsheba captured David's full attention with the threat to Solomon's succession. When he learned that others were attempting to nullify the promise he had made to her he roused to action. Understanding the urgency of the issues, he acted kingly once more and moved to put his house in order. Calling Bathsheba back into his presence (apparently she had stepped out of the room so Nathan could have full access to the king, see 1 Kings 1:23, 28), David vowed, "As surely as the Lord lives, who has rescued me from every danger, today I decree that your son Solomon will be the next king and will sit on my throne, just as I swore to you before the Lord, the God of Israel" (verses 29, 30, NLT). He addressed the words directly to her, intimating to us that it was a matter not only between king and queen, but also between husband and wife—father and mother.[23] I wonder if Bathsheba was a sight for David's tired eyes. Having captivated his attention on a moonlit night many years before, she had been *the* woman in his life ever since. Now after the passage of decades, it was she that he connected with personally.

Need has a way of breathing fresh life into a soul, if just for a moment. David, who had been chilled and powerless at the onset of the story, now assumed swift control, performing the will of God and fulfilling the desires of his wife's heart. Bathsheba had called on him for something that only he could do. In the end David lived no longer than the time it took to take care of his last few responsibilities. Rising from his bed, he formulated a plan to place Solomon on the throne.

"Then King David ordered, 'Call Zadok the priest, Nathan the prophet, and Benaiah son of Jehoiada.' When they came into the king's presence, the king said to them, 'Take Solomon and my officers down to Gihon Spring. Solomon is to ride on my personal mule. There Zadok the priest and Nathan the prophet are to anoint him king over Israel. Then blow the trumpets and shout, 'Long live King Solomon!' When you bring him back here, he will sit on my throne. He will succeed me as king, for I have appointed him to be ruler over Israel and Judah'" (verses 32-35, NLT).

David purposely called three specific men to escort Solomon to his rightful place of authority. Nathan was the primary prophet of the day, Zadok a prominent priest, and Benaiah the mighty warrior in charge of the royal body guard. For the nation to be strong, all four areas of authority needed to be present: prophet, priest, military, and king.

The dying king sent his most trustworthy warrior and his army to protect Solomon. They were to put him on King David's mule and escort him to his coronation. Customarily, a king rode on a mule to signify his intent to be a servant to the people. The mule often had a wreath of flowers around its neck or a royal drape over its back. Thus David placed Solomon on the throne—ruling as a coregent during David's last days. In the process he kept his family and nation strong.

Appointing Solomon as his successor was not the only thing David did. As the time of his death approached, he gave a special charge to his son:

"I am going where everyone on earth must someday go. Take courage and be a man. Observe the requirements of the Lord your God and follow all his ways. Keep each of the laws, commands, regulations, and stipulations written in the law of Moses so that you will be successful in all you do and wherever you go. If you do this, then the Lord will keep the promise he made to me: 'If your descendants live as they should and follow me faithfully with all their heart and soul, one of them will always sit on the throne of Israel'" (1 Kings 2:2-4, NLT).

"And you, my son Solomon, acknowledge the God of your father, and serve him with wholehearted devotion and with a willing mind, for the Lord searches every heart and understands every motive behind the thoughts. If you seek him, he will be found by you; but if you forsake him, he will reject you forever" (1 Chron. 28:9, NIV).

David's words to Solomon apply to us in every area of potential success. They are a legacy of passion passed from a father to his son—more than just a king to his successor. He gave his son four vital directives we would be wise to obey and leave as a legacy to others:

1. Be of courage and don't be wimpish or fearful. Be what God calls you to be and what duty demands. Take charge and lead.

2. Acknowledge God and His authority in your life. Follow all His ways. Don't be selective, but all-embracing in your obedience to the concrete things He has commanded. His Word and will must be paramount. Submit to Him as Lord in whatever circumstances. Consecrate your life to Him.

3. Serve God with wholehearted devotion. Don't give Him just a piece of your heart. A divided heart will place your entire life in jeopardy. Only God can be trusted with your heart. Wholehearted devotion will keep you out of trouble.

4. Serve God with a willing spirit. The Lord wants you to honor Him with a willing spirit, one that would choose no other way.

In other words, give God your whole heart, and life, and affections. That sounds like passion to me. Passion for God that captures one's whole self. David said it well in Psalm 86:11: "Teach me your way, O Lord, and I will walk in your truth; give me an undivided heart, that I may fear your name" (Ps. 86:11, NIV). We started our journey with David's passion. Here at the close we find it still strong and something to pass on to a son—the next generation of God's people.

During these times David also expressed his long-held desire for building the Temple. We learned about that in previous chapters. First, David charged Solomon to construct a house for the Lord (1 Chron. 22:6-16). Next, he commanded all the leaders of Israel to help his son to build for God's people (verses 17-19). Finally, David summoned all his officials to Jerusalem—the leaders of the tribes, the commanders of the 12 army divisions, the other generals and captains, the overseers of the royal property and livestock, the palace officials, the mighty men, and all the other warriors in the kingdom—and inspired them all with the vision of a completed Temple and expanding work for God, promising that the Lord would be with them and bless them (1 Chron. 28:1-10). There in front of all those leaders David gave Solomon the building plans, telling him to "be courageous and act" (verses 10, NASB).

It was at this time that David reminded them of his own commitment to this long-dreamed project and asked, "Who is willing to consecrate himself today to the Lord?" (1 Chron. 29:9, NIV). You'll remember that it was an incredible occasion of consecration as his people stepped forward with full hands to expand the work of God. It was a highly spiritual and moving moment that included prayer, sacrifices, worship of God, and eating before the Lord with great gladness (verses 10-22).

Finally, David did one more thing. He led the people in making Solomon king a second time. They anointed him as ruler for the Lord and Zadok as priest (verse 22). Then Solomon sat on the throne as king instead of David his father. And after all this, David finally died (verse 28).

"And the Lord exalted Solomon so the entire nation of Israel stood in awe of him, and he gave Solomon even greater wealth and honor than his father. So David son of Jesse reigned over all Israel. He ruled Israel for forty years in all, seven years from Hebron and thirty-three years from Jerusalem. He died at a ripe old age, having enjoyed long life, wealth, and honor. Then his son Solomon ruled in his place. All the events of King David's reign, from beginning to end, are written in *The Record of Samuel the Seer, The Record of Nathan the Prophet,* and *The Record of Gad the Seer.* These accounts include the mighty deeds of his reign and everything that happened to him and to Israel and to all the surrounding kingdoms" (verses 25-30, NLT).

I want you to catch what David did when once roused to action. 1. He handed the spiritual and moral leadership torch to his son Solomon. 2. He inspired his people with their spiritual heritage and a vision for God's work and divine redemption in the future. 3. He made sure the lion's share of his estate went to the Lord's work. 4. And he left no doubt in anyone's mind about his faith and relationship with God. David left a legacy of faith, hope, commitment, and vision. Most of all, he had passion for God—what it means to dance like a king.

The biblical record of David's life ends in a high note, with him handing on the torch. His final days illustrate how we ourselves are to live through the shadowlands of death. We must care for the important things before it is too late, saying what needs to be said, forgiving, reconciling, leaving a spiritual heritage and vision of God. Above all, we must leave no doubt in anyone's mind where our faith is or where we stand with God.

That's how my father ended things. Of all that he shared with me during his slow dying that summer, one sentence captured it best: "I want to die with my heart full of what I never had all my life." It was as much his acknowledgment of the emptiness and confusion that had driven his life as it was his last wish. He told me searing experiences of his childhood, the impact of war in the South Pacific, of drinking sprees, poolroom brawls, broken relationships, painful divorce, injustices too big to challenge, inexplicable pain, and insurmountable barriers to God. But now, at the end, through it all and in spite of it all, Dad was convinced that he could trust God. "I want to die with my heart full of what I never had all my life." God. Peace. Spiritual passion. And he felt compelled to show it publically.

So in answer to the hundreds of prayers that had gone up from caring hearts, in fulfillment of my lifelong dream and because of God's all-sufficient grace for every conceivable failure, I found myself in the baptistry of the Hamburg, Pennsylvania, Adventist Church. Dad gripped my arm to steady himself. Esta, his wife, stood quietly by, still dripping from her own baptism.

Most of the crowd gathered around the baptistry had never seen the likes before. Some were surprised to find a pool in a church. Many were skeptical about why Tom Lichtenwalter would switch ranks at the end.

Others were amazed that a proud man like "Papap" would do something so humiliating. Several realized for the first time that the blustering man they'd known was nothing more than a broken soul before God. A handful of Christian friends, including the Adventist couple who had given Dad and Esta Bible studies five years earlier, celebrated God's persistent grace. Mom, 30 years past their divorce, stood as close to the baptistry as possible. The back of her hand was wet with tears.

"Better hurry; I can't stand here much longer," he bellowed as he teetered in the water. For all the expletives he knew, it was a relatively gentle request. While I didn't want to rush the greatest moment of his life, I know it is also his weakest. The pain really was too hard to endure. He couldn't wait much longer. With few formalities, I lowered him into the water.

Weeks later I sat with him once more. Our tasks were more intimate, the end more imminent. He described what it will be like to be hugged by God. But he wanted to rest till then, though, because "dying is hell." I steadied him as we shuffled back to the darkness of his basement bedroom. I could hardly see his form under the worn sheet I pulled over him. When I found his hand and squeezed gently, he squeezed back.

The only thing left to say was the benediction I'd shared with him every time we'd parted the past few months: "The Lord bless you and keep you. . . . The Lord make his face to shine upon you . . . and give you peace." My father seemed to drift off even before I'd finished.

"Dad, you want me to let you sleep?"

"No . . . I'm thinking . . . how blessed . . . I am."

Tom Lichtenwalter fell asleep knowing he was finally at peace with God. The battle had raged a lifetime, the losses were high. But God won.

Need has a way of breathing fresh life into a soul, if just for a moment. As Bathsheba called on David for something that only he could do, and the request breathed enough life into his soul to finish the task, so God graciously but urgently called to Dad. During his final months he rose to meet the need—for himself and the important others in his life. Making things right. Letting go the hurts from the past. Forgiving. Being forgiven. Publically choosing Christ through baptism. Saying those ever so important words of love and personal goodbyes. Leaving no doubt as to where he was with God. Bequeathing a legacy—"This is the way to die, making things right. At peace with God in Christ. Awaiting the resurrection."

I never saw Dad's eyes dance quite like they did in the joy and peace of those last days. Undeniable passion. Dancing like a king.

God Did It!

When David received the news from his royal officials that Solomon had been anointed king, he bowed his head in worship as he lay in his bed and said, "Blessed be the Lord, the God of Israel, who today has chosen someone to sit on my throne while I am still alive to see it" (1 Kings 1:48, NLT). It is the last time the book of 1 Kings refers to David as *king*. God chose to have it penned in a sentence eternally linked to two responses: worship and praise. David's rule ended just as it had officially begun. His stiffened body bowed before God on his final day as king, with the same abandon he had demonstrated when he danced through the streets of Jerusalem. His actions were often contradictory, but one consistency he wove throughout his life and reign—passion for God.[24] He had but one overriding passion—an aspiration he was privileged to now experience—"I will sing to the Lord as long as I live. I will praise my God to my last breath!" (Ps. 104:33, NLT).

The book of Kings opens with David's health all but gone and quickly moves to a dramatic power struggle for the throne. It raises the burning question, "Who will sit upon the throne of David" (verses 20, 27) and then answers it decisively, "Long live King Solomon!" (verses 34, 39, NLT). Three times Solomon is said to sit on the throne (verses 32-35, 38-40, 41-48). The nine-part narrative of Solomon's succession to the throne of King David, his father, is the longest single story in 1 Kings.[25] Here we find an incredible picture of people behaving badly in the presence of death, of death bringing the very worst out in them as they treat the dying as problems and obstacles. Of people making sure the dying do everything they need to do so they're not left with a mess after they are gone.

In the end, Solomon is Israel's new king. On the surface it appears that the succession occurred only through shrewd and ruthless, even Machiavellian, political maneuvering. But in reality, God did it. His transcendence often operates behind unworthy human motives and plots (Gen. 50:20; Ruth 4:14; 2 Sam. 12:24, 25; 17:14; Esther). Here in David's life we see God's work in the seamy world of politics. The good news is that God is in charge even of political intrigue. He will work out things for good in spite of how poorly we might behave in the presence of death.

I believe the selection of Solomon displays a powerful lesson of grace and sovereign providence. "Solomon represented God's divine mercy. He was the embodiment of second chances. He was the innocence that came from guilt. He was God's choice, as history would prove."[26]

In pursuing His divine purposes, He works with what is available, with human beings as they are—their foibles and flaws as well as their wisdom. God does not perfect people before employing them. He can turn even evil to His divine purposes (see Gen. 50:20). That's why I read David's story and keep coming back to it. It tells me so much about God.

---

[1] E. H. Peterson, *Leap Over a Wall,* p. 217.

[2] "In Kings, David ends his career as a frail man surrounded by manipulative underlings and obsessed by old grudges (1 Kings 1-2). Chronicles presents a quite different picture. It reports in 1 Chron. 23:1 that when David was 'full of days' he made Solomon king. . . . [And] we get seven more chapters of David's arrangements for the temple and its staffing. An active and commanding David makes all arrangements for the crowning achievement of Solomon's reign (1 Chron. 22-29). Solomon meekly cooperates" (Marti J. Steussy, *David: Biblical Portraits of Power,* p. 114.).

[3] Jerome T Walsh, *1 Kings* (Collegeville, Minn.: Liturgical Press, 1996), p. 5.

[4] The Hebrew wordplay in the story of David "not knowing" Abishag (1 Kings 1:4) and later "not knowing" what Adonijah was doing (verse 18) heightens the implication that David was losing his grip. That physical impotence is symptomatic of his loss of control of public affairs. Matching his sexual incapacity, David is blissfully unaware of political developments.

[5] Paul R. House, *1, 2 Kings* (Broadman & Holman Publishers, 1995), p. 88. See E. G. White, *Patriarchs and Prophets,* p. 749.

[6] Terence E. Fretheim, *First and Second Kings* (Louisville: Westminster John Knox Press, 1999), p. 19. The family struggle no doubt included a bit of harem intrigue as Scripture mentions the two mothers of the contending candidates, and Bathsheba, who would have been in charge of the harem as queen mother, rises to make sure it was her son Solomon who won the struggle for power rather than Haggith's son Adonijah. After all, Bathsheba's own status and life were at stake.

[7] Walsh, p. 4.

[8] Peterson, p. 218.

[9] *Ibid.,* p. 219.

[10] *Ibid.,* p. 220.

[11] *Ibid.*

[12] *Ibid.,* pp. 221-223.

[13] *Ibid.,* pp. 221, 222.

[14] Adonijah's later request to marry Abishag is a prima-facie case of treason. No one who reads the story should think for a moment that Adonijah was in love with Abishag herself. He is infatuated with what she stands for—a powerful symbolic link with David, sexually and royally.

[15] Peterson, p. 222.

[16] *Ibid.*, p. 223.

[17] *Ibid.*

[18] Adonijah "now rebelled against the authority of God, who had appointed Solomon to the throne. Both by natural endowments and religious character Solomon was better qualified than his elder brother to become ruler of Israel; yet although the choice of God had been clearly indicated, Adonijah did not fail to find sympathizers" (E. G. White, *Patriarchs and Prophets*, p. 749).

[19] Nathan's strategy is clear. Bathsheba's question is to appear to assume that David has approved Adonijah's inauguration, though Nathan is well aware that this is not the case. The approach he counsels is calculated to stir up David's anger against Adonijah without endangering Bathsheba herself. It avoids suggesting that the old king is no longer in control of things, but will lead him to conclude that Adonijah thinks so and is acting as if it were the case. The question form itself implies that David must have reasons for naming Adonijah as his successor, and thus softens the tacit accusation that David has broken a promise. See Walsh, p. 11.

[20] Peterson, p. 220.

[21] *Ibid.*, pp. 218, 219.

[22] *Ibid.*, p. 229.

[23] B. Moore, *A Heart Like His*, p. 255.

[24] P. Yancey, *In Search of the Invisible God*, p. 192.

[25] Walsh, p. 3.

[26] Moore, p. 258.

Epilogue

DANCE FOREVER

One of the most well-documented lives in biblical history has ended. It has unfolded the realities of what God can mean in our life. The life of David shows how spiritual passion can claim one's whole being for God and how it involves both the meaning of our lives and the purpose of our existence in Him. It exhibits powerful facets of our inner private world.[1] And yet how very fragile such passion really is and how easily affected by life's experiences. Events can threaten it, numb it, or drain it away.

Following David through his *shepherd years,* his *fugitive years,* and now his *royal years,* we've learned how spiritual passion is like a well-written trilogy (or even a poorly written one that bombs). It opens with incredible potential and awesome experience with God. But then real life interferes. Not to say that passion for God is neither *real* nor *real life,* but that, as we have already said, life has a way of robbing us of spiritual passion. Sometimes we feel a difference in the passion itself. It may not be particularly energizing at every turn. But then again, What really is passion for God? And where are we going with it? How will we finish? Ultimately, what will our whole life story say about passion for God? Completing the story and ending well is challenging and daunting.

Thus the power of David's epic story. He reminds us who we are, whether it be at our best—or our worst. Israel's king was a person of passions like ours, shaped from the same substance as ourselves. Again and again David held back his bad passions and exhibited such noble passions that we almost want to worship him. But all the time his worst traits lurked in the background until finally they burst forth, reminding us that no flesh can glory in God's presence.[2]

When I read David's story, my spirit soars and my heart breaks. I climb to the most noble human emotions and behavior, only then to plummet to the depths of my own sinful nature. I see so many things in him I wish I had—and so many others I'm scared I do have. His story immerses me in a reality that embraces the entire range of humanness, stretching from the deep interior of my soul to the farthest reach of my imagination. Something in his story exposes my most guarded yearnings. No matter how many times I've been confronted with the biblical account of his life, I am still stirred, shocked, amazed, and forced to think a few hard thoughts once again. Throughout his life David hangs on, keeps his passion, and ends well. Why? And why do I want to end well, too?

Scripture allots a significant amount of space to chronicle David's life. He was the object of much love and continues to be the object of much learning. May our final look at him and his God be no exception. The Lord did not cast him away when he danced poorly, nor did He forsake the king when he was old. The God whose faithfulness endures to all generations completed the work He started in a little shepherd boy. David's story takes place against a background of measureless depth—that of God Himself! The Lord is ever present both in David's mind and his unfolding life. God was personal and present and required *response:* "I love You. I live in You. I run for dear life to You. I sing to You. I cry for help to You." David believed in, thought about, imagined, and prayed to God. The largest part of the king's existence wasn't David but God.[3] And he knew that God was good, compassionate, strong, forgiving, merciful, just, holy—and absolutely essential to life and its meaning.

During one of his most vulnerable moments, David passionately prayed: "Answer me, O Lord, out of the goodness of your love; in your great mercy turn to me" (Ps. 69:16, NIV). As his life came to an end, we see how God graciously answered. No wonder David remained passionate, dancing till the end.

"You have turned my mourning
into joyful dancing.
You have taken away my clothes of mourning
and clothed me with joy,
that I might sing praises to you
and not be silent.
O Lord my God,
I will give you thanks forever!" (Ps. 30:11, 12, NLT).

Some scholars suggest that David wrote the words of Psalm 71 in his old age as he confronted his approaching death.[4] While Scripture names no author, what we do know is that the words of the psalm are filled with Davidic expressions and that the writer is old or aging and has seen exceptional trouble. Against his failing strength he remembers God's faithfulness and a growing hope of His life-renewing power.

"O God, you have taught me
from my earliest childhood,
and I have constantly told others
about the wonderful things you do.
Now that I am old and gray,
do not abandon me, O God.
Let me proclaim your power to this new generation,
your mighty miracles to all who come after me.
Your righteousness, O God,
reaches to the highest heavens
You have done such wonderful things.
Who can compare with you, O God?
You have allowed me to suffer much hardship,
but you will restore me to life again
and lift me up from the depths of the earth.
You will restore me to even greater honor
and comfort me once again.
Then I will praise you with music on the harp,
because you are faithful to your promises, O God.
I will sing for you with a lyre,

O Holy One of Israel.
I will shout for joy and sing your praises,
for you have redeemed me" (Ps. 71:17-23, NLT).

I imagine the aged king still praising God. Once more his fingers wrapped around the strings of his harp. His hands, though, were no longer the calloused young ones of a hardy shepherd boy, but were bent with age and slowed with time. Although frail, they still brushed across the strings. His voice, once wavering with adolescence, now quavers from age. But no sweeter voice could be heard than the one that flowed from his sincere, ever-passionate heart. He sings his final song of hope. The One who would take him to the depths of the earth would bring him up (verse 20) in resurrection!

The one who peeked into the heart of God and danced through life in passion for God rejoiced in the incredible commitment that the Lord had made to him as His friend.

"These are the last words of David:
'David, the son of Jesse, speaks—
David, the man to whom God gave such wonderful success,
David, the man anointed by the God of Jacob,
David, the sweet psalmist of Israel.
The Spirit of the Lord speaks through me;
his words are upon my tongue.
The God of Israel spoke.
The Rock of Israel said to me:
"The person who rules righteously,
who rules in the fear of God,
he is like the light of the morning,
like the sunrise bursting forth in a cloudless sky,
like the refreshing rains that bring tender grass from the earth."
It is my family God has chosen!
Yes, he has made an everlasting covenant with me.
His agreement is eternal, final, sealed.
He will constantly look after my safety and success.
But the godless are like thorns to be thrown away,

for they tear the hand that touches them.
One must be armed to chop them down;
they will be utterly consumed with fire'"
(2 Sam. 23:1-7, NLT).

By the time David's story ends he has become the key figure in the life, memory, and imagination of Israel. Even more so, he has become the dominant figure in the whole biblical narrative. God chose to chisel David's reign into a kingdom that would last forever. His epic trilogy remains the ultimate quest, the ultimate personal battle between good and evil, and the ultimate stewardship of heart and life before God.

As we close our journey with David, let us ponder the words of Jeremiah, Luke, the Psalms, and Revelation. How certain is the covenant that God made with David? How indelibly is his name etched into passion for the God who's only passion is for us?

"'The day will come, says the Lord, when I will do for Israel and Judah all the good I have promised them.

"'At that time I will bring to the throne of David
a righteous descendant,
and he will do what is just and right throughout the land.
In that day Judah will be saved,
and Jerusalem will live in safety.
And their motto will be "The Lord is our righteousness!"

"'For this is what the Lord says: David will forever have a descendant sitting on the throne of Israel. And there will always be Levitical priests to offer burnt offerings and grain offerings and sacrifices to me.'

"Then this message came to Jeremiah from the Lord: 'If you can break my covenant with the day and the night so that they do not come on their usual schedule, only then will my covenant with David, my servant, be broken. Only then will he no longer have a descendant to reign on his throne'" (Jer. 33:14-21, NLT).

"And because Joseph was a descendant of King David, he had to go to Bethlehem in Judea, David's ancient home. He traveled there from the village of Nazareth in Galilee. He took with him Mary, his fiancée, who was obviously pregnant by this time. And while they were there, the time came for her baby to be born. She gave birth to her first child, a son. She wrapped him snugly in strips of cloth and laid him in a manger, because there was no room for them in the village inn" (Luke 2:4-7, NLT).

"You will become pregnant and have a son, and you are to name him Jesus. He will be very great and will be called the Son of the Most High. And the Lord God will give him the throne of his ancestor David. And he will reign over Israel forever; his Kingdom will never end!" (Luke 1:31-33, NLT).

The Gospels repeatedly refer to Jesus as the "Son of David." "That designation isn't an incidental detail of genealogy but a major item of theology—that is, it's about *God*. The David story anticipates the Jesus story. The Jesus story presupposes the David story."[5] Interestingly, among the very last words spoken by Jesus in Revelation—words of hope and promise just before the curtain of the ages fall—He identifies Himself with David. "I, Jesus, have sent My angel to testify to you these things in the churches. I am the Root and the Offspring of David, the Bright and Morning Star" (Rev. 22:16, NKJV). And Revelation's celebrated Lamb, who alone is worthy to open the sealed book of divine providence and human destiny, is not only the One who is slain, but the "Root of David" (Rev. 5:5). Jesus was the Son of David, yet in another sense He was David's ancestor. Jesus of Nazareth is at once David's Lord and Son (Mark 12:35-37).

I don't think this distant grandson of David was a surprise to him. God whispered these truths in his spirit and caused him to write them down for all eternity.

> "The Lord says to my Lord:
> 'Sit at My right hand
> Until I make Your enemies
> a footstool for Your feet'" (Ps. 110:1, NASB).

Someday the clouds will roll back, and the King of kings will burst through the sky. There will be a new heaven and a new earth. A holy city, the New Jerusalem, will come down from God out of heaven like a beautiful bride prepared for her husband. The home of God will be among His people. As He lives with them they will see His face. He will remove all their sorrows; and death, sorrow, and pain will cease forever. The old world and its evils will be gone forever. Christ Jesus—the Lamb, the Root and Offspring of David—will sit on the throne of David in the city of

Jerusalem. There we will join the one who said, "You turned my wailing into dancing; you removed my sackcloth and clothed me with joy, that my heart may sing to you and not be silent. O Lord my God, I will give you thanks forever" (Ps. 30:11, 12, NIV). With David, we will sing to One who is indeed worthy.

Oh, yes, I believe David will dance one more time (perhaps even throughout eternity) down the streets of Jerusalem—this time without an eye to despise him. Oblivious to anyone but God—the focus of his affections, the passion of his heart—he will dance his way to that same familiar throne, but this time it will be occupied by Another. David will see the Lord high and lifted up, and His train will fill the temple. He'll fall before the One who sits upon the throne, take the crown from his own head, and cast it at His feet. Lifting his eyes to the King of all kings and with the passion of an entire nation of redeemed gathered in one heart, he will cry, "Worthy!"[6]

---

[1]Again, see my discussion of passion in L. Lichtenwalter, *David: A Heart Like His*, pp. 12-15, and the development of nine facets of passion (pp. 125-127) that find expression in David's experience with God: 1. Passion *claims it all*. 2. Passion *yields it all*. 3. Passion is *imaginative*. 4. Passion *constantly renews itself*. 5. Passion *hears what it wants to hear*. 6. Passion *has purpose*. 7. Passion haunts the *imagination*. 8. Passion *evokes passion*. 9. Passion is *deeply personal*.

[2]Alexander Whyte, *Bible Characters* (Grand Rapids: Zondervan Pub. House, 1952, 1959), vol. 1, p. 252.

[3]E. H. Peterson, *Leap Over a Wall*, p. 206, 207.

[4]The writer and the occasion of the psalm are unknown. It is obviously an old man's psalm (verses 9, 17, 18). It has Davidic expressions ("my rock and my fortress"; "my enemies"; "make haste," etc.), but the writer may simply be drawing freely from earlier psalms. See Marvin E. Tate, *Psalms 51-100* (Dallas: Word Books, Publisher, 1990), p. 211; B. Moore, *A Heart Like His*, p. 277; D. Kidner, *Psalms 1-72*, p. 250.

[5]Peterson, p. 9.

[6]Moore, p. 280.